Seventh Edition

Be Prepared
for the

AP

Computer
Science
Exam in Java

Maria Litvin
Phillips Academy, Andover, Massachusetts

Gary Litvin
Skylight Publishing, Andover, Massachusetts

Skylight Publishing
Andover, Massachusetts

Library of Congress Control Number: 2019942212

ISBN 978-0-9972528-6-6

Skylight Publishing
9 Bartlet Street, Suite 70
Andover, MA 01810

web: www.skylit.com
e-mail: sales@skylit.com
            support@skylit.com

2 3 4 5 6 7 8 9 10   24 23 22 21

Printed in the United States of America

Brief Contents

About the Authors

Maria Litvin has taught computer science and mathematics at Phillips Academy in Andover, Massachusetts, since 1987. She is an AP Computer Science exam reader and Table Leader and, as a consultant for The College Board, provides AP training for high school computer science teachers. Maria is a recipient of the 1999 Siemens Award for Advanced Placement for Mathematics, Science, and Technology for New England and of the 2003 RadioShack National Teacher Award. Prior to joining Phillips Academy, Maria taught computer science at Boston University.

Maria has co-authored the earlier, C++ version of *Be Prepared* (Skylight Publishing, 1999) and several popular computer science textbooks: *C++ for You++: An Introduction to Programming and Computer Science*, which was the leading high school textbook for AP Computer Science courses in the C++ era, *Java Methods: Object-Oriented Programming and Data Structures*, now in its third AP Edition, and *Coding in Python and Elements of Discrete Mathematics* (Skylight Publishing, 2019).

Gary Litvin is a co-author of *C++ for You++*, the *Java Methods* series, and *Coding in Python and Elements of Discrete Mathematics*. Gary has worked in many areas of software development including artificial intelligence, pattern recognition, computer graphics, and neural networks. As the founder of Skylight Software, Inc., he developed SKYLIGHTS/GX, one of the first visual programming tools for C and C++ programmers. Gary led in the development of several state-of-the-art software products, including interactive touch screen development tools, OCR and handwritten character recognition systems, and credit card fraud detection software.

Contents

Preface to the Seventh Edition

The College Board has recently updated the *Computer Science A Course and Exam Description* (CED) that was in effect since 2014. The new course description is based on the more formal Understanding by Design model (Wiggins and McTighe): "big ideas," "enduring understandings," "learning objectives," and "essential knowledge." The Development Committee identified four "big ideas" for this course: Modularity, Variables, Control, and Impact of Computing. The format of the exam remains essentially the same, but the content is slightly simplified, with some of the more challenging topics (number systems, abstract classes and interfaces) dropped. Also, the four free-response questions in the exam are now linked to specific topics:

> Question 1: Methods and Control Structures
> Question 2: Class
> Question 3: Array / ArrayList
> Question 4: 2D Array

The College Board expects a typical AP CSA course to have a lab component. The Development Committee has made available sample labs to demonstrate the extent of lab work expected. These labs are samples only; they <u>will not be tested</u> on the AP exams.

Preface

The AP Computer Science A (AP CSA) exam tests your understanding of basic concepts in computer science as well as your fluency in Java programming. The exam covers roughly the material of a one-semester introductory college course in computer science (CS-1). In the past, the College Board offered two computer science exams: "A" and the more advanced "AB." Since 2010, the College Board has offered only AP Computer Science A and, more recently, the AP Computer Science: Principles (AP CSP) exam. Despite the College Board's claims to the contrary, AP CSP is a lower-level exam that does not require coding fluency in any programming language.

Exam questions are finalized by The College Board's AP Computer Science A Development Committee, and exams are administered by the Educational Testing Service (ETS). The College Board currently offers exams in 38 subjects. In 2018, 2,808,990 students took 5,090,324 exams. The most up-to-date information on the AP exams offered and participation statistics can be found on The College Board's website http://research.collegeboard.org/programs/ap/data.

In the spring of 2004, the computer science exams used Java for the first time. At the same time, the AP CS program's emphasis shifted from implementation of algorithms and coding proficiency to object-oriented programming (OOP) concepts. More recent exams, however, show renewed interest in algorithms and less in OOP. Future exams are likely to focus more on control structures (`if-else`, `for` and `while` loops), one- and two-dimensional arrays and `ArrayList`.

> **Answers to exam questions written in a programming language other than Java or in pseudocode will not receive credit.**

A working knowledge of Java is necessary but not sufficient for a good grade on the exam. You must also understand the basic concepts of computer science, OOP, and some common algorithms. As for Java: you don't have to know the whole language, just a subset.

This is a lot of material to cover, and it is certainly not the goal of this book to teach you everything you need to know from scratch. For that, you need a complete textbook with exercises and programming projects. Most students who take the exam are enrolled in an AP Computer Science course at their school. A determined student can prepare for the exam on his or her own; it may take anywhere between two and twelve months, and a good textbook will be even more important.

The goals of this book are:
- to describe the exam format and requirements
- to describe the Java subset
- to provide an effective review of what you should know with emphasis on the more difficult topics and on common omissions and mistakes
- to help you identify and fill the gaps in your knowledge
- to offer sample exam questions with answers, hints, and solutions for you to practice with and analyze your mistakes

The AP CSA exam is a paper-and-pencil affair. While you need a computer with a Java compiler to learn how to program and how to implement common algorithms in Java, this book does not require the use of a computer. In fact, it is a good idea not to use one when you work on practice questions, so that you can get used to the exam's format and environment. One-hundred-percent correct Java syntax is not the emphasis here. Small mistakes (a missed semicolon or a brace) that a compiler would normally help you catch will probably not affect your exam score. You'll need a computer only to access collegeboard.org and our website, www.skylit.com/beprepared/, for the latest updates and our solutions to the free-response questions from past exams.

Chapter 1 of this book explains the format, the required materials, and the Java subset for the exam and provides information about exam grading and exam-taking hints. Chapter 2 and Chapter 3 cover the elements of Java required for the exam. Chapter 4 deals with OOP topics (classes and inheritance). Chapter 5 reviews common searching and sorting algorithms. All review chapters contain sample multiple-choice questions with detailed explanations of all the right and wrong answers. Chapter 6 is actually on the web at this book's companion website, www.skylit.com/beprepared/. It offers our annotated solutions to the free-response questions from past exams. At the end of the book are five complete practice exams followed by answers and solutions.

❖   ❖   ❖

Our colleague and friend Dave Wittry passed away in a tragic accident while training for a triathlon, on February 5, 2008. He was 41. Dave contributed practice exam questions for the second and third editions of this book. Dave taught at Troy High School, a magnet school for science, math, and technology in Fullerton, California, and contributed to Troy's immense success in Computer Science. In 2005 Dave moved to Taiwan and taught AP Computer Science and mathematics at the Taipei American School. He was a Reader for the AP Computer Science Exams for several years. Dave was always ready to help friends, students, and colleagues, and he developed valuable resources for computer science teachers. We miss Dave!

❖   ❖   ❖

We are grateful to David Levine of St. Bonaventure University, who recommended many important improvements, helped us catch technical and stylistic mistakes, and pointed out questions that needed clarification in the first edition of *Be Prepared*, which came out in 1999.

Roger Frank and Judy Hromcik contributed practice questions to the second and third editions; some of the questions in this book are based on their ideas. Roger also went very thoroughly over the drafts of the earlier editions and recommended many corrections and improvements.

We thank teachers and students who alerted us to several mistakes in the earlier editions of this book.

Our special thanks to Margaret Litvin for making this book more readable with her thorough and thoughtful editing.

Finally, we thank the Boy Scouts of America for allowing us to allude to their motto in the book's title.

How to Use This Book

The companion website

      www.skylit.com/beprepared/

is an integral part of the book. It contains annotated solutions to free-response questions from past exams and relevant links. Check this website for the current information, and be sure you have the latest edition of *Be Prepared*.

Multiple-choice questions in the review chapters are marked by their number in a box:

Their solutions are delimited by ⬈ and ⬊.

> **Our practice exams may be slightly more difficult than the actual exams, so don't panic if they take more time.**

Braces like these on the margins in the free-response questions in our practice exams indicate suggestions for additional lab work based on our questions. Initial Java code for these labs is available at www.skylit.com/beprepared/. Complete solutions to the labs are available to teachers. To get access, e-mail support@skylit.com from your school e-mail account and include the school web page that lists your email address.

Chapter 1 Exam Format, Grading, and Tips

1.1 Exam Format and Materials

Figure 1-1 shows the format of the AP Computer Science exam. The exam takes 3 hours of test time, plus breaks and time for instructions. It is divided into two sections. Section I consists of 40 multiple-choice questions with a total allotted time of 1 hour and 30 minutes (2.25 minutes per question on average). Section II consists of four free-response questions with a total allotted time of 1 hour and 30 minutes (22.5 minutes per question on average). The free-response questions usually consist of two parts each (but occasionally might have three parts).

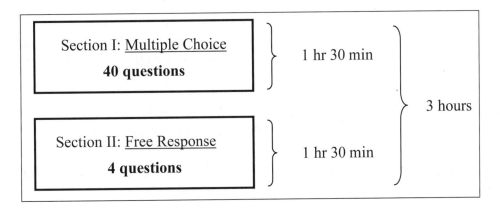

Figure 1-1. AP Computer Science exam format

> **No computers, calculators, other devices, books, or materials are allowed, only paper, pencil and an eraser.**

Pens are allowed, but we highly recommend that you use a pencil.

At the exam you will receive the *Quick Reference* page, both in your multiple-choice questions booklet and again in your free-response questions booklet (in other words, the same *Quick Reference* page will be given to you twice). The *Quick Reference* provides a list of the Java library classes and their methods included in the AP Java subset. Students and teachers can obtain a copy at the College Board's AP site (see www.skylit.com/cblinks.html). The *Quick Reference* is provided for reference — it is expected that you will already be very familiar and comfortable with the required Java library classes and their methods before the exam.

The multiple-choice section is a mixture of questions related to general computer science terms, program design decisions, specific elements of Java syntax, logical analysis of fragments of Java code, properties of classes, and some OOP concepts. Starting at the 2020 exam, the College Board has made the topics of the free-response questions more specific:

> Question 1: Methods and Control Structures
> Question 2: Class
> Question 3: Array / ArrayList
> Question 4: 2D Array

Each free-response question is graded out of 9 points, with all points weighted equally. The second part of the question often refers to the class or method implemented in the first part, but each part is graded separately, and your implementation of Part (a) does not have to be correct in order for you to receive full credit for Part (b).

In the free-response Question 2 you will be asked to write a complete small Java class. Your implementation will be graded based on the correctness of the implementation of your class, including the encapsulation principle (declaring all instance variables private), and other criteria.

In the past, the AP CSA exams included a specific case study, developed by the Exam Development Committee. In 2008-2014, the case study was GridWorld.

Starting with the 2015 exam, neither GridWorld nor any other case study was part of the exams, and they won't be in the future.

The College Board requires a typical AP CSA course to include at least 20 hours of computer lab work. The Development Committee has made available sample labs for practice.

These labs are only examples designed to illustrate the scope and difficulty of lab work in a typical AP CSA course. The content and code in these labs will not be tested on the AP CSA exams.

1.2   The Java Subset

The old course description included a table that defined the AP Java Subset. There is no such table in the new CED, but you can glean the elements of the subset from the *Essential Knowledge* components in the CED. The Java subset remains essentially the same, with the exception of abstract classes and interfaces.

So what is in the subset? Actually, quite a bit:

- Comments: `/* ... */`, `//`, and `/** ... */`, preconditions and postconditions.

- `boolean`, `int`, and `double` primitive data types. `(int)` and `(double)` casts. **Other primitive data types, including `char`, are not in the subset and should be avoided on the exam.**

- The assignment operator `=`. The arithmetic operators `+`, `-`, `*`, `/`, `%`. The increment/decrement operators `++` and `--` (**use only the postfix form `k++` or `k--`, and do not use them in expressions**). The compound assignment operators `+=`, `-=`, `*=`, `/=`, `%=`. The relational operators `<`, `>`, `<=`, `>=`, `==`, `!=`. The logical operators `&&`, `||`, `!`.

- `if-else` statements. The `true` and `false` keywords.

- Literal strings in double quotes. `\n`, `\\`, and `\"` escape characters in literal strings. The `+` and `+=` operators for concatenating strings. `String`'s `compareTo`, `equals`, `length`, `substring`, and `indexOf(String s)` methods.

- `System.out.print` and `System.out.println`.

- One-dimensional and two-dimensional (**rectangular only**) arrays. `array.length`. Arrays of objects. Initialized arrays such as
  ```
  int[] arr = {1, 2, 3};
  int[][] m = {{1, 2, 3}, {4, 5, 6}};
  ```
  Default values of elements for arrays defined using the `new` operator.

- `for` and `while` loops. The "enhanced" `for` loop ("for each" loop):
  ```
  for(type x : values)...
  ```

- Classes. Constructors. The `new` operator. `public` and `private` methods. `static` methods. Overloaded methods. The `return` statement. `void` methods.

- `static` instance variables and `static final` variables (constants). `null`. <u>All instance variables are `private`</u>.

- Inheritance, `extends`. Calling a superclass's constructor from a subclass, as in `super(...)`. Overriding a superclass's methods. Calling a superclass's method from a subclass, as in `super.someMethod(...)`. Passing `this` object to a method, as in `otherObject.someMethod(this)`.

- Understanding `ArithmeticException`, `NullPointerException`, `IndexOutOfBoundsException`, `ArrayIndexOutOfBoundsException`, `ConcurrentModificationException`.

- The `ArrayList<E>` class (see Section 2.6).

- Other library classes, methods, and constants:

  String: `length()`, `substring(...)`, `indexOf(String s)`
  Integer: `Integer(int x)`, `intValue()`;
  `Integer.MIN_VALUE` and `Integer.MAX_VALUE`
  Double: `Double(double x)`, `doubleValue()`
  Math: `abs(int x)`, `abs(double x)`,
  `pow(double base, double exp)`, `sqrt(double x)`,
  `random()`
  Object: `equals(Object other)`, `toString()`

  Also understand the `toString` and `equals` methods for all objects and the `compareTo` method for `String`, `Integer`, and `Double` objects.

  > **If you feel you must stray from this subset in your free-response solution, you might have misunderstood the problem and be making it harder than it is.**

At the same time, it is OK to use such out-of-the-subset features as `Math.min(x, y)` and `Math.max(x, y)` methods, `ArrayList`'s `contains` and `remove(object)` methods, `break` in loops, and other simple tools that all exam readers are familiar with.

Things that are <u>not</u> in the AP Java subset and should be avoided include the following:

- Java syntax abominations, such as the `?_:_` operator

- `++` and `--` in expressions (as in `a[i++]`)

- Primitive data types other than `boolean`, `int`, and `double` (`char`, `long`, `float` are <u>not</u> in the subset)

- Bitwise logical operators and shift operators: `~`, `&`, `|`, `^`, `<<`, `>>`.

Also <u>not</u> in the subset and will not be tested:

- The `switch` statement, the `do-while` loop, `break` and `continue` in loops

- The prefix form of `++` and `--` operators (`++k`, `--k`)

- Library classes and methods other than those mentioned above

- Abstract classes and interfaces

- Checked exceptions and `try-catch-finally` statements

- `System.in` and `Scanner`; any input and output other than `System.out.print` and `System.out.println`

- `enum` data types

1.3   Tested Terms, Concepts, and Algorithms

In addition to Java, you need to be familiar with the following terms, concepts, and algorithms mentioned in the *Essential Knowledge* components of the CED:

- Rounding: `(int)(x + 0.5)` for a positive `double x`; `(int)(x - 0.5)` for negative `x`

- *Autoboxing* / *unboxing*

- Constructor and method *signature* (name and data types of parameters)

- *Invoking* constructors, calling methods using the "dot" operator

- *Local* variables; *instance* variables

- *Formal parameters*

- Passing parameters *by value* (an object is passed as a copy of reference)

- *Accessor* and *mutator* (*modifier*) methods

- *Class, subclass*, the *IS-A* relationship between objects

- *Polymorphism*

- Array / `ArrayList` algorithms: traverse, find the minimum or maximum, find the sum or average of elements, examine all pairs of consecutive elements, find duplicates, examine all elements for a given property

- Sequential Search and iterative and recursive versions of Binary Search

- Selection Sort, Insertion Sort, and Mergesort

- Understand **(but not write)** recursive code

The Java subset features and the above terms, concepts, and algorithms are reviewed in the subsequent chapters.

1.4   Grading

The exam is graded on a scale from 1 to 5. Table 1-1 shows the College Board's college credit recommendations and grade equivalents for AP grades.

AP Grade	Credit Recommendation	College Grade Equivalent
5	Extremely well qualified	A
4	Well qualified	A-, B+, B
3	Qualified	B-, C+, C
2	Possibly qualified	n/a
1	No recommendation	n/a

Table 1-1. AP grades, credit recommendations, and college grade equivalents

Grades of 5 and 4 are called "extremely well qualified" and "well qualified," respectively, and usually will be honored by colleges that give credit or placement for AP CSA. A grade of 3, "qualified," may be denied credit or placement at some colleges. Grades of 2, "possibly qualified," and 1, "no recommendation," will not get you college credit or placement.

Table 1-2 presents published statistics and grade distributions for the 2017 and 2018 exams. 65,133 students took the exam in 2018; 45.9 percent of them scored 4 or 5.

AP Computer Science A	2018		2017	
	Number	%	Number	%
Students	65,133	100.0	60,519	100.0
Grade:				
5	16,105	24.7	14,623	24.2
4	13,802	21.2	12,650	20.9
3	14,222	21.8	13,271	21.9
2	7,738	11.9	6,970	11.5
1	13,266	20.4	13,005	21.5
4 or 5	29,907	45.9	27,273	45.1

Table 1-2. 2018 and 2017 grade distributions

| The multiple-choice and free-response sections weigh equally in the final grade.

The College Board uses a weighted combination of the multiple-choice (MC) and free-response (FR) scores to determine the final total score:

```
totalScore =
     MC_coeff * countCorrect + FR_coeff * FR_score;
```

One point is given for each correct answer to a multiple-choice question.

| There is no penalty for giving a wrong answer to a multiple-choice question, so it is a good strategy not to leave any answers blank.

Solutions to free-response questions are graded by a group of high school teachers and college professors. Scores are based on a *rubric* established by the Chief Reader, Exam Leader, and Question Leaders. Each free-response question is graded out of 9 points, with partial credit given according to a rubric.

The final score is obtained by adding the MC and FR weighted scores. The MC and FR coefficients are chosen in such a way that they give equal weights to the multiple-choice and free-response sections of the exam. For example, if the exam has 40 multiple-choice questions and 4 free-response questions, weights of 1.0 for multiple-choice and 1.1111 for free-response will give each section a maximum total of 40, for a maximum possible total score of 80.

The cut-off points are determined by the Chief Reader in consultation with the College Board and may vary slightly from year to year based on the score distributions and close examination of a sample of individual exams. Table 1-3 shows the cut-off points for the 2015 exam.

Composite score range	Percent range	Grade
62 - 80	77.5 - 100	5
44 - 61	55.0 - 77.4	4
31 - 43	38.8 - 54.9	3
25 - 30	31.3 - 38.7	2
0 - 24	0 - 31.2	1

Table 1-3. 2015 score cut-off points for grades

Over 98% of students who answer correctly at least 27 out of 40 questions on the multiple-choice section typically receive a 4 or a 5 for the whole exam.

The College Board releases the free-response questions 48 hours after the exam and posts them on their website. We post our annotated solutions at www.skylit.com/beprepared/ a few hours after the questions are posted. The College Board posts the scoring rubrics for the free-response questions sometime in the summer. Every few years the College Board releases a complete exam, including a diagnostic guide for the multiple-choice questions, grading rubrics for the free-response questions, and the cut-off points for grades. See www.skylit.com/beprepared/notes.txt for the latest updates.

1.5   College Credit

Most colleges will take your AP courses taken and exam grades into account in admission decisions. But acceptance of AP exam results for credit and/or placement varies widely among colleges. In general, the AP CSA course corresponds to a CS-1 course (Introductory Computer Science or Computer Programming I), a one-semester course for computer science majors. Some colleges may base their decision on your grade, and some may not give any credit at all. Consult the websites of the colleges you are interested in and the College Board's AP credit policies page https://apstudent.collegeboard.org/creditandplacement/search-credit-policies.

1.6   Exam Taking Tips

Some things are obvious:

- If you took the time to read a multiple-choice question and all the answer choices, take an extra ten seconds and guess. Most likely you have eliminated one or two wrong answers even without noticing. **Do not leave any multiple-choice answers blank: there is no penalty for wrong answers**.

- If a common paragraph refers to a group of questions and you took the time to read it, try each question in the group.

- Do read the question before jumping to the code included in the question. Notes to multiple-choice questions in our practice exams might show you some shortcuts.

- In questions with I, II, III options, work from the answers; for example, you might be able to eliminate two or three answer choices if you are sure that Option I doesn't work.

There are a few important things to know about answering free-response questions.

Remember that all free-response questions have equal weight. The first question is likely to be the easiest.

In a nutshell: be neat, straightforward, and professional; keep your exam reader in mind; don't show off.

More specifically:

1. Stay within the Java subset, except for a few obvious shortcuts, such as `Math.max(...)` and `Math.min(...)`.

2. Remember that the elegance of your code <u>does not</u> count. More often than not, a brute-force approach is the best. You may waste a lot of time writing tricky, non-standard code and trick yourself in the process or mislead your exam reader who, after all, is only human. Your exam reader will read your solution, but will not test it on a computer.

3. Superior efficiency of your code does not count, unless the desired performance of the solution is specifically stated in the question.

4. Remember that Parts (b) and (c) of a question are graded independently from the previous parts, and may actually be easier: Part (a) may ask you to write a method, while Part (b) or Part (c) may simply ask you to use it. It is not uncommon for method(s) specified in Part (a) to be called in subsequent parts. Do so, even if your Part (a) is incorrect or left blank. <u>Do not</u> re-implement code from earlier parts in later parts — you will waste valuable time and may lose points for doing so.

5. If a question presents a partial definition of a class with certain methods described but not implemented ("implementation not shown"), call these methods whenever appropriate in your code — do not write equivalent code yourself.

6. Bits of "good thinking" count. You may not know the whole solution, but if you have read and understood the question, go ahead and write fragments of code that may earn you partial credit points. On the free-response question #2, write the class, constructor, and method headers even if you are not sure how to implement them. But don't spend too much time improvising incorrect code.

7. Don't waste your time erasing large portions of work. Instead, cross out your work neatly, <u>but only after you have something better to replace it with</u>. Do not cross out a solution if you have no time to redo it, even if you think it is wrong. You <u>won't</u> be penalized for incorrect code and may get partial credit for it. Exam readers are instructed not to read any code that you have crossed out. But if you wrote two solutions, be sure to cross one out: otherwise only the first one on the page will be graded.

8. Read the comment above the method header quickly — it usually restates the task in a more formal way and sometimes gives valuable hints. <u>Assume that all preconditions are satisfied — do not add unnecessary checks to your code!</u>

9. One common mistake is to forget a `return` statement in a non-`void` method. Make sure the returned value matches the specified method return type.

10. Do not ignore hints in the question description. If an algorithm is suggested for a method (as in "you may use the following algorithm"), don't fight it, just use it!

11. Remember that the exam readers grade a vast number of exams in quick succession during a marathon grading session every June. Write as neatly as possible. Space out your code (don't save paper).

12. Always indent your code properly. This helps you and your exam reader. If you miss a brace but your code is properly indented, the reader (as opposed to a Java compiler) may accept it as correct. Similarly, if you put each statement on a separate line, a forgotten semicolon might not be held against you.

13. Follow the Java naming convention: the names of all methods, variables, and parameters start with a lowercase letter. Use meaningful, but not too verbose, names for variables. `count` may be better than `a`; `sum` may be better than `temp`; `row`, `col` or `r`, `c` may be better than `i`, `j`. But `k` is better than `loopControlVariable`. If the question contains examples of code with names, use the same names when appropriate.

14. Don't bother with comments; they do not count and you will lose valuable time. Occasionally you can put a very brief comment that indicates your intentions for the fragment of code that follows. For example:

```
// Find the first empty seat:
...
...
```

15. Don't worry about `imports` — assume that all the necessary Java library classes are imported.

16. Code strictly according to the specifications and preconditions and postconditions. Avoid extraneous "bells and whistles" — you will lose points. Never add `System.out.print/println` in solutions unless specifically asked to do so. <u>Never</u> read any data in your method — it is passed in as a parameter or is available as instance or static variables of the class.

17. Do not use in your code specific numbers, strings, or dimensions of arrays given as examples in explanations of questions. If the question says, "For example, a two-dimensional array `pixelValues` may contain the following image" and shows an array of 4 rows by 5 columns, do <u>not</u> use 4 and 5 in your code — make your code work with an array of any size.

18. Don't try to catch the exam authors on ambiguities: there will be no one to hear your case, and you'll waste your time. Instead, try to grasp quickly what was <u>meant</u> and write your answer.

19. Don't quit until the time is up. Use all the time you have and keep trying. The test will be over before you know it.

Chapter 2   Java Features, Part 1

2.1   Variables; Arithmetic, Relational, and Logical Operators

Primitive data types included in the subset are `boolean`, `int`, and `double`. In Java, an `int` always takes four bytes, regardless of a particular computer or Java compiler, and its range is from -2^{31} to $2^{31} - 1$. The smallest and the largest integer values are defined in Java as symbolic constants `Integer.MIN_VALUE` and `Integer.MAX_VALUE`; use these symbolic constants if you need to refer to the limits of the `int` range. A `double` takes 8 bytes and has a huge range, but its precision is about 15 significant digits.

Remember to declare local variables.

If you declare a variable inside a nested block, make sure it is used only in that block. If you declare a variable in a `for` loop, it will be undefined outside that loop.

For example:

```
public int countMins(int[] a)
{
  if (a.length > 0)
  {
    int iMin = 0;

    for (int i = 1; i < a.length; i++)
    {
      if (a[i] < a[iMin])
        iMin = i;
    }

    int count = 0;

    for (i = 0; i < a.length; i++)
    {
      if (a[i] == a[iMin])
        count++;
    }
  }
  return count;
}
```

Error: `i` *is undefined*

Error: `count` *is undefined here*

A safer version:

```java
public int countMins(int[] a)
{
  int iMin = 0;
  int count = 0;

  if (a.length > 0)
  {
    iMin = 0;
    for (int i = 1; i < a.length; i++)
    {
      if (a[i] < a[iMin])
        iMin = i;
    }

    count = 0;

    for (int i = 0; i < a.length; i++)
    {
      if (a[i] == a[iMin])
        count++;
    }
  }
  return count;
}
```

Do not declare count *here:*
`int` count = 0;
would be a mistake

You won't be penalized for declarations inside blocks of code, but if you declare important variables near the top of the method's code, it makes it easier to read and may help you avoid mistakes.

1

Which of the following statements is true?

(A)   In Java, data types in declarations of symbolic constants are needed only for documentation purposes.
(B)   When a Java interpreter is running, variables of the `double` data type are represented in memory as strings of decimal digits with a decimal point and an optional sign.
(C)   A variable's data type determines where it is stored in computer memory when the program is running.
(D)   A variable's data type determines whether that variable may be passed as a parameter to a particular method.
(E)   A variable of the `int` type cannot serve as an operand for the / operator.

☞ This question gives us a chance to review what we know about data types.

Choice A is false: the data type of a symbolic constant is used by the compiler. In this sense, symbolic constants are not so different from variables. The difference is that a constant declaration includes the keyword `final`. Class constants are often declared as `static final` variables. For example:

```
public static final double LBS_IN_KG = 2.20462262;
public static final int maxNumSeats = 120;
```

Choice B is false, too. While real numbers may be written in programs in decimal notation, a Java compiler converts them into a special "double" floating-point format that takes eight bytes and is convenient for computations.

Choice C is false. The data type by itself does not determine where the variable is stored. Its location in memory is determined by where and how the variable is declared: whether it is a local variable in a method or an instance variable of a class or a static variable.

Choice E is false, too. In Java, you can write `a/b`, where both `a` and `b` are of type `int`. The result is truncated to an integer.

Choice D is true. For example, a value of the type `String` cannot be passed to a method that expects an `int` as a parameter. Sometimes, though, a parameter of a different type may be promoted to the type expected by the method (for example, an `int` can be promoted to a `double` when you call, say, `Math.sqrt(x)` for an `int x`). The answer is D. ☜

Arithmetic operators

The most important thing to remember about Java's arithmetic operators is that the data type of the result, even each intermediate result, is the same as the data type of the operands. In particular, the result of division of one integer by another integer is truncated to an integer.

For example:

```
int n = 3;
double result;

result = (n + 1) * n / 2;        // result is 6.0
result = (n / 2) * (n + 1);      // result is 4.0
result = (1 / 2) * n * (n + 1);  // result is 0.0
```

To avoid truncation you have to watch the data types and sometimes use the *cast operator*. For example:

```
int a, b;
double ratio;
...
ratio = (double)a / b;        // Or: a / (double)b;
// But not ratio = (double)(a/b) -- this is a cast applied too late!
```

If at least one of the operands is a `double`, there is no need to cast the other one — it is promoted to a `double` automatically. For example:

```
int factor = 3;
double x = 2.0 / factor;  // Result: x = 0.6666...
```

2

Which of the following expressions does not evaluate to 0.4?

(A) `(int)4.5 / (double)10;`
(B) `(double)(4 / 10);`
(C) `4.0 / 10;`
(D) `4 / 10.0;`
(E) `(double)4 / (double)10;`

☞ In B the cast to `double` is applied too late — after the ratio is truncated to 0 — so it evaluates to 0. The answer is B. ↵

In the real world we have to worry about the range of values for different data types. For example, a method that calculates 3^n as an `int` may overflow the result, even for a relatively small *n*. In Java, arithmetic overflow is not reported in any way: there is no warning or exception. If an `int` result is greater than or equal to 2^{31}, the leftmost bit, which is the sign bit, may be set to 1, and the result becomes negative.

> **For the AP exam, you have to be aware of what overflow is, and you need to be aware of the `Integer.MIN_VALUE` and `Integer.MAX_VALUE` constants, but you don't have to know their specific values.**

Modulo division

> **The % (modulo division) operator usually applies to two integers: it calculates the remainder when the first operand is divided by the second.**

For example:

```
int r;
r = 17 % 3;   // r is set to 2
r = 8 % 2;    // r is set to 0
r = 4 % 5;    // r is set to 4
```

Compound assignments and ++ and --

Compound assignment operators are +=, -=, *= , /=, and %=. x += y is the same as x = x + y. Other operations follow the same pattern.

There are two forms of the ++ and -- operators in Java. The prefix form ("++k") increments (or decrements) the variable before its value is used in the rest of the expression; the postfix form increments (or decrements) it afterwards.

> **The AP CS Development Committee discourages the use of ++ and -- in expressions. Use ++ and -- only in separate statements and only in the postfix form, such as in k++ or k--.**

For example:

You won't lose points over ++ or -- in expressions if you use them correctly, but they won't earn you any extra credit, either.

> **It is bad style <u>not</u> to use increment or compound assignment operators where appropriate.**

For example:

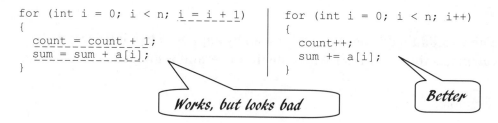

```
for (int i = 0; i < n; i = i + 1)      for (int i = 0; i < n; i++)
{                                       {
    count = count + 1;                     count++;
    sum = sum + a[i];                      sum += a[i];
}                                       }
```

> Works, but looks bad

> Better

Again, this incurs no penalty but doesn't look good.

Arithmetic expressions are too easy to be tested alone. You may encounter them in questions that combine them with logic, iterations, recursion, and so on.

Relational operators

In the AP Java subset, the relational operators ==, !=, <, >, <=, >= apply to `int`s and `double`s. Remember that "is equal to" is represented by == (not to be confused with =, the assignment operator). `a != b` is equivalent to `!(a == b)`, but != is stylistically better.

> **The == and != operators can also be applied to two objects, but their meanings are different from what you might expect: they compare the <u>addresses</u> of the objects. The result of == is true if and only if the two variables refer to exactly the same object. You rarely care about that: most likely you want to compare the <u>contents</u> of two objects, for instance two strings. Then you need to use the `equals` or `compareTo` method.**

For example:

```
if (str.equals("Stop")) ...
```

> **On the other hand, == or != must be used when you compare an object to `null`.**

`null` is a Java reserved word that stands for a reference with a zero value. It is used to indicate that a variable currently does not refer to any valid object. For example:

```
if (str != null && str.equals("Stop")) ...
// str != null avoids NullPointerException --
// can't call a null's method
```

You can write instead:

```
if ("Stop".equals(str)) ...
```

This works because `"Stop"` is not `null`; it works even if `str` is `null`.

Logical operators

The logical operators `&&`, `||`, and `!` normally apply to Boolean values and expressions. For example:

```
boolean found = false;          boolean found = false;
...                             ...
while (i >= 0 && !found)         while (i >= 0 && found == false)
{                               {
  ...                             ...
}                               }
```

Works, but is more verbose

Do not write

```
while (... && !found == true)
```

— this works, but "`== true`" is redundant.

3

Assuming that x, y, and z are integer variables, which of the following three logical expressions are equivalent to each other, that is, have equal values for all possible values of x, y, and z?

   I.   `(x == y && x != z) || (x != y && x == z)`

   II. `(x == y || x == z) && (x != y || x != z)`

   III. `(x == y) != (x == z)`

(A)   None of the three
(B)   I and II only
(C)   II and III only
(D)   I and III only
(E)   I, II, and III

☞ Expression III is the key to the answer: all three expressions state the fact that exactly one out of the two equalities, x == y or x == z, is true. Expression I states that either the first and not the second or the second and not the first is true. Expression II states that one of the two is true and one of the two is false. Expression III simply states that they have different values. All three boil down to the same thing. The answer is E. ☜

De Morgan's Laws

The exam is likely to include questions on De Morgan's Laws:

> !(a && b) is the same as !a || !b
> !(a || b) is the same as !a && !b

4

The expression !((x <= y) && (y > 5)) is equivalent to which of the following?

(A) (x <= y) && (y > 5)
(B) (x <= y) || (y > 5)
(C) (x >= y) || (y < 5)
(D) (x > y) || (y <= 5)
(E) (x > y) && (y <= 5)

☞ The given expression is pretty long, so if you try to plug in specific numbers you may lose a lot of time. Use De Morgan's Laws instead:

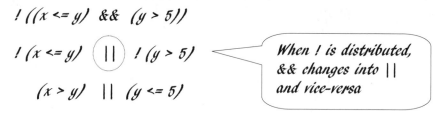

> *When ! is distributed, && changes into || and vice-versa*

The answer is D. ☜

Short-circuit evaluation

> **An important thing to remember about the logical operators && and || is *short-circuit evaluation*. If the value of the first operand is sufficient to determine the result, then the second operand is <u>not</u> evaluated.**

5

Consider the following code segment:

```
int x = 0, y = 3;
String op = "/";

if (op.equals("/") && (x != 0) && (y/x > 2))
{
  System.out.println("OK");
}
else
{
  System.out.println("Failed");
}
```

Which of the following statements about this code is true?

(A)   There will be a compile error because `String` and `int` variables are intermixed in the same condition.
(B)   There will be a run-time divide-by-zero error.
(C)   The code will compile and execute without error; the output will be `OK`.
(D)   The code will compile and execute without error; the output will be `Failed`.
(E)   The code will compile and execute without error; there will be no output.

☞   Choices A and E are just filler answers. Since `x` is equal to 0, the condition cannot be true, so C should be rejected, too. The question remains whether it crashes or executes. In Java, once `x != 0` fails, the rest of the condition, `y/x > 2`, won't be evaluated, and `y/x` won't be computed. The answer is D. ✍

The relational expressions in the above question are parenthesized. This is not necessary because relational operators always take precedence over logical operators. If you are used to lots of parentheses, use them, but you can skip them as well. For example, the Boolean expression from Question 5 can be written with fewer parentheses:

```
if (op.equals("/") && x != 0 && y/x > 2) ...
```

`&&` also takes precedence over `||`, but it's clearer to use parentheses when `&&` and `||` appear in the same expression. For example:

```
if ((0 < a && a < top) || (0 < b && b < top)) ...
```

_____ *Bitwise logical operators* _____

> **The bitwise logical operators, &, |, ^, and ~, are <u>not</u> in the AP Java subset and are <u>not</u> tested on the AP exam. You don't have to worry about them.**

Programmers use these operators to perform logical operations on individual bits, usually in `int` values. Unfortunately, Java also allows you to apply these operators to `boolean` values, and, when used that way, these operators do not comply with short-circuit evaluation. This may lead to a nasty bug if you inadvertently write `&` instead of `&&` or `|` instead of `||`. For example,

```
if (x != 0 & y/x > 2)
```

*Error: & instead of && *

results in a division by 0 exception when `x = 0`.

2.2   Conditional Statements and Loops

> **You can use simplified indentation for `if-else-if` statements.**

For example:

```
if (score >= 70)
  grade = 5;
else if (score >= 60)
  grade = 4;
...
else
  grade = 1;
```

But don't forget braces and proper indentation for nested `if`s. For example:

```
if (exam.equals("Calculus AB"))
{
  if (score >= 60)
    grade = 5;
  else if ...
    ...
}
else if (exam.equals("Calculus BC"))
{
  if (score >= 70)
    grade = 5;
  else if ...
    ...
}
```

6

Consider the following code segment, where m is a variable of the type int:

```
if (m > 0)
{
  if ((1000 / m) % 2 == 0)
    System.out.println("even");
  else
    System.out.println("odd");
}
else
  System.out.println("not positive");
```

Which of the following code segments are equivalent to the one above (that is, produce the same output as the one above regardless of the value of m)?

I.
```
if (m <= 0)
  System.out.println("not positive");
else if ((1000 / m) % 2 == 0)
  System.out.println("even");
else
  System.out.println("odd");
```

II.
```
if (m > 0 && (1000 / m) % 2 == 0)
  System.out.println("even");
else if (m <= 0)
  System.out.println("not positive");
else
  System.out.println("odd");
```

III.
```
if ((1000 / m) % 2 == 0)
{
  if (m <= 0)
    System.out.println("not positive");
  else
    System.out.println("even");
}
else
{
  if (m <= 0)
    System.out.println("not positive");
  else
    System.out.println("odd");
}
```

(A) I only
(B) II only
(C) I and II only
(D) II and III only
(E) I, II, and III

☞ Segment I can actually be reformatted as:

```
if (m <= 0)
  System.out.println("not positive");
else
{
  if ((1000 / m) % 2 == 0)
    System.out.println("even");
  else
    System.out.println("odd");
}
```

So it's the same as the given segment with the condition negated and `if` and `else` swapped. Segment II restructures the sequence, but gives the same result. To see that, we can try different combinations of true/false for `m <= 0` and `(1000 / m) % 2 == 0`. Segment III would work, too, but it has a catch: it doesn't work when `m` is equal to 0. The answer is C. ◪

_____ `for` *and* `while` *loops* _____

The `for` loop,

```
for (initialize; condition; change)
{
   ...   // Do something
}
```

is equivalent to the `while` loop:

```
initialize;
while (condition)
{
   ...   // Do something
   change;
}
```

change can mean any change in the values of the variables that control the loop, such as incrementing or decrementing an index or a counter.

`for` loops are often shorter and more idiomatic than `while` loops in many situations. For example:

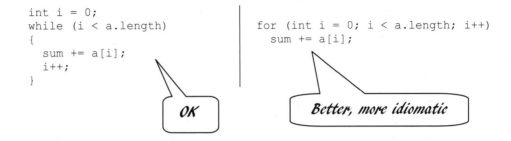

```
int i = 0;
while (i < a.length)
{
    sum += a[i];
    i++;
}
```
OK

```
for (int i = 0; i < a.length; i++)
    sum += a[i];
```
Better, more idiomatic

> **In a `for` or `while` loop, the condition is evaluated at the beginning of the loop and the program does not go inside the loop if the condition is false. Thus, the body of the loop may be skipped entirely if the condition is false at the very beginning.**

7

Consider the following methods:

```
public int fun1(int n)
{
    int product = 1;
    for (int k = 2; k <= n; k++)
    {
        product *= k;
    }
    return product;
}
```

```
public int fun2(int n)
{
    int product = 1;
    int k = 2;
    while (k <= n)
    {
        product *= k;
        k++;
    }
    return product;
}
```

For which integer values of n do `fun1(n)` and `fun2(n)` return the same result?

(A)   Only n > 1
(B)   Only n < 1
(C)   Only n == 1
(D)   Only n >= 1
(E)   Any integer n

☞   The best approach here is purely formal: since the initialization, condition, and increment in the `for` loop in `fun1` are the same as the ones used with the `while` loop in `fun2`, the two methods are equivalent. The answer is E.   ⏎

8

Consider the following code segment:

```
while (x > y)
{
  x--;
  y++;
}
System.out.println(x - y);
```

Assume that x and y are int variables and their values satisfy the conditions $0 \leq x \leq 2$ and $0 \leq y \leq 2$. Which of the following describes the set of all possible outputs?

(A)   0
(B)   –1, 1
(C)   –1, –2
(D)   0, –1, –2
(E)   0, –1, 1, –2, 2

☞ If $x \leq y$ to begin with, then the while loop is never entered and the possible outputs are 0, –1, and –2 (for the pairs (0, 0), (0, 1), (0, 2), (1, 1), (1, 2), (2, 2)). If $x > y$, then the loop is entered and after the loop we must have $x \leq y$, so $x - y$ cannot be positive. The answer is D.

OBOBs

When coding loops, beware of the so-called "off-by-one bugs" ("OBOBs"). These are mistakes of running through the loop one time too many or one time too few.

9

Suppose the `isPrime` method is defined:

```
// Returns true if p is a prime, false otherwise.
// Precondition: p >= 2
public static boolean isPrime(int p) { < implementation not shown > }
```

Given

```
int n = 101;
int sum = 0;
```

which of the following code segments correctly computes the sum of all prime numbers from 2 to 101, inclusive?

(A)
```
while (n != 2)
{
  n--;
  if (isPrime(n)) sum += n;
}
```

(B)
```
while (n >= 2)
{
  n--;
  if (isPrime(n)) sum += n;
}
```

(C)
```
while (n != 2)
{
  if (isPrime(n)) sum += n;
  n--;
}
```

(D)
```
while (n >= 2)
{
  if (isPrime(n)) sum += n;
  n--;
}
```

(E)
```
while (n >= 2 && isPrime(n))
{
  sum += n;
  n--;
}
```

☞ It is bad style to start the body of a loop with a decrement, so Choices A and B are most likely wrong. Indeed, both A and B miss 101 (which happens to be a prime) because n is decremented too early. In addition, Choice B eventually calls isPrime(1), violating isPrime's precondition. Choice C misses 2 — an OBOB on the other end. Choice E might look plausible for a moment, but it actually quits as soon as it encounters the first non-prime number. The answer is D. ☜

The "for each" loop

The "for each" loop (also known as "enhanced loop") has the form

```
for (SomeType x : a)  // read: "for each x in a"
{
   ...   // do something
}
```

where a is an array or an ArrayList (or another type of list or "collection") that holds values of *SomeType*.

For example:

```
int[] scores = {87, 95, 76};
for (int score : scores)
  System.out.print(score + " ");
```

works the same way as

```
int[] scores = {87, 95, 76};
for (int i = 0; i < scores.length; i++)
{
  int score = scores[i];
  System.out.print(score + " ");
}
```

Both will display

```
87 95 76
```

Another example:

```
ArrayList<String> plants = new ArrayList<String>();
plants.add("Bougainvillea");
plants.add("Hibiscus");
plants.add("Poinciana");

for (String name : plants)
  System.out.print(name + " ");
```

will display

```
Bougainvillea Hibiscus Poinciana
```

Notice that the "for each" loop traverses the array or list only in the forward direction and does not give you access to the indices of the values stored in the array or list. For example, a "for each" loop won't be very useful if you need to find the <u>position</u> of the first occurrence of a target value in a list.

If you need access to indices, use a `for` or `while` loop.

A "for each" loop does not allow you to set an element of an array to a new value, because it works with a <u>copy</u> of the element's value, and so the original values of an array will remain unchanged.

For example, given an `int` array `arr`,

```
for (int x : arr)
  x = 1;
```

will leave `arr` unchanged.

If you need to replace or delete elements in an array or `ArrayList`, use an indexed (regular) `for` or `while` loop.

If an array or `ArrayList` holds objects, then you can call an object's method inside a "for each" loop, so you can potentially change an object's state if the method changes it.

You cannot add or remove elements from an `ArrayList` while traversing it with a "for each" loop.

If you attempt to add an element to an `ArrayList` or remove an element from an `ArrayList` while traversing it with a "for each" loop, your code will throw a `ConcurrentModificationException`.

_____ break *and* return *in loops* _____

In Java it is okay to use break and return inside loops. return immediately quits the method from any place inside or outside a loop. This may be a convenient shortcut, especially when you have to quit a method from within a nested loop. For example:

```
// Returns true if all values in list are different, false otherwise
public boolean allDifferent(int[] list)
{
  for (int i = 0; i < list.length; i++)
    for (int j = i + 1; j < list.length; j++)
      if (list[i] == list[j])
        return false;
  return true;
}
```

You can also use break, but it may be dangerous and is not in the AP Java subset. Remember that in a nested loop, break takes you out of the inner loop but not out of the outer loop. Avoid redundant, verbose, and incorrect code such as this:

```
// Returns true if all values in list are different, false otherwise
public boolean allDifferent(int[] list)
{
  boolean foundDuplicates;

  for (int i = 0; i < list.length; i++)
  {
    for (int j = i + 1; j < list.length; j++)
    {
      if (list[i] == list[j])
      {
        foundDuplicates = true;
        break;
      }
      else
      {
        foundDuplicates = false;
      }
    }
  }
  if (foundDuplicates == true)
    return false;
  else
    return true;
}
```

Out of the inner for *but still in the outer* for.

If you insist on using Boolean flags, you need to be extra careful:

```java
// Returns true if all values in list are different, false otherwise
public boolean allDifferent(int[] list)
{
  boolean foundDuplicates = false;

  for (int i = 0; i < list.length; i++)
  {
    for (int j = i + 1; j < list.length; j++)
    {
      if (list[i] == list[j])
      {
        foundDuplicates = true;
        break;
      }
    }
  }
  return !foundDuplicates;
}
```

The `continue` statement is not in the AP Java subset and should be avoided.

2.3   Strings

In Java, a string is an object of the type `String`, and, as with other types of objects, a `String` variable holds a reference to (the address of) the string.

Strings are immutable: no string method can change the string.

An assignment statement

```java
str1 = str2;
```

copies the reference from `str2` into `str1`, so they both refer to the same memory location.

A *literal string* is a string of characters within double quotes. A literal string may include the "escape sequences" \n (newline), \" (a double quote), \\ (one backslash), and other escapes. For example,

```java
System.out.print("Hello\n");
```

has the same effect as

```java
System.out.println("Hello");
```

The `String` class supports the + and += operators for concatenating strings.

> **`String` is the only class in Java that supports special syntax for using operators on its objects (only + and +=).**

The operator

```
s1 += s2;
```

appends `s2` to `s1`. In reality it creates a new string by concatenating `s1` and `s2` and then sets `s1` to refer to the new string. It is equivalent to

```
s1 = s1 + s2;
```

10

What is the output of the following code segment?

```
String str1 = "Happy ";
String str2 = str1;
str2 += "New Year! ";
str2.substring(6);
System.out.println(str1 + str2);
```

(A)   Happy New Year!
(B)   Happy Happy New Year!
(C)   Happy New Year! New Year!
(D)   Happy New Year! Happy New Year!
(E)   Happy New Year! Happy

After `str2 = str1`, `str1` and `str2` point to the same memory location that contains `"Happy "`. But after `str2 += "New Year! "`, these variables point to different things: `str1` remains `"Happy "` (strings are immutable) while `str2` becomes `"Happy New Year! "`. `str2.substring(6)` does not change `str2` — it calls its `substring` method but does not use the returned value (a common beginner's mistake: again, strings are immutable). The answer is B.

String *methods*

The `String` methods included in the AP Java subset are:

```
int length()
boolean equals(Object other)
int compareTo(String other)
String substring(int from)
String substring(int from, int to)
int indexOf(String s)
```

> **Always use the `equals` method to compare a string to another string. The == and != operators, applied to two strings, compare their <u>addresses</u>, not their values.**

`str1.equals(str2)` returns `true` if and only if `str1` and `str2` have the same values (that is, consist of the same characters in the same order).

`str1.compareTo(str2)` returns a positive number if `str1` is greater than `str2` (<u>lexicographically</u>), zero if they are equal, and a negative number if `str1` is less than `str2`.

`str.substring(from)` returns a substring of `str` starting at the `from` position to the end, and `str.substring(from, to)` returns `str`'s substring starting at the `from` position and up to but <u>not including</u> the `to` position (so the length of the returned substring is `to - from`). Positions are counted from 0. For example, `"Happy".substring(1, 4)` would return `"app"`.

`str.indexOf(s)` returns the starting position of the first occurrence of the substring `s` in `str`, or `-1` if not found.

11

Consider the following method:

```
public String process(String msg, String delim)
{
    int pos = msg.indexOf(delim);
    while (pos >= 0)
    {
        msg = msg.substring(0, pos) + " "
                        + msg.substring(pos + delim.length());
        pos = msg.indexOf(delim);
    }
    return msg;
}
```

What is the output of the following code segment?

```
String rhyme = "Twinkle\ntwinkle\nlittle star";
String rhyme2 = process(rhyme, "\n");
System.out.println(rhyme + "\n" + rhyme2);
```

(A) little star
     Twinkle twinkle little star

(B) little star
     Twinkle
     twinkle
     little star

(C) Twinkle
     twinkle
     little star
     Twinkle winkle ittle tar

(D) Twinkle
     twinkle
     little star
     Twinkle twinkle
     little star

(E) Twinkle
     twinkle
     little star
     Twinkle twinkle little star

➢ process receives and works with a <u>copy</u> of a reference to the original string (see Section 3.3). The method can reassign the copy, as it does here, but the original reference still refers to the same string. This consideration, combined with the immutability of strings, assures us that rhyme remains unchanged after the call process(rhyme).

The rhyme string includes two newline characters, and, when printed, it produces

```
Twinkle
twinkle
little star
```

So the only possible answers are C, D, or E. Notice that we can come to this conclusion before we even look at the process method! This method repeatedly finds the first occurrence of delim in msg, cuts it out, and replaces it with a space. No other characters are replaced or lost. The resulting message prints on one line. The answer is E. ⬦

2.4 Integer and Double Classes

In Java, variables of primitive data types (int, double, and so on) are not objects. In some situations it is convenient to represent numbers as objects. For example, you might want to store numeric values in an ArrayList (see Section 2.6), but the elements of an ArrayList must be objects. The java.lang package provides several "wrapper" classes that represent primitive data types as objects. Two of these classes, Integer and Double, are in the AP Java subset.

The Integer class has a constructor that takes an int value and creates an Integer object representing that value. The <u>intValue</u> method of an <u>Integer</u> object returns the value represented by that object as an int. For example:

```
Integer obj = new Integer(123);
...
int num = obj.intValue();   // num gets the value of 123
```

Likewise, Double's constructor creates a Double object that represents a given double value. The method doubleValue returns the double represented by a Double object:

```
Double obj = new Double(123.45);
...
double x = obj.doubleValue();   // x gets the value of 123.45
```

The `Integer` class also provides two symbolic constants that describe the range for `int` values:

```
public static final int MIN_VALUE = -2147483648;
public static final int MAX_VALUE = 2147483647;
```

> **Use the `equals` method of the `Integer` or of the `Double` class if you want to compare two `Integer` or two `Double` variables, respectively.**

For example:

```
Integer a = new Integer(...);
Integer b = new Integer(...);
...
if (a.equals(b))
   ...
```

If you apply a relational operator `==` or `!=` to two `Integer` or two `Double` variables, you will compare their addresses, not values. This is rarely, if ever, what you want to do.

Both `Integer` and `Double` classes have a `compareTo` method. As usual, `obj1.compareTo(obj2)` returns a positive integer if `obj1` is greater than `obj2` (that is, `obj1`'s numeric value is greater than `obj2`'s numeric value), a negative integer if `obj1` is less than `obj2`, and zero if their numeric values are equal.

Autoboxing/unboxing

The Java compiler in certain situations automatically converts values of primitive data types (`int`, `double`, and so on) into the corresponding wrapper types (`Integer`, `Double`, and so on). This feature is called *autoboxing*. For example, in

```
ArrayList<Integer> numbers = new ArrayList<Integer>();
numbers.add(5);
```

the second line is compiled as

```
numbers.add(new Integer(5));
```

Likewise, where appropriate, the compiler performs *unboxing*. For example,

```
int num = numbers.get(0);
```

in effect compiles as

```
int num = numbers.get(0).intValue();
```

> **Autoboxing and unboxing are included in the AP Java subset, but are unlikely to be tested separately.**

2.5   Arrays

There are two ways to declare and create a one-dimensional array:

```
SomeType[] a = new SomeType[size];
SomeType[] b = {value_0, value_1, ..., value_{n-1}};
```

For example:

```
double[] samples = new double[100];
int[] numbers = {1, 2, 3};
String[] cities = {"Atlanta", "Boston", "Cincinnati", "Dallas"};
```

The first declaration declares an array of `double`s of size 100. Its elements get default values (zeros). The second declaration creates an array of `int`s of size 3 with its elements initialized to the values 1, 2, and 3. The third declaration declares and initializes an array of four given strings.

We can refer to `a`'s elements as `a[i]`, where `a` is the name of the array and `i` is an index (subscript), which can be an integer constant, variable, or expression.

> **Indices start from 0.**

`a.length` refers to the size of the array. (In an array, `length` is not a method, but rather works like a public instance variable, hence <u>no parentheses</u>.)

> **`a[a.length-1]` refers to the last element.**

Once an array is created, its size cannot be changed. The only way to expand an array is to create a bigger array and copy the contents of the original array into the new one. The old array is discarded (or, more precisely, recycled by a process called *garbage collection*).

For example:

```
int[] a = new int[100];
...
int[] temp = new int[a.length * 2];

for (int i = 0; i < a.length; i++)
  temp[i] = a[i];

a = temp;    // reassign a to the new array; the old array is discarded
```

If a and b are arrays, a = b does not copy elements from b into a: it just reassigns the reference a to b, so that both a and b refer to the same array.

The following method reverses the order of elements in an array of strings:

```
public void reverse(String[] words)
{
  int i = 0, j = words.length - 1;

  while (i < j)
  {
    String temp = words[i]; words[i] = words[j]; words[j] = temp;
    i++;
    j--;
  }
}
```

The Java Virtual Machine (the run-time interpreter) checks that an array index is within the valid range, from 0 to `array.length-1`. If an index value is invalid, the interpreter "throws" an `ArrayIndexOutOfBoundsException` — reports a run-time error, the line number for the offending program statement, and a trace of the method calls that led to it.

An *exception* is a run-time error, not a compile-time error.

The compiler cannot catch errors that will be caused by certain circumstances that occur during program execution, such as a variable used as an array index whose value has gone out of the allowed range.

12

Suppose the method `int sign(int x)` returns 1 if x is positive, −1 if x is negative, and 0 if x is 0. Given

```
int[] nums = {-2, -1, 0, 1, 2};
```

what are the values of the elements of nums after the following code is executed?

```
for (int k = 0; k < nums.length; k++)
{
  nums[k] -= sign(nums[k]);
  nums[k] += sign(nums[k]);
}
```

(A) −2, −1, 0, 1, 2
(B) −1, 0, 0, 0, 1
(C) 0, 0, 0, 0, 0
(D) −2, 0, 0, 2, 3
(E) −2, 0, 0, 0, 2

👉 Remember that the first statement within the loop changes nums[k], which may change the sign of nums[k], too. Jot down a little table:

Before		After −=		After +=
a[k]	sign of a[k]	a[k]	sign of a[k]	a[k]
-2	-1	-1	-1	-2
-1	-1	0	0	0
0	0	0	0	0
1	1	0	0	0
2	1	1	1	2

The answer is E. 🔖

13

Consider the following method:

```
// Returns true if there are no two elements among
// counts[0], ... counts[n-1], whose values are the same
// or are consecutive integers; otherwise, returns false.
// Precondition: counts contains n values, n > 1
public boolean isSparse(int[] counts, int n)
{
  < missing code >
}
```

Which of the following code segments can be used to replace < *missing code* > so that the method isSparse works as specified?

I.
```
for (int j = 0; j < n; j++)
{
  for (int k = j + 1; k < n; k++)
  {
    int diff = counts[j] - counts[k];
    if (diff >= -1 && diff <= 1)
      return false;
  }
}
return true;
```

II.
```
for (int j = 1; j < n; j++)
{
  for (int k = 0; k < j; k++)
  {
    int diff = counts[j] - counts[k];
    if (diff >= -1 && diff <= 1)
      return false;
  }
}
return true;
```

III.
```
for (int j = 0; j < n; j++)
{
  for (int k = 1; k < n; k++)
  {
    int diff = counts[j] - counts[k];
    if (Math.abs(diff) <= 1)
      return false;
  }
}
return true;
```

(A)   I only
(B)   II only
(C)   I and II only
(D)   I and III only
(E)   I, II, and III

☞   Notice that in this question not all `counts.length` elements of `counts` are used, just the first n. Their subscripts range from 0 to n-1. The precondition states that n > 1, so there is no need to worry about an empty array or an array of just one element. Looking at the inner loop in each segment you can quickly see that they work the same way. So the difference is how the loops are set up; more precisely, the limits within which the indices vary. In Option I the outer loop starts with the first item in the list; the inner loop compares it with each of the subsequent items. In Option II the outer loop starts with the second item in the list; the inner loop compares it with each of the preceding items. Both of these are correct and quite standard in similar algorithms. This eliminates A, B, and D. Option III at first seems harmless, too, but it has a catch: the inner loop doesn't set a limit for k that depends on j, so when j is greater than 0, k may eventually take the same value as j (such as j = 1, k = 1). The method will erroneously detect the same value in `counts` when it is actually comparing an item to itself. The answer is C.   ☜

Array return type

Occasionally you may need to return an array from a method. Suppose you want to restructure the `reverse` method above so that it <u>returns</u> a new array containing the values from a given array in reverse order. The original array remains unchanged. The method can be coded as follows:

```
public String[] reverse(String[] words)
{
  String[] result = new String[words.length];

  for (int i = 0; i < words.length; i++)
    result[i] = words[words.length - 1 - i];

  return result;
}
```

Two-dimensional arrays

The AP Java subset includes rectangular two-dimensional arrays. These are similar to one-dimensional arrays but use two indices, one for the row and one for the column. For example:

```
double[][] matrix = new double[3][5]; // 3 rows by 5 cols
int r, c;
...
matrix[r][c] = 1.23;
```

> **In fact, a two-dimensional array is an array of arrays, its rows. If m is a two-dimensional array, m[0] is its first row, m[1] is the second row, and so forth.**

Therefore,

> **if m is a two-dimensional array, m.length represents the number of rows.**

m[k].length represents the length of the *k*-th row.

> **Only rectangular 2D arrays are considered in the AP Java subset; therefore, the lengths of all the rows are the same. m[0].length represents the number of columns.**

The following method calculates the sums of the values in each column of a 2D array, places these sums into a new 1D array of sums, and returns that array:

```
// Returns a 1D array containing sums of all the values
// in each column of table
public double[] totalsByColumn(double[][] table)
{
  int nRows = table.length;
  int nCols = table[0].length;
  double[] totals = new double[nCols];

  for (int c = 0; c < nCols; c++)
  {
    totals[c] = 0.0;   // optional: default
    for (int r = 0; r < nRows; r++)
      totals[c] += table[r][c];
  }
  return totals;
}
```

14

Consider the following code segment:

```
String[][] m = new String[6][3];
                  for each row
for (int k = 0; k < m.length; k++)
{
  m[k][m[0].length - 1] = "*";
}
```

Which of the following best describes the result when this code segment is executed?

(A)   All elements in the first row of m are set to "*"
(B)   All elements in the last row of m are set to "*"
(C)   All elements in the last column of m are set to "*"
(D)   The code has no effect
(E)   `ArrayIndexOutOfBoundsException` is reported

☞   The first index is the row, and the `for` loop is set up for all rows. The answer is C. ☜

> **Since a two-dimensional array is an array of one-dimensional arrays, a naive "for each" loop won't work for traversing a 2D array.**

To make a "for each" loop work on a 2D array, you need nested loops. For example:

```
int[][] a = {{1, 2, 3}, {4, 5, 6}};

for (int[] row : a)
{
  for (int x : row)
    System.out.print(x + " ");

  System.out.println();
}
```

2.6   The `ArrayList` Class

`java.util.ArrayList<E>` is a Java library class that defines a list of objects of some type *E*.[*]

For example, assuming the class `Student` is defined,

```
ArrayList<Student> list = new ArrayList<Student>();
```

defines an `ArrayList` of `Student` objects.

> **An `ArrayList` cannot hold values of a primitive data type. For instance, `ArrayList<int>` or `ArrayList<double>` will result in a syntax error.**

However, an `int` or `double` value can be added to an `ArrayList<Integer>` or `ArrayList<Double>`, respectively, due to autoboxing. For example:

```
ArrayList<Double> prices = new ArrayList<Double>();
prices.add(29.95);
```

`ArrayList` provides methods for getting and setting the value of a particular element, adding a value at the end of the list, removing a value, and inserting a value at a given position. As in standard arrays, indices start from 0.

An `ArrayList` is automatically resized when it runs out of space for added elements. `ArrayList`'s "no-args" constructor (that is, the constructor that takes no parameters) allocates an array of some default initial capacity and sets the size to 0 (no values stored in the `ArrayList` yet). As values are added, their number may exceed the current capacity. Then a new array is allocated with twice the capacity, the old values are copied into the new array, and the old array is discarded. All this happens behind the scenes — you don't have to worry about any of it.

The AP Java subset includes the following methods of `ArrayList<E>`:

---

[*] Another Java library class that represents a list, `java.util.LinkedList<E>`, is not included in the AP Java subset and not tested on AP CSA exams.

`int size()`	Returns the number of values currently stored in the list
`boolean add(E x)`	Adds x at the end of the list; returns `true`
`E get(int index)`	Returns the value stored at `index`
`E set(int index, E x)`	Sets the value of the element at `index` to x; returns the old value stored at `index`
`E remove(int index)`	Removes the value at `index` and shifts the subsequent values toward the beginning of the list; reduces the size by one; returns the old value stored at `index`
`void add(int index, E x)`	Inserts x at `index`, shifting the current value stored at `index` and all the subsequent values toward the end of the list; increases the size by one

The `add` and `remove` methods adjust the size of the `ArrayList` appropriately. The methods that take an `index` parameter check that the index is in the valid range, from 0 to `size()-1` (or 0 to `size()` for `add(x)`) and "throw" an `IndexOutOfBoundsException` if the index is not in that range.

It might be helpful for you to know and use on the AP exam three additional methods of `ArrayList`, which are not in the AP Java subset:

`boolean contains(Object obj)`	Returns `true` if one of the elements in the list is equal to `obj`
`int indexOf(Object obj)`	Returns the index of the first occurrence of `obj` in the list, or –1, if the list does not contain `obj`
`boolean remove(Object obj)`	If the list contains `obj`, removes the first occurrence of `obj` and returns `true`; otherwise returns `false`

Since the compiler knows what type of objects are stored in an `ArrayList`, it automatically casts values retrieved from the list into their type. For example:

```
ArrayList<Fish> list = new ArrayList<Fish>();
...
Fish f = list.get(i);
```

15

What is the output of the following code segment?

```
ArrayList<String> list = new ArrayList<String>();
list.add("A");
list.add("B");
list.add("C");
list.add("D");
list.add("E");

for (int k = 1; k <= 3; k++)
{
  list.remove(1);
}

for (int k = 1; k <= 3; k++)
{
  list.add(1, "*");
}

for (String word : list)
{
  System.out.print(word + " ");
}
```

(A)   A C D E * * *
(B)   * * * B C D E
(C)   A * * * E
(D)   A E * * *
(E)   IndexOutOfBoundsException

☞   This question is not as tricky as it might seem. First we create an empty list and add five values to it: "A", "B", "C", "D", "E". Then we remove the value at index 1 three times. This is the second element and each time we remove it, the subsequent values are shifted toward the beginning by one position. "A" and "E" remain. Then we insert three asterisks. Notice that we always insert at index 1. After the first insertion we get "A", "*", "E". After the second we get "A", "*", "*", "E". The third insertion produces "A", "*", "*", "*", "E". The third loop (a "for each" loop) traverses the list and prints out the values. The answer is C. ☈

Chapter 3   Java Features, Part 2

3.1   Classes

A Java program consists of classes. The term *class* refers to a class of objects.

You should know the following concepts and terms:

Class
Object
Instance of a class
Constructor
new operator
Instance variables
Private and *public* instance variables
    and methods

Encapsulation and *information hiding*
Static methods and variables
Public static final constants
Accessor method
Mutator (*modifier*) method
Client of a class

An <u>object</u> that belongs to a <u>particular class</u> is also called an *instance* of that class, and the process of creating an object is called *instantiation*.

A class definition includes *constructors*, *methods*, and instance or static variables (data fields). The constructors describe how objects of the class can be created; the methods describe what an object of this class can do; the *instance variables* describe the object's attributes — the current state of an object.

Constructors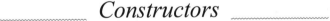

Constructors describe ways to create an object of a class and initialize the object's instance variables.

> **All constructors have the same name as the class. Constructors do not have any return data type, not even void.**

A constructor may take parameters that help define a new object. A constructor that takes no parameters is called a "no-args" constructor.

> **The term *parameter* is often interchangeable with the term *argument* (as in *function argument* in math), especially when it refers to the actual values passed to a constructor or method.**

Hence such usage as "no-args" constructor, `IllegalArgumentException`, or `main(String[] args)`. The CED seems to favor "parameter," and so do we.

A new object is created using the `new` operator. For example, suppose you have defined a class `School`:

```
public class School
{
  // constructor
  public School(String name, int numStudents) { < code not shown > }
  ...
}
```

Then you can create a `School` object in a *client class* (a class that uses `School` objects), declare a variable of the type `School`, and set it equal to a reference to the newly created object. For example:

```
School sch1 = new School("Gifted and Talented Magnet", 1200);
```

If a class has instance variables `name` and `numStudents` —

```
public class School
{
  ...
  private String name;
  private int numStudents;
}
```

— the constructor can set them to the values of the parameters passed to it:

```
public School(String nm, int num)
{
  name = nm;
  numStudents = num;
}
```

Objects that are no longer accessible in the program, that is, no longer referred to by any variable, are automatically destroyed and the memory they occupy is recycled. This mechanism is called *garbage collection*.

public *and* private

Data fields (static and instance variables) and methods may be *public* or *private*.

> **Private fields and methods can be referred to only within the source code of the class they are defined in.**

Public fields and methods are accessible anywhere in the code.

> **The concept of "privacy" applies to the source code of <u>the class as a whole</u> and not to individual objects. Different objects of the same class <u>have full access</u> to each other's fields and methods, and can even modify the values of each other's fields.**

In the AP Java subset, constructors are always public.

> **It is a common practice in OOP (and a requirement on the AP exam) to make <u>all instance variables private</u>.**

Private fields and methods hide the implementation details of a class from other classes, its clients. This concept is known as *encapsulation*. A *client* class uses your class by invoking constructors and calling public methods of your class. In general, it is a good idea to supply as little information to client classes as possible. This concept is known as *information hiding*. For example, if a method is used only internally within a class, it should be made <u>private</u>.

Accessors and mutators

Since all instance variables are private, they are not directly accessible in client classes. It is common to provide special public methods, called *accessors*, that return the values of instance variables. For example:

```
public class School
{
  ...
  public String getName()
  {
    return name;
  }
  ...
}
```

Accessors' names often start with "get." Accessors can have any name, but starting with "get" makes their purpose easier to remember. Accessors do not change the state of the object.

A public method that sets a new value of an instance variable is called a *mutator* (or *modifier*). Mutators' names often start with "set." For example:

```
public class School
{
  ...
  public void setName(String nm)
  {
    name = nm;
  }
  ...
}
```

The "accessor" and "mutator" designations are somewhat informal — a class may have a method that sets an instance variable to a new value and at the same time returns the old value.

─────────────── this ───────────────

The Java keyword this refers to the object whose constructor or method is running. You can pass this as a parameter to a method. For example, suppose a class Student is defined and it has a method that registers this student for a course, which is an ArrayList of students. Something like this:

```
public class Student
{
  ...
  public void register(ArrayList<Student> course)
  {
    course.add(this);
  }
}
```

16

Consider the following class:

```
public class Clock
{
  private int hours;
  private int mins;

  public Clock(int h, int m)
  {
    hours = h;
    mins = m;
  }

  // moves this clock one minute forward
  public void move()
  {
    < missing code >
  }

  public void set(int h, int m)
  {
    hours = h;
    mins = m;
    normalize();
  }

  private void normalize()
  {
    while (mins >= 60)
    {
      mins -= 60;
      hours++;
    }
    hours %= 12;
  }
}
```

Which of the following could replace < *missing code* > in the move method?

I.   `this = new Clock(hours, mins + 1);`

II. `mins++;`
     `normalize();`

III. `set(hours, mins + 1);`

(A) I only
(B) II only
(C) I and II only
(D) II and III only
(E) I, II, and III

☞ Option I is wrong: it attempts to replace `this` with a new object instead of changing this one, which results in a syntax error. The other two options are acceptable: it is okay to access private instance variables and call private and public methods inside the same class. The answer is D.

(Notice that it would be better to add a call to `normalize` in `Clock`'s constructor, too, just to make sure the clock is set correctly, even if `mins` ≥ 60. Alternatively, the constructor could throw an `IllegalArgumentException` if its parameters didn't make sense.) ☜

3.2   Static Variables and Methods

Sometimes an attribute belongs to a class as a whole, not to individual objects (instances) of that class. Such an attribute is represented by a variable called a *static variable*, which is declared with the keyword `static`.

Static variables are used to keep track of a property or quantity shared by all objects of the class. For example:

```
public class School
{
  private static int numSchools = 0; // = 0 is optional: initialized to 0
                                     // by default
  private static int[] totalNationalEnrollmentByGrade;
  ...
}
```

A static variable can also be used to define a public symbolic constant. In that case, the keyword `final` is used in its declaration. For example:

```
public class School
{
  public static final int HIGHEST_GRADE = 12;
  ...
}
```

A class may also have static methods — methods that do not involve any particular instances of a class. For example:

```
public class School
{
  public static final int HIGHEST_GRADE = 12;
  private static int numSchools;
  private static int[] totalNationalEnrollmentByGrade;
  ...
  public static void initializeStatistics()
  {
    numSchools = 0;
    totalNationalEnrollmentByGrade = new int[HIGHEST_GRADE + 1];
                  // +1 for kindergarten
  }
  ...
}
```

Static variables can be initialized in a class constructor and they can be accessed and modified in instance methods. For example:

```
public class School
{
  // Static variables:
  public static final int HIGHEST_GRADE = 12;
  private static int numSchools;
  private static int[] totalNationalEnrollmentByGrade;

  // Static methods:
  public static int getNationalEnrollment(int grade)
  {
    return totalNationalEnrollmentByGrade[grade];
  }
  ...

  // Instance variables:
  private int[] enrollmentByGrade;
  ...

  // Constructor:
  public School(int[] numStudents)
  {
    numSchools++;

    enrollmentByGrade = new int[HIGHEST_GRADE + 1];

    for (int grade = 0; grade <= HIGHEST_GRADE; grade++)
    {
      enrollmentByGrade[grade] = numStudents[grade];
      totalNationalEnrollmentByGrade[grade] += numStudents[grade];
    }
    ...
  }

  // Instance methods:
  public void enrollOneStudent(int grade)
  {
    enrollmentByGrade[grade]++;
    totalNationalEnrollmentByGrade[grade]++;
  }
  ...
}
```

> **Static methods cannot access or modify any instance variables and cannot refer to this, because this is undefined when a static method is running.**

17

Consider a class with the following fields:

```
public class TestPow2
{
  private static int[] powersOfTwo = {1, 2, 4, 8, 16};
  private int num;
  ...
}
```

Which of the following methods inside the TestPow2 class will compile with no errors?

I.
```
public int pow2()
{
  return powersOfTwo[num];
}
```

II.
```
public static int pow2(int x)
{
  return powersOfTwo[x];
}
```

III.
```
public static int pow2()
{
  return powersOfTwo[num];
}
```

(A) I only
(B) II only
(C) I and II only
(D) II and III only
(E) I, II, and III

☞ The code in Option I would compile, because here an instance (non-static) method pow2 can work with both the instance variable num and the static variable powersOfTwo. The code in Option II would compile, too, because here a static method pow2 works only with its own parameter and the static variable powersOfTwo. The code in Option III would cause a syntax error, because a static method pow2 attempts to access the instance variable num. The answer is C.

The Java library class `Math` has static methods `abs`, `sqrt`, `pow`, `random`. For your convenience, it also includes the `public static final` "variables" `Math.PI` (which represents π, the ratio of a circle's circumference to its diameter) and `Math.E` (which represents e, the base of the natural logarithm). It might be useful (but not required) for you to know that `Math` also has static methods `min` and `max`, which return the smaller and the larger, respectively, of two numbers (`int`s or `double`s).

Outside the class, public static methods are called and public static constants are accessed using the dot notation, with the class's name as the prefix. For example:

```
double volume = 4.0 / 3.0 * Math.PI * Math.pow(r, 3);
```

3.3   Calling Methods

In Java, all methods belong to classes.

> **It is universal Java style that all method names start with a lowercase letter.**

An *instance* method is called for a particular object; then the object's name and a dot are used as a prefix in a call, as in `obj.someMethod(...)`. If an object's method calls another method of <u>the same object</u>, the prefix is not needed and you write simply `otherMethod(...)`, which is the same as `this.otherMethod(...)`.

Static methods belong to the class as a whole and are called using the class's name with a dot as a prefix. For example: `Math.max(x, y)` or `School.getNationalEnrollment(...)`.

A method takes a specific number of parameters of specific data types. (A method can be defined with a variable number of parameters, as in `System.out.printf`; however, this feature is not in the AP Java subset.) Some methods take no parameters, such as `ArrayList`'s `size()` or `String`'s `length()`. A method call may include a whole expression as a parameter; then the expression is evaluated first and the result is passed to the method. An expression may include calls to other methods. For example:

```
double x, y;
...
x = Math.sqrt(Math.abs(2*y - 1));
```

A method usually returns a value of the specified data type, but a `void` method does not return any value. The return type is specified in the method's header. The return <u>value</u> is specified in the `return` statement.

> It is considered a serious error (1 point deduction) to read the new values for a method's parameters from `System.in` inside the method. It is also a serious error to print the return value to `System.out` inside a method (when it is not requested) and another serious error to omit a `return` statement in a non-`void` method.

For example:

```
// Returns the sum of all integers from 1 to n.
// Precondition: n >= 1
public int addNumbers(int n)
{
  int sum = 0;

  n = System.in.read();

  for (int k = 1; k <= n; k++)
  {
    sum += k;
  }

  System.out.println(sum);

  return sum;
}
```

Error: n is passed to this method from `main` *or from another calling method*

Error: Not specified in the method description

18

`Math`'s static method `min` returns the value of the smaller of two integers. If a, b, c, and m are integer variables, which of the following best describes the behavior of a program with the following statement?

```
m = Math.min(Math.min(a, c), Math.min(b, c));
```

(A)   The statement has a syntax error and will not compile.
(B)   The program will run but go into an infinite loop.
(C)   a will get the smaller value of a and c; b will get the smaller value of b and c; m will get the smallest value of a, b, and c.
(D)   m will be assigned the smallest of the values a, b, and c.
(E)   None of the above

☞ Any expression of the appropriate data type, including a method call that returns a value of the appropriate data type, may be used in a larger expression or as a parameter to a method. The code above is basically equivalent to:

```
int temp1 = Math.min(a, c);
int temp2 = Math.min(b, c);
m = Math.min(temp1, temp2);
```

So m gets the smallest of the three values. The answer is D. ⏎

Parameters of primitive data types

> **In Java, all parameters of primitive data types are passed to methods "by value."**

When a parameter is passed by value, the method works with a copy of the variable passed to it, so it has no way of changing the value of the original.

19

Consider the following method:

```
public void fun(int a, int b)
{
    a += b;
    b += a;
}
```

What is the output from the following code?

```
int x = 3, y = 5;
fun(x, y);
System.out.println(x + " " + y);
```

(A)   3 5
(B)   3 8
(C)   3 13
(D)   8 8
(E)   8 13

☞ x and y are ints, so they are passed to fun by value. fun works with copies of x and y, named a and b. What is happening inside fun is irrelevant here because x and y do not change after the method call. The answer is A. ⏎

Objects passed to methods

> **All objects are passed to methods as references. A method receives a <u>copy</u> of a reference to (the address of) the object.**

When a variable gets an "object" as a value, what it actually holds is a reference to (the address of) that object. Likewise, when an object is passed to a method, the method receives a copy of the object's address, and therefore it potentially <u>can</u> change the original object. Usually all instance variables of an object are private, so to change the object, the method would have to call one of the object's *mutator* methods.

But notice that the `String`, `Integer`, and `Double` classes represent *immutable* objects, that is, objects without mutator methods. Even though these objects are passed to methods as references, no method can change them. For example, there is no way in Java to write a method

```
// Converts s to upper case
public void toUpperCase(String s)
{
    ...
}
```

because the method has no way of changing the string passed to it. For immutable objects, the method has to create and return a new object with the desired properties:

```
// Returns s converted to upper case
public String toUpperCase(String s)
{
    ...
}
```

Arrays passed to methods

A one- or two-dimensional array is passed to a method as a copy of a reference to the array. So an array is treated like an object.

> **A method can change the values of the elements of an array passed to it as a parameter, but cannot change the size of the array.**

(A method can change the size of an `ArrayList` passed to it as a parameter.)

20

Consider the following method:

```
public void accumulate(int[] a, int n)
{
  while (n < a.length)
  {
    a[n] += a[n-1];
    n++;
  }
}
```

What is the output from the following code?

```
int[] a = {1, 2, 3, 4, 5};
int n = 1;
accumulate(a, n);
for (int k = 0; k < a.length; k++)
  System.out.print(a[k] + " ");
System.out.println(n);
```

(A) 1 2 3 4 5 1
(B) 1 2 3 4 5 5
(C) 1 3 5 7 9 1
(D) 1 3 5 7 9 5
(E) 1 3 6 10 15 1

☞ n is passed to accumulate by value, so accumulate cannot change it. This rules out Choices B and D. (Inside accumulate, n acts like a local variable.) a is passed to accumulate as a reference, so accumulate can change its values. Starting at n = 1, it adds the value of the previous element to the current one. As the name of the method implies, this sets a[k] to the sum of all the elements up to and including a[k] in the original array. The answer is E. ⏎

——————————— return ———————————

A method that is not void must return a value of the designated type using the return statement. return works with any expression, not just variables. For example:

```
return (-b + Math.sqrt(b*b - 4*a*c)) / (2*a);
```

An often overlooked fact is that a boolean method can return the value of a Boolean expression. For example, you can write simply

```
return x >= a && x <= b;
```

as opposed to the redundant and verbose

```
if (x >= a && x <= b)
  return true;
else
  return false;
```

A `void` method can use a `return` (within `if` or `else`) to quit early, but there is no need for a `return` at the end of the method. It is OK to have multiple `return` statements in a method, and often advisable. For example, the following recursive method is well-written:

```
// Returns the index of target in a sorted array
// among a[i], ..., a[j] or -1 if not found
public static int binarySearch(int[] a, int i, int j, int target)
{
  if (i > j)
    return -1;

  int m = (i + j) / 2;
  if (target == a[m])
    return m;

  if (target < a[m])
    return binarySearch(a, i, m-1, target);
  else
    return binarySearch(a, m+1, j, target);
}
```

Returning objects

A method's return type can be a class, and a method can return an object of that class. Often a new object is created in the method and then returned from the method. For example:

```
public String getFullName(String firstName, String lastName)
{
  return firstName + " " + lastName;
}
```

Or:

```
public Location adjacentSouth(Location loc)
{
  int r = loc.getRow(), c = loc.getCol();
  return new Location(r+1, c);
}
```

A method whose return type is a class can also return a `null` (a reference with a zero value, which indicates that it does not refer to any valid object). For example:

```
/** Precondition: listOfNames and listOfAddresses (instance variables
 *  of this class) hold valid data
 */
public String getAddress(String name)
{
  for (int i = 0; i < listOfNames.length; i++)
  {
    if (listOfNames[i].equals(name))
      return listOfAddresses[i];
  }
  return null; // not found
}
```

If a method returns an `ArrayList`, write the full `ArrayList` type, including its elements' type in angle brackets, as the method's return type. For example:

```
public ArrayList<Integer> getCourseNumbers()
{
  ArrayList<Integer> courseNumbers = new ArrayList<Integer>();
  ...
  return courseNumbers;
}
```

Overloaded methods

Methods of the same class with the same name but different numbers or types of parameters are called *overloaded* methods. (The order of different types of parameters is important, too.)

> **The compiler treats overloaded methods as different methods. It figures out which one to call depending on the number, the types, and the order of the parameters.**

The `String` class, for example, has two forms of the `substring` method:

```
String substring(int from)
String substring(int from, int to)
```

If you call `"Happy".substring(2)` then the first overloaded method will be called, but if you call `"Happy".substring(1, 3)` then the second overloaded method will be called. Another example of overloading is `Math.abs(x)`, which has different versions of the static method `abs`, including `abs(int)` and `abs(double)`. `System.out.print(x)` has overloaded versions for all primitive data types as well as for `String` and `Object`.

The ArrayList class has two overloaded add methods: add(obj), which adds an object obj at the end of the list, and add(index, obj), which inserts obj at a specified index.

Overloading methods is basically a stylistic device. You could instead give different names to different forms of a method, but it would be hard to remember them. Overloaded methods do not have to have the same return type, but often they do, because they perform similar tasks. A different return type alone is not enough to make an overloaded method.

> **All constructors of a class have the same name, so they are overloaded by definition and must differ from each other in the number and/or types of their parameters.**

21

Consider the following class declaration:

```
public class Date
{
  public Date()
  { < implementation not shown > }

  public Date(String monthName, int day, int year)
  { < implementation not shown > }

  public void setDate(int month, int day, int year)
  { < implementation not shown > }

    < fields and other constructors and methods not shown >
}
```

Consider modifying the Date class to make it possible to initialize variables of the type Date with month (given as a month name or number), day, and year information when they are declared, as well as to set their values later using the method setDate. For example, the following code segment should define and initialize three Date variables:

```
Date d1 = new Date();
d1.setDate("May", 11, 2006);
Date d2 = new Date("June", 30, 2010);
Date d3 = new Date(6, 30, 2010);
```

Which of the following best describes the additional features that should be present?

(A)   An overloaded version of `setDate` with three `int` parameters
(B)   An overloaded version of `setDate` with one `String` and two `int` parameters
(C)   A constructor with three `int` parameters
(D)   Both an overloaded version of `setDate` with three `int` parameters and a constructor with three `int` parameters
(E)   Both an overloaded version of `setDate` with one `String` and two `int` parameters and a constructor with three `int` parameters

☞ This is a wordy but simple question. Just match the declarations against the provided class features:

```
Date d1 = new Date();              ──────────  ✓ Date()

Date d2 = new Date("June", 30, 2010);  ───  ✓ Date(String, int, int)

Date d3 = new Date(6, 30, 2010);   ─────────   Date(int, int, int)

d1.setDate("May", 11, 2004);       ─────────   void setDate(String, int, int)

            not used               ─────────  ✓ void setDate(int, int, int)
```

As we can see, what's missing in the class definition is a constructor with three `int` parameters and a version of `setDate` with one `String` and two `int` parameters. The answer is E. ↩

Three review questions

Questions 22-24 refer to the following partial class definition:

```
public class TicketSales
{
  private String name;
  private double[] sales;
        /** sales[0], ..., sales[51] hold sales totals for 52 weeks */

  public TicketSales(String movieName) { < implementation not shown > }

  /** Sets box office receipts for a given week.
   *  Precondition: 1 <= week <= 52
   */
  public void setWeekSales(int week, double dollars)
  { < implementation not shown > }

  /** Finds and returns the week with best sales
   */
  private int findBestWeek() { < implementation not shown > }

  < Other methods not shown >
}
```

22

The method `findBestWeek` is declared `private` because

(A)   `findBestWeek` is not intended to be used by clients of the class.
(B)   `findBestWeek` is intended to be used only by clients of the class.
(C)   Methods that work with private instance variables of the `array` type cannot be public.
(D)   Methods that have a loop in their code cannot be public.
(E)   Methods that return a value cannot be public.

☞   In this question only the first two choices deserve any consideration — the other three are fillers. You might get confused for a moment about what a "client" means, but common sense helps: a client is anyone who is not yourself, so if a client needs to use something of yours, you have to make it public. Private things are for your class, not for clients. The answer is A. ☜

23

The constructor for the `TicketSales` class initializes the `sales` array to hold 52 values. Which of the following statements will do that?

(A)   `double sales[52];`
(B)   `double sales = new double[52];`
(C)   `double[] sales = new double[52];`
(D)   `sales = new double[52];`
(E)   `sales.setSize(52);`

☞   This is a syntax question. Choice A has invalid syntax. Choice E is absurd: an array does not have a `setSize` method (or any other methods). Choice B assigns an array to a `double` variable — a syntax error. Both Choices C and D appear syntactically plausible and in fact either one will compile with no errors. But C, instead of initializing an instance variable `sales`, will declare and initialize a local variable with the same name. This is a very common nasty bug in Java programs. The answer is D. ☜

[24]

Given the declaration

```
TicketSales movie = new TicketSales("Monsters, Inc.");
```

which of the following statements sets the third week sales for that movie to 245,000?

(A) `movie = TicketSales(3, 245000.00);`
(B) `setWeekSales(movie, 3, 245000.00);`
(C) `movie.setWeekSales(3, 245000.00);`
(D) `movie(setWeekSales, 3, 245000.00);`
(E) `setWeekSales(3, 245000.00);`

☞ This is another syntax question. The variable `movie` of the type `TicketSales` is defined outside the class, in a client of the class. The key word in this question is "sets." It indicates that a method, a modifier, is called, and the way to call a method from a client class is with dot notation. (Besides, Choice A assumes that there is a constructor with two parameters; Choices B and D look like calls to non-existing methods; Choice E forgets to mention `movie` altogether.) The answer is C. ↵

3.4   Random Numbers

Random numbers simulate chance in computer programs. For example, if you want to simulate a roll of a die, you need to obtain a random number from 1 to 6 (with any one of these values appearing with the same probability). "Random" numbers are not truly random — their sequence is generated using a certain formula — but they are good enough for many applications.

One way to get random numbers in a Java program is to call the static method `random` of the `Math` class. It returns a random `double` from 0 (inclusive) to 1 (exclusive). To get a random integer from 1 to *n* use:

```
int r =  (int)(n * Math.random()) + 1;
```

25

Which of the following is a list of all possible outputs of the following code segment?

```
String memo = "MEMO";
System.out.print("[" +
    memo.substring((int)(3 * Math.random()),
                            (int)(3 * Math.random()) + 2) +
        "]");
```

(A)   [ME], [EM]
(B)   [ME], [EM], [MO]
(C)   [EM], [MO], [O], []
(D)   [], [M], [ME], [EM], [MO]
(E)   [], [M], [E], [ME], [EM], [MO], [MEM], [EMO], [MEMO]

☞   The two calls to Math.random() look the same, but they return different values — two successive values in the random number sequence. The "from" parameter of memo.substring can be 0, 1, or 2, and the "to" parameter can be 2, 3, or 4. Any combination of these from/to values results in a valid substring (including substring(2,2), which returns an empty string). The answer is E.

> **Another way to get random numbers relies on the `java.util.Random` class, but it is not in the AP Java subset and should be avoided.**

3.5   Input and Output

The AP Java subset does not include any classes or methods for data input. In particular, the Scanner class is not in the subset. If a question involves user input it may be stated as follows:

```
double x = < call to a method that reads a floating-point number >
```

or

```
int x = IO.readInt();  // Reads user input
```

Output is limited to System.out.print and System.out.println calls.

You do not have to worry about formatting numbers. Java converts an int or a double value passed to System.out.print or System.out.println into a string using default formatting.

The `System.out.printf` method with a variable number of parameters can be used for more precisely formatted output of one or several numbers and strings.

`printf` is <u>not</u> in the AP Java subset and should not be used in your exam solutions.

You can pass any object to `System.out.print`, `System.out.println`. These methods handle an object by calling its `toString` method. Both `Integer` and `Double` classes have reasonable `toString` methods defined. If you are designing a class, it is a good idea to supply a reasonable `toString` method for it. For example:

```
public class Fraction
{
  ...
  public String toString()
  {
    return num + "/" + denom;
  }
}
```

Otherwise, your class inherits a generic `toString` method from `Object`, which returns the object's class name followed by the object's address.

The `System.out.print` and `System.out.println` methods take only <u>one</u> parameter.

If you need to print several things, use the + operator for concatenating strings. You can also concatenate a string and an `int` or a `double`: the latter will be converted into a string. For example:

```
System.out.println(3 + " hours " + 15 + " minutes.");
```

The displayed result will be

```
3 hours 15 minutes.
```

You can also concatenate a string and an object: the object's `toString` method will be called to convert it into a string. For example:

```
int n = 3, d = 4;
Fraction f = new Fraction(n, d);
System.out.println(f + " = " + (double)n / (double)d);
```

The displayed result will be

```
3/4 = 0.75
```

Just be careful not to apply a + operator to two numbers or two objects other than strings: in the former case the numbers will be added rather than concatenated; the latter will cause a syntax error.

3.6 Exceptions

An exception is a <u>run-time</u> event that signals an abnormal condition in the program. Some run-time errors, such as invalid user input or an attempt to read past the end of a file, are considered fixable. The `try-catch-finally` syntax allows the programmer to catch and process the exception and have the program recover. This type of exception is called a *checked exception*.

> **Checked exceptions and the `try-catch` statements are <u>not</u> in the Java subset and won't be tested.**

Other errors, such as an array index out of bounds or an attempt to call a method of a non-existing object (null reference) are considered fatal: the program displays an error message with information about where the error occurred, then quits. This type of exception is called an *unchecked exception*.

In Java, an exception is an object of one of the Java exception classes. The Java library implements many types of exceptions, and, if necessary, you can derive your own exception class from one of the library classes. For an AP CS exam, you are expected to understand when `ArithmeticException`, `IndexOutOfBoundsException`, `ArrayIndexOutOfBoundsException`, `NullPointerException`, and `ConcurrentModificationException` happen.

We say that a program "throws" an exception.

An `ArithmeticException` is thrown when an arithmetic error, such as integer division by zero, occurs. (You would expect `Math.sqrt(x)` to throw an `ArithmeticException` for a negative x, but it doesn't — it returns NaN, "not a number," instead. Java exception handling is inconsistent at times.)

`ArrayIndexOutOfBoundsException` is self-explanatory: it is thrown at run time when an array index is negative or is greater than `array.length-1`. `ArrayList` methods throw a similar `IndexOutOfBoundsException`.

`NullPointerException` is thrown when you forget to initialize an object-type instance variable or an element of an array and then try to call its method. For example:

```
public class MyClass
{
  private String name;  // name is set to null
    ...
    // the following statement is inside a method:
    int n = name.length();   // if name has not been initialized
                             // by MyClass's constructor, this statement
                             // will throw a NullPointerException
  ...
}
```

Another example:

```
        Integer[] a = new Integer[10];
        int x = a[0].intValue();      // a[0] is null -- Java interpreter
                                      // throws a NullPointerException
```

A third example:

```
public class DeckOfCards
{
  private Card[] cards;

  public DeckOfCards()
  {
    cards = new Card[52];     // all elements set to null
          // Forgot to initialize each element
  }

  public Card getCard(int k) { return cards[k]; }
}
```

In a client class,

```
        DeckOfCards deck = new DeckOfCards();
        int r = deck.getCard(0).getRank();
```

will throw a `NullPointerException`, because `deck.getCard(0)` returns `null`.

A `ConcurrentModificationException` is thrown if you attempt to add or remove elements of an `ArrayList` while traversing it in a "for each" loop.

Chapter 4   Program Design and OOP Concepts

4.1   Program Design and Development Methodology

Computer science courses try to emphasize problem solving, as opposed to just programming in a particular language or using specific hardware platforms. The exam topics related to general software design and development methodology emphasize *procedural* and *data abstraction*, *functional decomposition*, and the *reusability* of code. These topics are discussed in the context of *object-oriented* software design and development. Here is a very brief glossary of the relevant terms:

Specifications — a detailed description of what a piece of software should accomplish and how it should behave and interact with the user. Specifications may be given for a whole system, one module, or even one class or method.

Object-oriented programming (*OOP*) — a programming methodology based on designing the program as a world of interacting objects arranged in hierarchies of classes and using encapsulation and polymorphism.

Top-down design — a design methodology in which you first define the general structure of the program, laying out high-level classes and their interactions, and then refine the design of each class, identifying subtasks and smaller classes or methods. Then you refine the design of subtasks, individual methods, and so on.

Top-down development — similar to top-down design: you first lay out your code at a high level, defining general classes and methods. These methods may call lower-level methods, which are not yet implemented. You can compile and sometimes even test high-level pieces of your code by substituting "stubs" — empty or greatly simplified placeholders — for low-level methods that are still not implemented.

Data structure — a way of organizing data combined with methods of accessing and manipulating the data. For example, a two-dimensional array, together with methods or operators for accessing and modifying the values of its elements, is a data structure that may be useful for representing tables, grids, matrices, or images.

Encapsulation and *information hiding* — the practice of making all instance variables and helper methods that are used only inside the class private. The clients of a class can use such a class only through its public constructors and public methods.

Procedural abstraction — specifying and using procedures and functions (methods) without knowing the details of their implementation.

Reusable code — debugged and tested libraries, classes, or fragments of code that are somewhat general in nature and ready to be reused in other projects. Reusing code speeds up software development, no matter what methodology is being employed.

Team project development — object-oriented languages, such as Java, allow you to conveniently split a project into separate pieces and assign their development to different team members. Encapsulation and information hiding facilitate teamwork on a project by limiting the amount of interaction needed between developers.

User interface — the behavior of a program as it interacts with a user: screens, menus, commands, messages, graphics, sounds, and so on.

These are very general concepts, and it is not easy to come up with multiple-choice or free-response questions that test in-depth understanding of these concepts. In past exams, design and implementation questions have been limited to specific data structures and algorithms, which sometimes used some of these terms in their descriptions.

4.2   Inheritance

Inheritance allows a programmer to state that one class *extends* another class, inheriting its features. In Java terminology, a *subclass* extends a *superclass*. `extends` is a Java reserved word. For example:

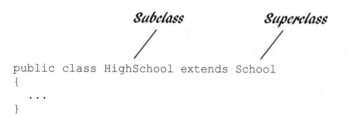

```
public class HighSchool extends School
{
   ...
}
```

Inheritance implements the *IS-A* relationship between objects: an object of a subclass type IS-A(n) object of the superclass. A high school is a kind of school. A `HighSchool` object IS-A (kind of) `School` object. Technically this means that in your program you can use an object of a subclass whenever an object of its superclass is expected. For example:

```
School sch = new HighSchool(...);
```

If a constructor or a method in a client class expects a `School` type of parameter to be passed to it, you can call it with a `HighSchool` type of parameter. Objects of a subclass inherit the data type of the superclass.

In Java, a class can directly extend only one superclass — there is no *multiple inheritance* for classes. But more than one subclass can be derived from the same superclass:

```
public class HighSchool extends School ...
public class ElementarySchool extends School ...
public class DrivingSchool extends School ...
```

The IS-A relationship of inheritance is not to be confused with the HAS-A relationship between objects. That *X* "has a" *Y* simply means that *Y* is a data field (an instance variable) in *X*. For example, you might say that a `HighSchool` HAS-A `MarchingBand`, but not that a `HighSchool` IS-A `MarchingBand`.

Subclass methods

A subclass inherits all the public methods of its superclass, and you can call an inherited method of the same object without any "dot prefix." For example, if `School` has a method

```
public String getName() { ... }
```

then `HighSchool`'s method `registerForAP` can call it directly:

```
public class HighSchool extends School
{
  ...
  public void registerForAP()
  {
    String registrationForm = getName() + ...;
    ...
  }
  ...
}
```

`HighSchool`'s clients can call `getName`, too, for any `HighSchool` object:

```
HighSchool hs = new HighSchool(...);
String name = hs.getName();
```

A subclass can add its own methods. It can also *override* (redefine) a method of the superclass by providing its own version with exactly the same *signature* (the same name and the same number, types, and order of parameters). For example, `School` may have a `toString` method, and `HighSchool`'s `toString` may override it.

> **Occasionally it may be necessary to make an explicit call to a superclass's public method from a subclass. This is accomplished by using the super-dot prefix.**

For example:

```
public class HighSchool extends School
{
  ...
  public String toString()
  {
    return super.toString() + collegeAcceptance() + ...;
  }
  ...
}
```

> **The superclass's <u>private</u> methods are not callable in its subclasses.**

Subclass constructors

> **<u>Constructors are not inherited; a subclass has to provide its own or rely on the default no-args constructor.</u>**

A subclass's constructors can explicitly call the superclass's constructors using the keyword `super`. For example:

```
public class School
{
  private String name;
  private int numStudents;

  public School(String nm, int num)
  {
    name = nm;
    numStudents = num;
  }
  ...
}

public class ElementarySchool extends School
{
  private int highestGrade;

  public ElementarySchool(String nm, int num, int grade)
  {
    super(nm, num); // calls School's constructor
    highestGrade = grade;
  }
  ...
}
```

If `super(...)` is used, it must be the <u>first</u> statement in the subclass's constructor (as in the above example). If `super` is not used, then the superclass's no-args constructor is called by default, and it must exist, or the compiler will report an error.

Subclass's instance variables

A subclass inherits all the class (static) variables and instance variables of its superclass. However, the instance variables are usually declared private (always private in the AP Java subset) and so cannot be referenced directly in the subclass.

> **The superclass's private variables are <u>not</u> directly accessible in its subclass. So you must use public accessors and mutators to get and set the values of instance variables declared in the superclass.**

Superclass's <u>public</u> constants (`public static final` variables) are accessible everywhere.

A subclass can add its own static or instance variables. For example, the class `ElementarySchool` above, a subclass of `School`, adds an instance variable

```
private int highestGrade;
```

26

Consider the following partial definitions:

```
public class MailingList
{
    private ArrayList<String> people;

    public MailingList() { people = new ArrayList<String>(); }
    public void add(String name) { people.add(name); }
    public ArrayList<String> getPeople() { return people; }

    < Other methods not shown >
}

public class Subscribers extends MailingList
{
    public Subscribers() { }   // Calls super() by default

    // Returns the number of names in people
    private int size()
    {
        return < expression >;
    }

    < Other methods not shown >
}
```

Which of the following should replace < *expression* > in the `size` method of the `Subscribers` class so that the method works as specified?

(A)   `super.size();`
(B)   `people.size();`
(C)   `super.people.size();`
(D)   `getPeople().size();`
(E)   None of the above

☞ The `MailingList` class HAS-A(n) `ArrayList<String> people` as an instance variable, but `MailingList` is not an `ArrayList`: it does not extend `ArrayList`. The programmer has not provided a `size` method for the `MailingList` class (a design mistake), so Choice A is wrong. Choices B or C might look plausible at first, but `people` is private in `MailingList`, so it is not directly accessible in `Subscribers`. But `MailingList` has a public method `getPeople`, and this method is inherited and accessible in the `Subscribers` class. `getPeople` returns an `ArrayList<String>`, which has a method `size` that returns the size of the list. The answer is D.

Also notice that

```
return getPeople().size();
```

is equivalent to

```
ArrayList<String> temp = getPeople();
return temp.size();
```

☜

4.3   Class Hierarchies

If you have a class, you can derive one or several subclasses from it. Each of these classes can in turn serve as a superclass for other subclasses. You can build a whole tree-like hierarchy of classes, in which each class has one superclass. For example:

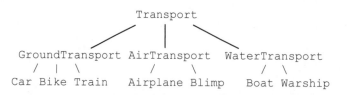

```
                        Transport
                       /    |    \
   GroundTransport AirTransport  WaterTransport
      /  |  \        /    \         /  \
   Car Bike Train  Airplane Blimp  Boat Warship
```

In fact, in Java all classes belong to one big hierarchy; it starts at a class called `Object`. If you do not specify that your class extends any particular class, then it extends `Object` by default. Therefore, every object IS-A(n) `Object`. The `Object` class provides a few common methods, including `equals` and `toString`, but these methods are not very useful and usually get redefined in classes lower in the hierarchy.

Class hierarchies exist to allow reuse of code from higher classes in the lower classes without duplication and to promote a more logical design. A class lower in the hierarchy inherits the data types of all classes above it.

For example, if we have classes

```
public class Animal { ... }
public class Dog extends Animal { ... }
public class Spaniel extends Dog { ... }
```

all of the following declarations are legal:

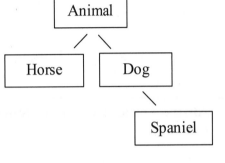

```
Spaniel s = new Spaniel(...);
Dog d = new Spaniel(...);
Animal a = new Spaniel(...);
```

But if you also define

```
public class Horse extends Animal { ... }
```

then

```
Horse x = new Spaniel(...);
```

is an error, of course: `Spaniel` does not extend `Horse`.

Abstract classes

Classes closer to the top of the hierarchy are more abstract — the properties and methods of their objects are more general. As you proceed down the hierarchy, the classes become more specific and the properties of their objects are more concretely spelled out. Java syntax allows you to define a class that is officially designated `abstract`. For example:

```
public abstract class Solid { ... }
```

An abstract class can have constructors and methods; however, some of its methods may be declared `abstract` and left without code. For example:

```
public abstract class Solid
{
  ...
  public abstract double getVolume();
  ...
}
```

This indicates that every `Solid` object has a method that returns its volume, but the actual implementation may depend on the specific type of solid. For example, the `Sphere` and `Cube` subclasses of `Solid` will define `getVolume` differently.

A class in which all the methods are defined is called *concrete*. Naturally, abstract classes appear near the top of the hierarchy and concrete classes sit below. You cannot instantiate an abstract class, but you can declare variables or arrays of its type. For example:

```
Solid s1 = new Sphere(radius);
Solid s2 = new Cube(side);
Solid[] solids = { new Sphere(100), new Cube(100) };
```

> **Abstract classes are not included in the AP Java subset and won't be tested.**

4.4   Polymorphism

Polymorphism is a mechanism that ensures that the correct method is called for an object disguised as a more generic type. In our "solids" example, if we write

```
double volume = solids[0].getVolume();
```

the compiler does not know whether `solids[0]` is a `Sphere` or a `Cube`. The decision of which `getVolume` method to call is postponed until run time. In Java implementation, each object holds a pointer to a table of entry points to its methods; thus the object itself "knows" what type of object it is. This technique is called *dynamic method binding* — which method to call is decided at run time, not compile time.

> **Polymorphism is a feature of Java and other object-oriented languages; all you have to do is understand it and use it correctly.**

One common situation in which polymorphism comes into play occurs when different types of objects are mixed together in an array or list, as shown in the above example. The code

```
for (Solid solid : solids)
   totalVolume += solid.getVolume();
```

works no matter what `Solids` are stored in the `solids` array because the appropriate `getVolume` method is called for each element of the array. This is true even if several different types of `Solids` are in the `solids` array, such as `Sphere`, `Cube`, or `Pyramid`.

Another situation for polymorphism occurs when a method takes a more generic type of parameter and a client class passes a more specific type of parameter to the method. For example, one of the overloaded versions of `System.out`'s `print` method takes an `Object` type as a parameter. This method may be implemented as follows:

```
public void print(Object x)
{
  if (x != null)
    print(x.toString());
  else
    print("<null>");
}
```

This method works for any type of object x with a reasonable `toString` method defined (including `Integer`, `Double`, and so on). Polymorphism assures that the appropriate `toString` method is called for each type of x.

27

Given

```
public class Person
{
  private String name;

  public Person(String nm) { name = nm; }
  public String getName() { return name; }
  public String toString { return getName(); }
}

public class OldLady extends Person
{
  private int age;

  public OldLady(String nm, int yrs) { super(nm); age = yrs; }
  public String getName() { return "Mrs. " + super.getName(); }
  public int getAge() { return age; }
}
```

what is the output of the following statements?

```
Person p = new OldLady("Robinson", 92);
System.out.println(p + ", " + ((OldLady)p).getAge());
```

(A) Mrs. Robinson, 92
(B) Robinson, 92
(C) Robinson
(D) ClassCastException
(E) No output due to infinite recursion

⬧ In this question we have to restore a somewhat convoluted sequence of events:

1. The variable `p` is disguised as a `Person` type, but it is actually an `OldLady`.

2. `p + ", "` calls p's `toString` method. `OldLady` inherits `toString` from `Person`, so `Person`'s `toString` is called.

3. `toString` in turn calls `getName`. Which one? This is the trickiest part. Both `Person` and `OldLady` have a `getName` method, but, due to polymorphism, `OldLady`'s `getName` will be called (notwithstanding the fact that we call it from `Person`'s `toString` method).

4. `OldLady`'s `getName` takes `"Mrs. "` and appends to it the result of `super.getName()`. The latter explicitly calls `Person`'s `getName`, which simply returns the name.

5. Finally we cast `p` back to the `OldLady` type — we need this to call its `getAge` method. A `Person` does not have `getAge`, and the compiler does not keep track of what type we assigned to `p`. `getAge`'s result is appended to the output string.

Choice B tries to make you forget about polymorphism or suggests that polymorphism does not apply here. It does. Choice C lacks the comma. Choice D is an awkward attempt to confuse you about p's data type. Deep inside, `p` is not just a `Person` but an `OldLady`, so it does have a `getAge` method once we cast it to `OldLady`. If p were only a `Person`, the cast to `OldLady` would cause a `ClassCastException`, as suggested in Choice D. Choice E hints that `getName` infinitely calls itself. This does not happen here: `OldLady`'s `getName` explicitly calls `Person`'s `getName` as indicated by the super-dot prefix. We would have infinite recursion only if we forgot the super-dot prefix. The answer is A. ⬧

4.5   The "Class" Question

The free-response Question 2 of the exam is a "class" question, which may ask you to design and write a short class or a subclass of a given class.

> **In writing a subclass of a given class, avoid duplicating code of the superclass's constructors or methods — use `super(...)` or `super.someMethod(...)` calls whenever possible.**

In designing and writing your class, pay special attention to the following:

- Use reasonable and consistent style with proper indentation and generous spacing between statements.

- Do not include comments — they are not required and will waste your time.

- Choose meaningful names for your class, its methods and their parameters, and fields and local variables. A class name starts with an uppercase letter; the names of all methods, their parameters, and instance variables start with a lowercase letter. Make sure that all constructors have the same name as the class.

- Make all instance variables private and group them together at the top of the class.

- Make all methods public (unless there is a specific hint in the question that some of them are "helper" methods used only inside this class — in which case, make them private).

- Specify appropriate return types for all methods. Recall that constructors do not have a return type, not even `void`.

- Provide public "accessor" methods only if requested in the question. An accessor returns the value of the respective instance variable. Accessor names may start with "get." For example:

```
public double getBalance() { ... }
```

- Provide "mutator" (modifier) methods only if requested in the question. Mutators set the values of instance variables. Mutator names often start with "set". For example:

```
public void setPrice(double amount) { ... }
```

The "class" question is likely to consist of only one part.

But we cannot completely exclude the possibility of a Part (b). It may ask you to write a fragment of code from a client class that uses your class written in Part (a). In answering this part of the question, pay special attention to the following:

- Use constructors and call public methods of your Part (a) class with appropriate numbers, types, and order of parameters, consistent with what you wrote in Part (a). Use this opportunity to double-check the code you wrote in Part (a).

- Never refer directly to private instance variables of your Part (a) class in the client class; rather, call accessors or mutators.

- It is allowed (and often desirable) to reuse in the client class the same names for variables as you used for similar formal parameters in methods in Part (a). For example, if in Part (a) you wrote

```
public void setPrice(double amount) { ... }
```

then in Part (b) you may write

```
double amount = ...;
...
item.setPrice(amount);
```

Chapter 5   Algorithms

5.1   Iterations

Most programming languages provide iteration control structures, such as the `while` and `for` loops in Java. Simple loops are good for iterating (repeating the same operation) over a range of numbers or over the elements of a one-dimensional array or a list.

A `for` loop is a convenient and idiomatic way to *traverse* a one-dimensional array:

```
for (int k = 0; k < a.length; k++)
{
  System.out.println(a[k]);        // ... or do whatever you need to do
                                   //       with each element
}
```

or

```
for (T x : a)
{
  System.out.println(x);
}
```

where T is the data type of the elements of `a`.

Working with two-dimensional arrays usually requires *nested* loops. The following code, for example, traverses a two-dimensional array `m`:

```
int nRows = m.length, nCols = m[0].length;

for (int r = 0; r < nRows; r++)
{
  for (int c = 0; c < nCols; c++)
  {
    System.out.println(m[r][c]);   // ... or do whatever...
  }
}
```

Notice that braces are optional if the body of the loop has only one statement:

```
for (int i = 1; i < n; i++)
  for (int j = 0; j < i; j++)
    if (a[i] == a[j])
      count++;
```

In "triangular" nested loops, the outer loop may run, say, for i from 1 to $n-1$ and the inner loop may run for j from 0 to $i-1$. In the above example the inner loop runs i times for $i = 1, ..., n-1$, so the total number of comparisons is

$$1 + 2 + ... + (n-1) = \frac{n(n-1)}{2}$$

The "for each" loop (also known as "enhanced" loop) makes it easy to traverse an array or `ArrayList`:

```
ArrayList<String> list = new ArrayList<String>();
...
for (String s : list)
{
   ...
}
```

Max and min

A common example of using loops is to find a maximum or a minimum value (or its position) in an array:

```
/** Returns maxValue such that maxValue >= a[k] for any 0 <= k <= n-1
 *   and maxValue = a[k] for some k.
 *   Precondition: array a holds values a[0], ..., a[n-1]; n >= 1
 */
public double max(double[] a, int n)
{
  double maxValue = a[0];

  for (int k = 1; k < n; k++)
  {
    if (a[k] > maxValue)
      maxValue = a[k];
  }
  return maxValue;
}
```

28

Consider the following method:

```java
public int mysteryMax(int[] a)
{
   int m = 0;

   for (int i = 0; i < a.length; i++)
   {
      int sum = 0;

      for (int k = i; k < a.length; k++)
      {
         sum += a[k];
         if (sum > m)
            m = sum;
      }
   }

   return m;
}
```

(-1, -3, 2, -3, 2, 1]

sum

If a contains -1, -3, 2, -3, 2, 1, what value will be returned by `mysteryMax(a)`?

(A) -2
(B) -1
(C) 1
(D) 2
(E) 3

☞   The method returns the largest sum of any number of consecutive elements in a (or 0 if all the sums are negative). The answer is E.

29

Consider the following method:

```
/** Returns the largest sum of any two elements.
 *  Precondition: n >= 2; a[0] ... a[n-1] are filled with values
 */
public double maxSum(double[] a, int n)
{
    < missing code >
}
```

Which of the following code segments can replace < *missing code* > so that the method works as specified?

I.
```
double max = a[0] + a[1];

for (int i = 1; i < n; i++)
  for (int j = 0; j < i; j++)
    if (a[i] + a[j] > max)
      max = a[i] + a[j];
return max;
```

II.
```
double max1 = a[0], max2 = a[0];

for (int i = 1; i < n; i++)
  if (a[i] > max1)
    max1 = a[i];

for (int i = 1; i < n; i++)
  if (a[i] != max1 && a[i] > max2)
    max2 = a[i];

return max1 + max2;
```

III.
```
double max1 = a[0], max2 = a[1];

if (a[1] > a[0])
{
  max1 = a[1];
  max2 = a[0];
}

for (int i = 2; i < n; i++)
{
  if (a[i] > max1)
  {
    max2 = max1;
    max1 = a[i];
  }
  else if (a[i] > max2)
    max2 = a[i];
}

return max1 + max2;
```

(A)   I only
(B)   II only
(C)   I and II only
(D)   I and III only
(E)   I, II, and III

☞   This is a lot of code for one question, so we need to focus on the key points. The code in Option I is inefficient but most straightforward: using triangular nested loops we generate sums for all the different pairs of elements and choose the largest of them. Option II is based on a different idea: finding the largest value and then the second largest value in two separate traversals of the array. But it has two problems. First, if the largest value happens to be `a[0]`, then the second `for` loop will never update `max2`. Second, it will fail if the largest value appears in the array more than once. The method description states that the method is looking for the largest sum of any two elements, but these can have the same value.

To work, Option II would need a couple of minor fixes:

```
int iMax1 = 0, iMax2 = 0;

for (int i = 1; i < n; i++)
  if (a[i] > a[iMax1])
    iMax1 = i;

if (iMax1 == 0)
  iMax2 = 1;

for (int i = 1; i < n; i++)
  if (i != iMax1 && a[i] > a[iMax2])
    iMax2 = i;

return a[iMax1] + a[iMax2];
```

In Option III we find both the largest and the second largest elements in one sweep (and these can have the same value). Notice how the largest element becomes the second largest when we find another one with a greater value. It works fine. The answer is D.   ☜

Insert in order

Many applications, including Insertion Sort, require you to insert a value into a sorted array while preserving the order:

```
/** Shifts values a[k], ..., a[n-1] appropriately into
 *   a[k+1], ..., a[n] and inserts newValue into a[k] so that the
 *   ascending order is preserved.
 *   Precondition:  a[0] <= a[1] <= ... <= a[n-1]; n < a.length
 */
public void insertInOrder(int[] a, int n, int newValue)
{
  // Shift values to the right by one until you find the
  //     place to insert:

  int k = n;              // Start at the end
  while (k > 0 && a[k-1] > newValue)
  {
    a[k] = a[k-1];
    k--;
  }
  a[k] = newValue;
}
```

In the above code, we shift the values in the array to the right by one to create a vacant slot and then insert the new value into the vacancy thus created. Notice that the shifting has to proceed from the end, so that each shifted value is placed into a vacant slot and does not overwrite any data (Figure 5-1).

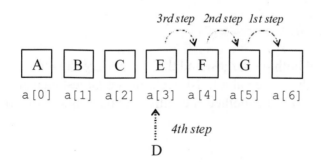

Figure 5-1. Inserting a new value in the middle of a sorted array

30

Consider an array `a` that contains `n` integer values sorted in ascending order
(`n < a.length`). Which of the following code segments correctly inserts
`newValue` into a, preserving the ascending order?

I.
```
for (int k = n; k > 0; k--)
{
  if (a[k-1] <= newValue)
  {
    a[k] = newValue;
    k = 0;
  }
  else
    a[k] = a[k-1];
}
```

II.
```
int k = n;
while (k > 0 && a[k-1] > newValue)
{
  a[k] = a[k-1];
  k--;
}
a[k] = newValue;
```

III.
```
int k = 0;

while (k < n && a[k] < newValue)
  k++;

for (int j = n-1; j >= k; j--)
{
  a[j+1] = a[j];
}
a[k] = newValue;
```

(A)   I only
(B)   II only
(C)   III only
(D)   I and II only
(E)   II and III only

☞   When you have to decide whether such code is correct, check the boundary
conditions first: does it work if you have to insert the value at the very beginning or at
the very end of the array? The code in Option I, for example, looks good at first —
similar to the `insertInOrder` method described above. But if `newValue` is smaller
than all the values in the array, nothing is inserted. Option II is equivalent to the
`insertInOrder` code above. Option III uses a more step-wise approach: first find
the place to insert, then shift the values above that place, then insert. In Option III, it
is sufficient to check that this code works for `newValue` being the smallest and the
largest — that means there are no tricks. The answer is E. ↵

5.2   Sequential Search and Binary Search

A typical application of a simple loop is *Sequential Search*:

```
/** Returns the first value of pos, such that
 *   0 <= pos < n and a[pos] == target;
 *   returns -1 if target is not among a[0], ..., a[n-1].
 *   Precondition: a.length >= n
 */
public int sequentialSearch(int[] a, int n, int target)
{
  for (int k = 0; k < n; k++)
  {
    if (a[k] == target)
      return k;
  }
  return -1;
}
```

Sequential Search works for any array: the values in the array may be in random order. If an array is sorted (that is, if its elements are arranged in ascending or descending order), then Binary Search is a much more efficient searching method.

Binary Search is a "divide and conquer" method for quickly finding a target value in a sorted array. Suppose the array is sorted in ascending order. We take an element in the middle (or approximately in the middle) of the remaining search range (the whole array at the start) and compare that element to the target. If they are equal, we're done. If the target is greater, we continue the search in the right half of the remaining search range; if it's smaller, we continue in the left half.

For example:

```
/** Returns the position of the element equal to target or -1 if target
 *  is not in the array.
 *  Precondition: array a contains n values sorted in ascending order
 */
public int binarySearch(int[] a, int n, int target)
{
  int left = 0;
  int right = n - 1;

  while (left <= right)
  {
    int middle = (left + right) / 2;
    if (target == a[middle])
      return middle;
    else if (target < a[middle])
      right = middle - 1;     // continue search in the left half
    else
      left = middle + 1;      // continue search in the right half
  }
  return -1;
}
```

Binary Search in an array of $2^k - 1$ elements requires at most k iterations. In other words, Binary Search in an array of n elements requires $\log_2 n$ iterations. Thus in an array of 1,000,000 elements it would need at most 20 iterations. By comparison, Sequential Search in an array of n elements takes, on average, $n/2$ iterations, and in the worst case it may take n iterations.

31

Suppose that two programs, one using Binary Search and the other using Sequential Search, take (on average) the same amount of time to find a random target value in a sorted array of 30 elements. Roughly how much faster than the Sequential Search program will the Binary Search program run on an array of 1000 elements?

(A)   2 times faster
(B)   10 times faster
(C)   16 times faster
(D)   33 times faster
(E)   50 times faster

☞   Binary Search takes 5 iterations for 30 elements ($32 = 2^5$) and 10 iterations for 1000 elements ($1024 = 2^{10}$). So Binary Search will run roughly two times longer on a 1000-element array than on a 30-element array. Sequential search will run roughly 33 times longer ($1000 \approx 30 \cdot 33$). On 1000 elements, Binary Search will be $33/2 = 16.5$ times faster. The answer is C. ☟

32

An e-mail address is a string made up of alphanumeric characters, one or several "dots," and one "@" character. The short substring after the last dot is called the domain name suffix. For example, in `jane.lee@math.thebestschool.edu`, "edu" is the suffix. Which of the following methods can be used to find the position of the suffix?

I. A modified Sequential Search in which we scan through the whole array keeping track of the last occurrence of a given character

II. A modified Sequential Search that proceeds backward, starting at the end of the array

III. A modified Binary Search in which each alphanumeric character is treated as '0' and a dot and @ are treated as '1'

(A) I only
(B) II only
(C) III only
(D) I and II only
(E) II and III only

The task is basically to find the last dot in a string. Method I is not the most efficient, but it works:

```
for (int k = 0; k < email.length(); k++)
  if (email.charAt(k) == '.')
     dotPos = k;

// Characters, charAt, and char constants are not
// in the AP Java subset

return dotPos;
```

Method II works a bit faster:

```
for (int k = email.length() - 1; k >= 0; k--)
  if (email.charAt(k) == '.')
    return k;
```

The description of Method III tries to confuse you with the binary number system, which has no relation to Binary Search. The latter won't work here because the string is not sorted and dots are scattered among alphanumeric characters. The answer is D.

5.3   Selection and Insertion Sorts

Sorting means arranging a list of items in ascending or descending order, according to the values of the items or some key that is part of an item. Sorting algorithms are usually discussed for lists represented as arrays.

> **Selection Sort** and **Insertion Sort** are called *quadratic sorts* because they use two straightforward nested loops and the number of required comparisons is approximately proportional to n^2.

Selection Sort

In *Selection Sort* we iterate for k from n down to 2: we find the largest among the first k elements and swap it with the k-th element.

```java
/** Sorts n values in array a in ascending order.
 *  Precondition: array a contains a[0], ..., a[n-1] (n >= 1)
 */
public void selectionSort(int[] a, int n)
{
  for (int k = n; k >= 2; k--)
  {
    int maxPos = 0;
    for (int i = 1; i < k; i++)
    {
      if (a[i] > a[maxPos])
        maxPos = i;
    }
    // Swap a[maxPos], a[k-1]:
    int temp = a[maxPos]; a[maxPos] = a[k-1]; a[k-1] = temp;
  }
}
```

Or we can use a `while` loop:

```java
public void selectionSort(int[] a, int n)
{
  while (n > 1)
  {
    int maxPos = 0;
    for (int i = 1; i < n; i++)
    {
      if (a[i] > a[maxPos])
        maxPos = i;
    }
    int temp = a[maxPos]; a[maxPos] = a[n-1]; a[n-1] = temp;
  }
  n--;
}
```

In another variation of Selection Sort we find the smallest among the elements a[k], ..., a[n-1] and swap it with a[k] (for $k = 0, ..., n-2$).

In Selection Sort, the inner loop runs $k-1$ times, for $k = n, n-1, ..., 2$.

The total number of comparisons in Selection Sort is always the same:

$$(n-1) + (n-2) + ... + 1 = \frac{n(n-1)}{2}$$

Insertion Sort

In *Insertion Sort*, we iterate for k from 1 up to $n-1$. We keep the first k elements — a[0], a[1], ..., a[k-1] — sorted and insert a[k] among them, where it belongs:

```
/** Sorts n values in array a in ascending order
 *  Precondition: array a contains a[0], ..., a[n-1] (n >= 1)
 */
public void insertionSort(int[] a, int n)
{
  for (int k = 1; k < n; k++)
  {
    int temp = a[k];
    int i = k;
    while (i > 0 && a[i-1] > temp)
    {
      a[i] = a[i-1];
      i--;
    }
    a[i] = temp;
  }
}
```

In this version of Insertion Sort, if the array is already sorted, then the inner loop runs just one comparison and we immediately break out of it. Then the method needs a total of $n-1$ comparisons. This is the best case: instead of *quadratic* time, the method executes in *linear* time.

The worst case for this implementation of Insertion Sort is when the array is sorted in reverse order. Then the inner loop runs $k-1$ times and the whole method will need as many comparisons as Selection Sort:

$$1 + 2 + \ldots + (n-1) = \frac{n(n-1)}{2}$$

The average case is about half that number, still approximately proportional to n^2.

The methods above are just examples of how Selection Sort and Insertion Sort can be implemented. Other variations are possible.

[33]

Consider the task of sorting the elements of an array in ascending order. Which of the following statements are true?

    I.   Selection Sort always requires more comparisons than Insertion Sort.
   II.   Insertion Sort always requires more moves than Selection Sort.
  III.   Insertion Sort, on average, requires more moves than Selection Sort.

(A)   I only
(B)   II only
(C)   III only
(D)   I and II only
(E)   II and III only

👉 This question gives us a chance to review the properties of these two quadratic sorts. As we have seen, Statement I is false: although, on average, Selection Sort requires more comparisons, Insertion Sort in the worst case (an array sorted in reverse order) will take as many comparisons as Selection Sort. Statement II is false, too: in the best case, when the array is already sorted, Insertion Sort does not require any moves at all. (Selection Sort, too, with a slight modification, can avoid any moves when the array is already sorted.) Statement III is the vague part: what do we mean by "on average"? First, our array must be large enough to support some conclusions. Sorting an array of three elements will not be representative. Let's assume that we set up an experiment where we generate a fairly large array of random numbers, sort it using each of the two algorithms, and count the number of moves. Intuition tells us that Insertion Sort, on average, needs more moves. Indeed, the k-th iteration through the outer loop may require anywhere from 0 to k moves, $k/2$ moves on average. In Selection Sort, each iteration through the outer loop requires one swap, which can be counted as three moves. The answer is C. 🔁

5.4   Recursion

You may find recursion pleasant or difficult, depending on your taste. If you happen to hate it, you can still take a stab at the multiple-choice questions on recursion.

34

Consider the following method:

```
public void mystery(int n)
{
  if ( n <= 0)
    return;

  for (int i = 0; i < n; i++)
  {
    System.out.print("-");
  }

  for (int i = 0; i < n; i++)
  {
    System.out.print("+");
  }

  System.out.println();

  mystery(n-1);
}
```

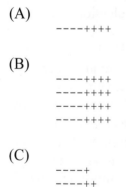

What is the output when `mystery(4)` is called?

(A)

```
----++++
```

(B)

```
----++++
----++++
----++++
----++++
```

(C)

```
----+
----++
----+++
----++++
```

(D)
```
-+
--++
---+++
----++++
```

(E)
```
----++++
---+++
--++
-+
```

This method calls itself — that's what recursion is. Notice two things about it. First, if n <= 0, the method doesn't do anything. An exit from a recursive method, perhaps after some work but without recursive calls, is called the *base case* (or the *stopping case*). In this method the base case does nothing. Second, when the method calls itself, it calls itself with a parameter whose value is one less than the original. The parameter of a recursive call must be different from the parameter of the original call, usually decreased in some way in the direction of the base case, if the recursion is to terminate at some point.

Instead of trying to unwrap and trace all the recursive calls in this method, first try to reason more formally about its properties. The method prints some minuses followed by the same number of pluses. When called with $n = 4$, the method right away prints one line with 4 minuses and 4 pluses. But that is not all: after printing the first line, the method calls mystery(3), which must do the same thing as mystery(4) but on a smaller scale. The answer is E.

Now suppose we change the mystery method in the previous question, placing the recursive call above the for loops:

35

Consider the following method:

```java
public void mystery(int n)
{
  if (n <= 0)
    return;

  mystery(n-1);

  for (int i = 0; i < n; i++)
  {
    System.out.print("-");
  }

  for (int i = 0; i < n; i++)
  {
    System.out.print("+");
  }

  System.out.println();
}
```

What is the output when `mystery(4)` is called?

< Same answer choices as in Question 34 >

This question is a bit trickier, but D and E are still the only plausible answers:

(D)	(E)
`-+`	`----++++`
`--++`	`---+++`
`---+++`	`--++`
`----++++`	`-+`

We have to choose D because the last thing `mystery(4)` does is print `----++++`.

(If you are more mathematically inclined, you can reason as follows. `mystery(4)` prints a triangle pointing either up or down. Let's take a guess at this method's general behavior: say, "`mystery(n)` prints a triangle with *n* rows that points up." Suppose it's true for *n* = 3. Then `mystery(4)` first prints a triangle with 3 rows in the recursive call, then adds the longest fourth row. Our guess fits, so the answer should be D.)

36

*[handwritten: mM("la-la-la!"
0 1 2 3 4 5 6 7 8
↳ mM (0, 3)
↳ mM (6, 1)
print (*]*

Consider the following method:

```java
public void mysteryMix(String str)
{
  int len = str.length();
  if (len >= 3)
  {
    mysteryMix(str.substring(0, len / 3));
    System.out.print (str.substring(len / 3, 2*len / 3));
    mysteryMix(str.substring(2*len / 3));
  }
}
```

What is the output when `mysteryMix("la-la-la!")` is called?

(A) `la-la-la!`
(B) `ala-a`
(C) `ala-la-la-l`
(D) `lla-l`
(E) `a-la-a!`

☞ Many AP questions mix unrelated topics. This tough question tests both recursion and strings. We start with a string of nine characters, but immediately call `mysteryMix` recursively for a string of three characters. So it makes sense to first see what happens when we call, say, `mysteryMix("xyz")`. This call just prints the middle character, `"y"`, and does nothing else: when `len` is 3 the two recursive calls do nothing. Now back to the original string of nine characters. The two recursive calls print one character each and `System.out.print` prints three characters, so the output must have five characters. This eliminates Choices A, C, and E. The first character printed is the middle character in the first one-third of the string, which is `"a"`. The answer is B. ☚

Recursive implementation of Binary Search

The description of the Binary Search algorithm is recursive in nature, and it can be implemented recursively with ease.

37

Consider the following incomplete recursive implementation of Binary Search:

```
/** Returns the position of the element equal to target or -1,
 *  if target is not among the values a[left], ..., a[right].
 *  Precondition: array a contains values stored from a[left]
 *                to a[right], sorted in ascending order
 */
public int binarySearch(int[] a, int left, int right, int target)
{
  int targetPos = -1;

  < statement 1 >
  {
    int middle = (left + right) / 2;
    if (target == a[middle])
      < statement 2 >
    else if (target < a[middle])
      targetPos = binarySearch(a, left, middle - 1, target);
    else
      targetPos = binarySearch(a, middle + 1, right, target);
  }

  return targetPos;
}
```

Which of the following could be used to replace < *statement 1* > and < *statement 2* > so that the `binarySearch` method works as intended?

< *statement 1* >	< *statement 2* >
(A) while (left <= right)	return targetPos;
(B) while (left <= right)	return middle;
(C) while (left < right)	targetPos = middle;
(D) if (left <= right)	targetPos = middle;
(E) if (left < right)	return middle;

☞ In the choice between `while` and `if`, `if` wins, because this is a <u>recursive</u> solution and recursion <u>replaces</u> iterations. This eliminates A, B, and C. In D and E either choice works for Statement 2, but Statement 1 in E misses the case when `left == right`. The answer is D. ☜

5.5   Mergesort

Mergesort is a recursive sorting algorithm based on the "divide and conquer"
principle. It takes, on average, $n \log n$ comparisons, as opposed to order of n^2
comparisons in quadratic sorts. This difference can be very significant for large
arrays. For example, for 1024 elements, Mergesort may run 100 times faster than
Selection Sort and Insertion Sort.

The idea of *Mergesort* is simple: divide the array into two approximately equal halves;
sort (recursively) each half, then merge them together into one sorted array
(Figure 5-2). Mergesort usually requires a temporary array for holding the two sorted
halves before they are merged back into the original space.

Split the array into two halves	→	A: 1 7 4 9 ⋮ 3 5 8 6 2
Sort each half (recursively) and copy into *temp*	→	temp: 1 4 7 9 ⋮ 2 3 5 6 8
Merge elements in ascending order from the two sorted halves back into the array	→	temp: 1 4 7 9 ⋮ 2 3 5 6 8 A: 1 2 3 _ _ _ _ _ _

Figure 5-2.   Mergesort

38

Consider the following implementation of Mergesort:

```
/** Sorts values a[n1], ..., a[n2] in ascending order.
 * Precondition: 0 <= n1 <= n2 < a.length
 */
public void sort(int[] a, int n1, int n2)
{
  if (n1 == n2)
    return;

  int m = (n1 + n2) / 2;
  sort(a, n1, m);
  sort(a, m+1, n2);
  if (a[m] > a[m+1])          // Optional line
    merge(a, n1, m, n2);
}
```

Compare it with a more conventional version with the if statement on the "optional line" removed. Suppose a has 8 elements and sort(a, 0, 7) is called. For which of the following values in a will the version with if work faster than the version without?

  I.   1 2 3 4 5 6 7 8
  II.   5 6 7 8 2 1 4 3
 III.   2 1 4 3 6 5 8 7

(A) I only
(B) I and II only
(C) I and III only
(D) I, II, and III
(E) None of the three

A typical implementation of Mergesort doesn't skip the work even when the array is already sorted. The slight change proposed in this question allows Mergesort to skip all the merging and quickly establish that an array is already sorted, as in Option I. This version also avoids merging when the array is partially sorted, namely when all the values in the left half of the array are smaller than any value in the right half, as in Option III. In that case, after the two recursive calls to sort, the array becomes sorted and the call to merge is skipped.

Since the algorithm is recursive, it will also save time when some portions of the array have these properties — are either sorted or partially sorted — even when the whole array isn't. In Option II, for example, the left half is sorted and the right half is partially sorted. The answer is D.

Chapter 6   Annotated Solutions to Past Free-Response Questions

The material for this chapter is on our website:

`www.skylit.com/beprepared/fr.html`

That page includes links to free-response questions from recent years, an annotated solution for each question, and executable files for all questions.

Practice Exams

A blank multiple-choice answer form is available at

www.skylit.com/beprepared/MCAnswerForm.pdf

Remember the topics of the free-response questions in each exam:

Question 1: Call provided methods and use `if-else` statements and `for` and/or `while` loops; work with strings.

Question 2: Write a complete Java class.

Question 3: Work with an array and/or an `ArrayList`.

Question 4: Work with a 2D array.

No need to use an array or an `ArrayList` in free-response Questions 1 and 2.

Practice Exam #1

SECTION I

Time — 1 hour and 30 minutes
Number of questions — 40
Percent of total grade — 50

1. What is printed when the following statement is executed?

   ```
   System.out.println(17 / 5 % 3 + 17 * 5 % 3);
   ```

   (A) 1
   (B) 4
   (C) 9
   (D) 42
   (E) 42.5

2. Assume that a and b are properly declared and initialized boolean variables. Consider the following expression.

   ```
   !(!a || b) || (!a && b)
   ```

   When does the expression evaluate to true?

   (A) When a and b have different values
   (B) When a and b have the same value
   (C) When both a and b have the value true and only then
   (D) When both a and b have the value false and only then
   (E) Never

3. Consider the following statement.

   ```
   System.out.println("yes\\no".indexOf("\no"));
   ```

   What is printed when the statement is compiled and executed?

   (A) 3
   (B) 4
   (C) 5
   (D) −1
   (E) Nothing, due to a syntax error

4. Consider the following method.

    ```
    public void printSomething(String s)
    {
      int n = s.length();
      if (n < 1)
        return;
      String s1 = s.substring(1, n);
      printSomething(s1);
      System.out.println(s);
      printSomething(s1);
    }
    ```

    How many A's and how many letters total will be printed when
    `printSomething("ABCD")` is called?

	A's	Total
(A)	1	10
(B)	4	10
(C)	1	26
(D)	4	26
(E)	15	26

5. What are the smallest and the largest possible values of x after the following statement
    has been executed?

    ```
    int x = (int)(Math.sqrt(4*Math.random()) + 0.5);
    ```

    (A) 0 and 1
    (B) 0 and 2
    (C) 0 and 3
    (D) 1 and 2
    (E) 1 and 3

6. Which of the following expressions evaluate to `true`?

    ```
    I.    "Boston".equals(new String("Boston"));
    II.   "Bos" + "ton" == new String("Boston");
    III.  (new String("Boston")).substring(3) == "ton";
    ```

    (A) I only
    (B) I and II only
    (C) II and III only
    (D) I, II, and III
    (E) None of the three

7. What is printed when the following code segment is executed?

```
double pi = 3.14159;
int r = 100;
int area = (int)(pi * Math.pow(r, 2));
System.out.println(area);
```

(A) 30000
(B) 31415
(C) 31416
(D) 314159
(E) Depends on the particular computer system

8. Assume that the String variables str1 and str2 have been properly declared and initialized. Which of the following conditions correctly tests whether the value of str1 is greater than or equal to the value of str2 (in lexicographical order)?

(A) str1 >= str2
(B) str1.compareTo(str2) >= 0
(C) str1.compareTo(str2) == true
(D) str1.length() > str2.length() || str1 >= str2
(E) str1.equals(str2) || str1.compareTo(str2) == 1

9. Consider the following recursive method.

```
public static int fun(int n)
{
  int product = 2;
  for (int k = 2; k < n; k++)
    product *= fun(k);
  return product;
}
```

What does fun(5) return?

(A) 2
(B) 24
(C) 120
(D) 256
(E) Nothing. The method exceeds the maximum allowed recursion depth and the program is aborted, because the method does not specify a base case.

10. Consider the following class `Test` with an incomplete `main` method.

```
public class Test
{
  private static int year = 2020;

  public Test(int yr) { year = yr; }

  public void increment() { year++; }

  public String toString() { return year + ""; }

  public static void main(String[] args)
  {
    < missing statements >
  }
}
```

Which of the following replacements of *< missing statements >* will result in a syntax error or print something other than 2020 when `main` is executed?

(A)
```
System.out.println(this);
```
(B)
```
Test x = new Test(2020);
System.out.println(x);
```
(C)
```
Test x = new Test(20);
System.out.println("" + x + x);
```
(D)
```
year = 2020;
System.out.println(year);
```
(E)
```
Test x = new Test(2019);
x.increment();
System.out.println(x);
```

11. Which of the following statements print 1234?

```
I.    System.out.print(12 * 100 + 34);
II.   System.out.print("12" + 34);
III.  System.out.print(1 + "2" + 3 + 4);
```

(A)   None of the above
(B)   I only
(C)   I and II only
(D)   II and III only
(E)   I, II, and III

12. Consider the following code segment.

```
int i = 2;
for (int k = 0; k <= 12; k += i)
{
  System.out.print(k + " ");
  i++;
}
```

What is printed when the statement is executed?

(A) 0 3 7
(B) 0 3 7 12
(C) 2 5 8 11
(D) 0 3 6 9 12
(E) 0 2 4 6 8 10

13. Consider the following class.

```
public class Monster
{
  private String x;

  public void feed(String number)
  {
    if (x == null || x.compareTo(number) < 0)
      x = number;
  }

  public String get()
  {
    return x;
  }
}
```

What is printed when the following code in Monster's client class is executed?

```
Monster bfg = new Monster();
String[] numbers = {"One", "Two", "Three", "Four", "Five",
                    "Six", "Seven", "Eight", "Nine", "Ten"};
for (String number : numbers)
  bfg.feed(number);
System.out.println(bfg.get());
```

(A)   One
(B)   Two
(C)   Eight
(D)   Ten
(E)   NullPointerException

14. What is printed when the code segment is executed?

```
int[] a = {0, 1};
int[] b = a;
a[0] = 1;
b[0] = 2;
System.out.println(a[0] + b[0] + a[1] + b[1]);
```

(A) 3
(B) 4
(C) 5
(D) 6
(E) None of the above

15. What are the values of a and b after two iterations through the for loop?

```
int a = 1, b = 2;
for (int k = 1; k <= 20; k++)
{
  int oldA = a;
  a = b;
  b = (1 + b)/oldA;
}
```

(A) 2 and 2
(B) 2 and 3
(C) 3 and 2
(D) 3 and 3
(E) 3 and 6

16. Consider the following method.

```
public void mystery(int a, int b)
{
  System.out.print(a + " ");
  if (a <= b)
    mystery(a + 5, b - 1);
}
```

What is printed when mystery(0, 16) is called?

(A) 0
(B) 0 5
(C) 0 5 10
(D) 0 5 10 15
(E) 0 5 10 15 20

17. Consider the following method.

```
/** Precondition: a != null; a.length > 0 */
private static void doIt(double[] a)
{
  for (int k = 0; k < a.length / 2; k++)
  {
    double temp = a[k];
    a[k] = a[a.length - 1 - k];
    a[a.length - 1 - k] = temp;
  }
}
```

Which of the following best describes the task performed by this method?

(A)   Sorts an array in ascending order
(B)   Sorts an array in descending order
(C)   Swaps the first and last elements of an array
(D)   Reverses the order of elements in an array
(E)   None of the above tasks is implemented correctly

18. Assume that the int variables a and b have been properly declared and initialized. For which of the following pairs of values of a and b is the value of the following expression true?

```
(a > 20 && a < b) || (a > 10 && a > b)
```

(A)   5 and 0
(B)   5 and 10
(C)   15 and 10
(D)   15 and 20
(E)   None of the above

19. Brad has derived his class from the library class JPanel. JPanel's paintComponent method prints a blank picture in a panel. Brad has overridden JPanel's paintComponent to display his own picture. Brad's class compiles with no errors, but when he runs the program, only a blank background is displayed. Which of the following hypotheses CANNOT be true in this situation?

(A)   Brad misspelled "paintComponent" in his method's name.
(B)   Brad specified an incorrect return type for his paintComponent method.
(C)   Brad chose the wrong type for a parameter in his paintComponent method.
(D)   Brad specified two parameters for his paintComponent method, while JPanel's paintComponent takes only one parameter.
(E)   Brad has a logic error in his paintComponent code that prevents it from generating the picture.

20. Consider the following code segment. It is supposed to calculate and print the sum $1 + 2 + ... + 20$.

```
int count = 0, sum = 0;
while (count < 20)
{
   sum += count;
}
System.out.println(sum);
```

Which of the following statements best describes the result?

(A) The total printed will be correct.
(B) The total printed will be too small by 20.
(C) 0 is printed.
(D) 20 is printed.
(E) Nothing is printed, because the program goes into an infinite loop.

21. Consider the following code segment.

```
ArrayList<Integer> list = new ArrayList<Integer>();

for (int i = 1; i <= 8; i++)
{
   list.add(i);
}

for (int i = 0; i < list.size(); i++)
{
   list.remove(i);
}

for (Integer x : list)
{
   System.out.print(x + " ");
}
```

What is printed when the code segment is executed?

(A)   IndexOutOfBoundsException
(B)   1 3 5 7
(C)   2 4 6 8
(D)   1 2 3 4 5 6 7 8
(E)   No output, because the resulting list is empty

22. Consider the following code segment with a missing `for` loop.

```
ArrayList<String> letters = new ArrayList<String>();

letters.add("A");
letters.add("B");
letters.add("C");

< missing "for" loop >

System.out.println(letters);
```

The code segment, when executed, prints

```
[A*, B*, C*]
```

Which of the following can replace < *missing "for" loop* >?

I.
```
for (int i = 0; i < letters.size(); i++)
{
   letters.set(i, letters.get(i) + "*");
}
```

II.
```
for (int i = 0; i < letters.size(); i++)
{
   String s = letters.get(i);
   s = s + "*";
}
```

III.
```
for (String s : letters)
{
   s = s + "*";
}
```

(A) I only
(B) II only
(C) I and II only
(D) II and III only
(E) I, II, and III

Questions 23 and 24 refer to a project that includes the following classes.

```
public class Cake
{
  private String name;
  private int price;

  public Cake(String _name, int _price)
  {
    name = _name;
    price = _price;
  }

  public int getPrice() { return price; }

  < other constructors and methods not shown >
}

public class Sale
{
  private ArrayList<Cake> items;

  public Sale() { items = new ArrayList<Cake>(); }
  public void add(Cake cake) { items.add(cake); }

  public int getTotal()
  {
    int total = 0;

    for (Cake cake : items)
      total += cake.getPrice();

    return total;
  }
}
```

The project designer has instructed the programmer to modify the code as follows: to introduce

```
public class PricedItem
{
  int getPrice() { return 0; }
}
```

into the project, add extends PricedItem to the header of the class Cake, and replace Cake with PricedItem everywhere in the Sale class.

23. Which design principle is applied here, and which Java feature makes it possible for the modified code to work?

    (A) Modularity and recursion
    (B) Modularity and encapsulation
    (C) Abstraction and encapsulation
    (D) Encapsulation and polymorphism
    (E) Abstraction and polymorphism

24. Which of the following are good reasons for this change?

    I. In a future version of the project, the `items` list in a `Sale` object may hold items of the type of a subclass of `Cake`.

    II. In a future version of the project, different types of `PricedItem` objects can be intermixed in the `items` list in a `Sale` object.

    III. The `Cake` class can be reused in other projects dealing with a different type of `PricedItem` items.

    (A) I only
    (B) II only
    (C) I and II only
    (D) II and III only
    (E) I, II, and III

25. Consider the following code segment.

```
ArrayList<String> list = new ArrayList<String>();
list.add("A");
list.add("B");
list.add("C");
for (String s : list)
{
  String t = list.get(list.size() - 1);
  list.set(list.size() - 1, s);
  s = t;
}
```

Which of the following represents the contents of `list` after the code segment has been executed?

    (A) ["A", "B", "C"]
    (B) ["C", "B", "A"]
    (C) ["C", "A", "B"]
    (D) ["C", "C", "C"]
    (E) ["A", "B", "B"]

26. Consider the following class.

```java
public class FrequentFlyer
{
  private int miles = 0;

  public FrequentFlyer(int m) { miles = m; }
  public void addMiles(int m) { miles += m; }
  public int getMiles() { return miles; }
}
```

What is printed when the following code segment in a client class is executed?

```java
FrequentFlyer akshay = new FrequentFlyer(20000);
FrequentFlyer bruno = new FrequentFlyer(10000);
FrequentFlyer cindy = new FrequentFlyer(0);
FrequentFlyer[] friends = {akshay, bruno, cindy};
int total = 0;
for (FrequentFlyer p : friends)
{
  p.addMiles(1000);
  total += p.getMiles();
}
System.out.println(total);
```

(A) 0
(B) 3000
(C) 30000
(D) 33000
(E) None of the above

27. What is printed when the following code segment is executed?

```java
String url = "http://www.usa.gov";
int pos = url.indexOf("http://");
if (pos >= 0)
{
  System.out.println("<" + url.substring(0, pos) + ">");
}
else
{
  System.out.println("not found");
}
```

(A) <www.usa.gov>
(B) <http://www.usa.gov>
(C) <>
(D) not found
(E) StringIndexOutOfBoundsException

28. The statement

```
Animal a = new Mammal("Elephant");
```

compiles with no errors. Which of the following situations will permit that?

(A) Mammal is a class with a constructor that takes one parameter of the String type, and Animal is its subclass.
(B) Animal is a class with a constructor that takes one parameter of the String type, and Mammal is its subclass that has no constructors defined.
(C) Mammal is a class with a constructor that takes one parameter of the String type, and Animal is a superclass of Mammal.
(D) Animal has a public static data field String Mammal.
(E) None of the above

29. Consider the following code segment.

```
ArrayList<String> list = new ArrayList<String>();
list.add("One");
list.add("Two");
String[] msg = new String[2];
list.add(msg[0]);
< another statement >
```

Which of the following choices for < *another statement* > will cause a NullPointerException when the code is compiled and executed?

(A) msg[0] = "Three";
(B) msg[0] = list.get(list.size());
(C) msg[1] = msg[0].substring(0, 2);
(D) list.add(2, msg[0]);
(E) if (!"Three".equals(list.get(2))) msg[0] = "Three";

30. At a county fair, prizes are awarded to the five heaviest cows. More than 2000 cows are entered, and their records are stored in an array. Which of the following algorithms provides the most efficient way of finding the records of the five heaviest cows?

(A) Selection Sort
(B) Insertion Sort
(C) Mergesort
(D) Insertion Sort terminated after the first five iterations
(E) Selection Sort terminated after the first five iterations

Questions 31 and 32 refer to the following class.

```java
public class Sample
{
  private double[][] amps;

  public Sample(int n)
  {
    < missing statements >
  }

  public double get(int j, int k)
  {
    return amps[j][k];
  }
}
```

31. Which of the following code segments can replace < *missing statements* > in `Sample`'s constructor so that it initializes `amps` to hold a table of values with `n` rows and `n` columns and fills them with random values $0.0 \leq$ `amps[j][k]` < 1.0?

    I.
```java
        amps = new double[n][n];
```

    II.
```java
        amps = new double[n][n];
        for (int j = 0; j < n; j++)
        {
          for (int k = j; k < n; k++)
          {
            amps[j][k] = Math.random();
            amps[k][j] = Math.random();
          }
        }
```

    III.
```java
        amps = new double[n][n];
        for (double[] r : amps)
        {
          for (int k = 0; k < n; k++)
          {
            r[k] = Math.random();
          }
        }
```

(A)   I only
(B)   II only
(C)   I and II only
(D)   II and III only
(E)   I, II, and III

32. Given

```
int size = 100;
Sample s = new Sample(size);
```

which of the following statements in a client class of Sample assigns to x the value in the last row and the first column of amps in s?

(A)   double x = s[99][0];
(B)   double x = s.get(size - 1, 0);
(C)   double x = s.get[s.length - 1, 0];
(D)   double x = s.get(s.amps.length - 1, 0);
(E)   double x = s.amps[s.amps.length - 1][0];

33. Consider an incomplete definition of the class C.

```
public class C
{
  private int value;

    < other fields, constructors, and methods not shown >
}
```

Suppose we have a method

```
public static int compare(C x, C y)
{
   return x.value - y.value;
}
```

and we need to find a "home" for it: place it into some class. Where can we place this method so that it compiles with no errors?

(A)   Only into C
(B)   Only into C or any subclass of C
(C)   Only into C or any superclass of C
(D)   Into any class
(E)   This method will always cause a syntax error, no matter what class we place it in.

34. Consider the following class.

```
public class ArrayProcessor
{
  public static void run(int[] arr)
  {
    for (int i = 0; i < arr.length; i++)
    {
      for (int j = arr.length - 1; j > i; j--)
      {
        if (arr[j] < arr[i])
        {
          swap(arr, i, j);
        }
      }
    }
  }

  private static void swap(int[] arr, int i, int j)
  {
    int temp = arr[i];
    arr[i] = arr[j];
    arr[j] = temp;
  }
}
```

How many times will `ArrayProcessor`'s `swap` method be called when the following code segment is executed?

```
int[] counts = {1, 2, 3, 4, 5, 0};
ArrayProcessor.run(counts);
```

(A)   5
(B)   10
(C)   15
(D)   30
(E)   35

35. Suppose it takes about 18 milliseconds to sort an array of 80,000 random numbers using Mergesort. Suppose for an array of 160,000 numbers, Mergesort runs for 40 milliseconds. For approximately how much time will Mergesort run on an array of 320,000 numbers? Choose the closest estimate.

(A)   88 milliseconds
(B)   96 milliseconds
(C)   126 milliseconds
(D)   160 milliseconds
(E)   192 milliseconds

36. The Binary Search algorithm is designed to work with an array sorted in ascending order. Under which of the following circumstances will the algorithm find a given target value even if the array is not sorted?

    I.   The array has an odd number of elements and the target value is located exactly in the middle of the array.

    II.   The array is partially sorted: the left third of the array has values all in ascending order and the target value is among them.

    III.   The array is partially sorted: all the values to the left of the target are smaller than the target, and all the values to the right of the target are larger than the target.

(A)   I only
(B)   I and II only
(C)   I and III only
(D)   II and III only
(E)   I, II, and III

37. Consider the following code segment.

```
ArrayList<Integer> lst = new ArrayList<Integer>();
int k = 2;

while (lst.size() < 5)
{
  boolean found = false;

  for (Integer n : lst)
    if (k % n == 0)
      found = true;

  if (!found)
    lst.add(k);

  k++;
}

System.out.println(lst);
```

What is printed when the code segment is executed?

(A)   [2, 3, 4, 5, 6]
(B)   [2, 3, 5, 7, 11]
(C)   [2, 3, 4, 5, 6, 7]
(D)   [2, 3, 5, 7, 11, 13]
(E)   Nothing is printed — the program goes into an infinite loop.

Questions 38 and 39 refer to the following class `Game` and the incomplete class `ChessGame`.

```java
public class Game
{
  private String gameName;
  private ArrayList<String> players;

  public Game(String name)
  {
    gameName = name;
    players = new ArrayList<String>();
  }

  public Game(String name, String[] people)
  {
    gameName = name;
    players = new ArrayList<String>();
    for (String nm : people)
      players.add(nm);
  }

  public void addPlayer(String name)
  {
    players.add(name);
  }

  public String getPlayer(int k)
  {
    return players.get(k - 1);
  }

  public String toString()
  {
    return gameName + " game " + players.toString();
  }
}


public class ChessGame extends Game
{
  public ChessGame(String black, String white)
  {
    < missing code >
  }
}
```

38. Consider the following code segment in a client class of Game.

```
String[] players = {"Annette", "Bertrand",
                              "Claude", "Danielle"};

Game game = new Game("Bauernschnapsen", players);

System.out.println( < missing expression >);
```

Which of the following can replace < *missing expression* > so that the code prints "Annette"?

(A)   `game.getPlayer(0)`
(B)   `game.getPlayer(1)`
(C)   `game.players.get(0)`
(D)   `game.players.get(1)`
(E)   `game.getPlayers().get(0)`

39. Suppose the statement

```
System.out.println(new ChessGame("Deep Blue", "Kasparov"));
```

prints

```
Chess game [Deep Blue, Kasparov]
```

Which of the following can replace < *missing code* > in ChessGame's constructor?

I.   `super("Chess", black, white);`

II.   `super("Chess");`
          `super.addPlayer(black);`
          `super.addPlayer(white);`

III.   `String[] players = {black, white};`
          `super("Chess", players);`

(A)   I only
(B)   II only
(C)   I and II only
(D)   II and III only
(E)   I, II, and III

40. Consider the following three implementations of a method `rotate90degrees` and the code segments (in the same class) used to test them.

I.
```
public int[] rotate90degrees(int[] v)
{
  int[] w = new int[2];
  w[0] = -v[1];
  w[1] = v[0];
  return w;
}

int[] v = {1, 2};
v = rotate90degrees(v);
System.out.println(v[0] + ", " + v[1]);
```

II.
```
public void rotate90degrees(int[] v)
{
  int  temp  = v[0];
  v[0] = -v[1];
  v[1] = temp;
}

int[] v = {1, 2};
rotate90degrees(v);
System.out.println(v[0] + ", " + v[1]);
```

III.
```
public int[] rotate90degrees(int[] v)
{
  int  temp  = v[0];
  v[0] = -v[1];
  v[1] = temp;
  return v;
}

int[] v = {1, 2};
rotate90degrees(v);
System.out.println(v[0] + ", " + v[1]);
```

Which of these implementations will compile with no errors and print $-2, 1$?

(A) I only
(B) II only
(C) I and II only
(D) II and III only
(E) I, II, and III

Practice Exam #1

Time — 1 hour and 30 minutes
Number of questions — 4
Percent of total grade — 50

1. Many websites have strict requirements for login passwords. The class `Password` provides methods that help verify that the password requirements are met and can also generate a password from a secret phrase and a number.

```
public class Password
{
  /** Returns true if password contains an uppercase letter;
   *  otherwise returns false.
   */
  private static boolean hasUpper(String password)
  { /* implementation not shown */ }

  /** Returns true if password contains a lowercase letter;
   *  otherwise returns false.
   */
  private static boolean hasLower(String password)
  { /* implementation not shown */ }

  /** Returns true if password contains a digit;
   *  otherwise returns false.
   */
  private static boolean hasDigit(String password)
  { /* implementation not shown */ }

  /** Returns true if password is valid, as described
   *  in part (a)
   */
  public static boolean isValid(String  password)
  {
    /* to be implemented in part (a) */
  }

  /** Returns a string made of the first letters of the words
   *  in phrase.
   *  Precondition: phrase is not null.
   */
  public static String makePasswordLetters(String phrase)
  { /* implementation not shown */ }
```

Continued ☞

127

```
/** Generates a password from phrase and n, as described in
 *   part (b).
 */
public static String makePassword(String phrase, int n)
{ /* to be implemented in part (b) */ }

/* constructors, other methods, and fields not shown */
}
```

(a) Write a method isValid that checks whether the given string meets the following password requirements: has between 8 and 16 characters; contains an uppercase letter; contains a lowercase letter; contains a digit. For example, "Tttoajaf0" is a valid password; "TrdiaywAsIcntb5191" is not valid, because it is too long — more than 16 characters. Use the methods provided in the Password class to determine whether a given string includes an uppercase letter, a lowercase letter, and a digit; you will not receive full credit if you write your own code to check for these occurrences.

Complete the method isValid below.

```
/** Returns true if password is 8 to 16 characters long and
 *   includes an uppercase letter, a lowercase letter, and a
 *   digit; otherwise returns false.
 *   Precondition: password is not null.
 */
public static boolean isValid(String password)
```

(b) Many internet users find it difficult to remember passwords for various websites. So they take a secret phrase and make a string of the first letters of the words in that string. Password's method makePasswordLetters(phrase) (whose implementation is not shown) returns the string of the first letters of the words in a given phrase. For example,

```
makePasswordLetters("Then took the other, as just as fair")
```

returns "Tttoajaf".

The method makePassword(phrase, n) takes a string of the first letters of the words in phrase and appends to it the digits of n taken in reverse order. So if phrase is "Then took the other, as just as fair", then makePassword(phrase, 1915) returns "Tttoajaf5191". makePassword returns null if the password generated that way is not a valid password.

Complete the method `makePassword` below.

```
/** Generates a password by taking the first letters
 *  of the words in phrase followed by the digits of n
 *  taken in reverse order. Returns the generated
 *  password if it is valid; otherwise returns null.
 *  Precondition: phrase is a non-empty string; n >= 0.
 */
public static String makePassword(String phrase, int n)
```

For additional practice, write the `makePasswordLetters` method. The consecutive words in `phrase` are separated by one or several spaces. Also add the necessary `String` constants for uppercase and lowercase letters and for digits and implement the `hasUpper`, `hasLower`, and `hasDigit` methods. Once your `Password` class is complete, test your code written in Parts (a) and (b).

2. The class `Shopping` helps a consumer choose the best option for buying a particular item. `Shopping`'s constructor initializes an `int` constant that represents the maximum distance (in miles) the consumer is willing to travel to a store. The `Shopping` class has three methods:

    - `addShoppingOption` — presents a shopping option to the consumer.

    - `streetPrice` — returns the average price of the item (a `double`) across all the shopping options presented to the consumer (regardless of the distance to the store), rounded to the nearest cent.

    - `toString` — returns a string that combines the store name, the item price at that store, and the distance from the consumer's home for the best shopping option (that is, the store within the maximum distance that offers the best price)

    `addShoppingOption` takes three parameters: the store name (a `String`), the item price (a `double`), and the distance from the consumer's home to that store (an `int`).

    For example, the following statements in a client of the `Shopping` class —

    ```
    Shopping kayak = new Shopping(20);
    kayak.addShoppingOption("JMart", 225.95, 18);
    kayak.addShoppingOption("Jest Buy", 189.00, 24);
    kayak.addShoppingOption("Tarjet", 220.95, 19);
    System.out.println(kayak);
    System.out.println(kayak.streetPrice());
    ```

    — print

    ```
    Tarjet 220.95 19
    211.97
    ```

    because the best shopping option presented to the consumer, within the 20-mile radius, is Tarjet, at \$220.95, and the average price for the three shopping options, $(225.95 + 189.00 + 220.95)/3$, rounded to the nearest cent, is \$211.97.

    Write the complete class `Shopping`, including the required instance variables, a constructor, and the three methods described above. Your implementation must meet the specifications and conform to the above example. **Do not use arrays, `ArrayLists`, or other data structures in your solution.**

    For additional practice, allow the consumer to order the item online, using 0 distance in `addShoppingOption` calls. For "brick-and-mortar" (not online) shopping options, add to the item price the cost of gas at \$0.45 per mile for traveling to the store and back.

    Another possible project is to allow the consumer to shop for three items at once, replacing the price parameter in the `addShoppingOption` method and the return value of the `streetPrice` method with an array of three `double` values and recommending the best option based on the sum of the prices for the three items.

3.   Memory Lane is a one-dimensional version of the popular card matching game Memory. Several cards are arranged face down in a row on the table. Each card contains a word or a picture, and there are two identical cards for each word or picture (so the number of cards is even). A player opens any two cards; if they have the same word or picture on them, the player removes both cards and shifts the remaining cards to the left to fill the gaps. If the cards are different, the player puts them back, face down.

In the computer model of the game, a card is represented by an object of the class Card. The Card class has a constructor that takes a String as a parameter and stores the string in an instance variable. The Card class also defines an equals method, which compares this card to another based on the strings they hold.

The class MemoryLane supplies several methods for playing the game. A partial implementation of this class is shown below.

```
public class MemoryLane
{
  /** The array of cards */
  private Card[] cards;

  /** The number of cards remaining to pair up */
  private int numCards;

  /** Returns true if for each card among the first
   *  numCards cards in the cards array there is exactly one
   *  other card equal to the first one; otherwise
   *  returns false.
   */
  public boolean isValidArrangement()
  { /* to be implemented in part (a) */ }

  /** Removes the card with index k from the cards array,
   *  shifting the subsequent cards "to the left" (toward the
   *  the beginning of the cards array) to close the gap;
   *  reduces numCards by one.
   *  Precondition: 0 <= k < numCards
   */
  public void removeCard(int k)
  { /* to be implemented in part (b) */ }

  /** If cards with the indices k1 and k2 are equal, removes
   *  these two cards and returns true; otherwise leaves
   *  the cards array unchanged and returns false.
   *  Precondition: 0 <= k1 < k2 < numCards
   */
  public boolean openTwoCards(int k1, int k2)
  { /* to be implemented in part (c) */ }

  /* constructors and other methods not shown */
}
```

(a)   Write a `boolean` method `isValidArrangement` that checks whether numCards cards at the beginning of the array cards represent a valid configuration for the game, that is, for each card there is exactly one other card equal to it.

Complete the method `isValidArrangement` below.

```
/** Returns true if for each card among the first
 *  numCards cards in the cards array there is exactly one
 *  other card equal to the first one; otherwise
 *  returns false.
 */
public boolean isValidArrangement()
```

(b)   Write a method `removeCard` that removes a card with the given index from the array `cards`, shifting the subsequent cards, if any, by one position toward the beginning. The method also decrements `numCards` by 1.

Complete the method `removeCard` below.

```
/** Removes the card with index k from the cards array,
 *  shifting the subsequent cards by one toward the
 *  beginning to close the gap; reduces numCards by one.
 *  Precondition: 0 <= k < numCards
 */
public void removeCard(int k)
```

(c)   Write a method `openTwoCards` that "opens" two cards with given indices. If the cards are equal, the method removes both cards and returns `true`; otherwise the array of cards remains unchanged and the method returns `false`. In writing this method, assume that the method `removeCard` from Part (b) works as specified, regardless of what you wrote there. You may not receive full credit if you duplicate `removeCard`'s code here.

Complete the method `openTwoCards` below.

```
/** If the cards with the indices k1 and k2 are equal,
 *  removes these two cards and returns true; otherwise
 *  leaves the cards array unchanged and returns false.
 *  Precondition: 0 <= k1 < k2 < numCards
 */
public boolean openTwoCards(int k1, int k2)
```

For additional practice, write the Card class. In addition to the constructor and the equals method explained in the introduction to this question, supply a toString method that returns the word on the card.

Also write and test a constructor for the MemoryLane class:

```
public MemoryLane(ArrayList<String> words)
```

The constructor should initialize the array cards by producing a valid configuration of randomly ordered pairs of cards. The words on the cards come from the list words; two cards are created for each word in the list words, so the size of the array cards will be 2*words.size(). numCards should be set to the same value. Write a helper method shuffle that arranges the elements of an array of cards in random order in such a way that each card can end up in any location with equal probability.

4. The picture below shows a few points connected by lines.

Such a structure is called a *graph*; the points are called *vertices*, and the lines are called *edges*. Graphs are useful for modeling all kinds of things: computer networks, airline routes, connections in social media apps, and board game rules and strategies, to name a few. We will consider only simple graphs in which any two vertices can be connected by at most one edge and a vertex cannot be connected to itself.

In some algorithms dealing with graphs, it is convenient to represent a graph as an *n*-by-*n* two-dimensional array of integers, where *n* is the number of vertices. Such a square array is called the *adjacency matrix* of the graph. If the vertices with indices i and j are connected by an edge, then m[i][j] and m[j][i] are both set to 1; otherwise these elements of m are set to 0 (where m is the name of the adjacency matrix).

(a) A simple graph is called *complete* if any two of its vertices are connected by an edge. For example:

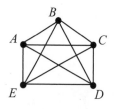

Write a boolean method isComplete that takes an adjacency matrix of a graph as a parameter and returns true if the corresponding graph is complete; otherwise the method returns false. (The adjacency matrix of a complete graph has 0's on the NW-SE diagonal and 1's everywhere else.)

Write the method isComplete below.

```
/** Returns true if the graph represented by the
 *  given adjacency matrix is a complete graph; otherwise
 *  returns false.
 */
public static boolean isComplete(int[][] m)
```

for (int r=0; r< m.

(b)   To represent a graph in a computer program, we can label its vertices with numbers or letters. Here we will use the letters "A", "B", ... as labels and represent the edges as pairs of letters in one long string. For example:

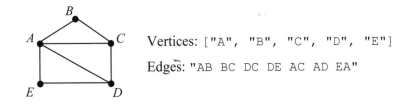

Vertices: ["A", "B", "C", "D", "E"]

Edges: "AB BC DC DE AC AD EA"

To find out whether an edge connects two vertices, we combine their letters into a two-letter string in two ways (first+second and second+first) and check whether one of these two combinations can be found in the string that represents the edges.

Write a method `makeAdjacencyMatrix` that takes two parameters, an `ArrayList` of vertices (single-letter strings) and a `String` of edges (two-letter substrings, separated by spaces), and returns the adjacency matrix of that graph.

Complete the method `makeAdjacencyMatrix` below.

```
/** Returns the adjacency matrix of the graph represented by
 *  a list of its vertices and a string of its edges. The
 *  vertices are single letters, and the edges are
 *  two-letter substrings of edges, separated by spaces.
 */
public static int[][] makeAdjacencyMatrix(
            ArrayList<String> vertices, String edges)
```

A graph is called a *cycle* if its vertices are arranged in one cycle with each vertex connected to two neighbors. For example:

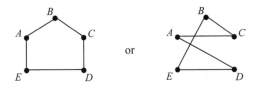

or

For additional practice, write a `boolean` method `isCycle` that takes the adjacency matrix of a graph and determines whether the graph is a cycle.

28/40

Practice Exam #2

−12

SECTION I

Time — 1 hour and 30 minutes
Number of questions — 40
Percent of total grade — 50

2/20 → 7:40 −
8:10

1. Assume that the `boolean` variables x, y, and z have been properly declared and initialized. Given that x is `true`, y is `true`, and z is `false`, which of the following expressions will evaluate to false?

    (A)   `(x && y) || z`
    (B)   `(x || y) && z`
    (C)   `y || (x && z)`
    (D)   `x || (y && z)`
    (E)   `x && (y || z)`

$2(1 + \frac{6}{1}) \rightarrow 2(1 + 6) \rightarrow 14$

2. Given two initialized `int` variables a and b, which of the following expressions evaluates to the same result as `2*(1 + (3*b)/a)` for all positive values of a and b?

    (A)   `2 + 6*b/a`
    (B)   `2*(1 + b/a*3)`
    (C)   `2 + 2*(b*3/a)`
    (D)   All of the above
    (E)   None of the above

$2(1 + \frac{6}{2})$

$2(1+3) = 8$

$2 + \frac{12}{2} = 2+6 = 8$

$2 \cdot (1 + 1 \cdot 3)$

$2(1+3) \rightarrow 2(4) = 8$

a=2
b=2

a=1
b=2

$2 + 2(\frac{6}{2})$

$2 + 2(3) = 6+2$

$2 + 2(\frac{6}{1}) \rightarrow 2+12 = 14$

3. Consider the following statement.

```
System.out.println("\\\"hello\"".substring(1));
```

What is printed when the statement is executed?

    (A)   `hello`
    (B)   `\hello`
    (C)   `\\hello`
    (D)   `"hello"`
    (E)   `\\"hello"`

4. Consider the following code segment.

```
String[] a = {"A", "B"};
String[] b = a;
String[] c = {a[0], a[1]};

String letter = a[0]; a[0] = a[1]; a[1] = letter;

System.out.println(a[0] + a[1] + b[0] + b[1] + c[0] + c[1]);
```

What is printed when the code segment is executed?

(A) BAABAB
(B) BAABBA
(C) BABAAB
(D) BABABA
(E) BBBBBB

5. Given

```
String s = "ALASKA";
int index = s.substring(1, 4).indexOf("A");
```

what is the value of index?

(A) 0
(B) 1
(C) 2
(D) 5
(E) -1

6. What is the value of v[4] after the following code segment is executed?

```
int d = 1;
int[] v = {1, 1, 1, 1, 1};
for (int i = 0; i < v.length; i++)
{
   d *= 2;
   v[i] += d;
}
```

(A) 16
(B) 32
(C) 33
(D) 64
(E) 65

7. Consider the following method fun2.

```
public int fun2(int x, int y)
{
  y -= x;
  return y;
}
```

What are the values of the variables a and b after the following code segment is executed?

```
int a = 3, b = 7;
b = fun2(a, b);
a = fun2(b, a);
```

(A) -1 and 4
(B) -4 and 7
(C) -4 and 4
(D) 3 and 7
(E) 3 and 4

$a = 3$
$b = 7$

$b = fun2(3,7)$
$b = 7-3$
return 4 (b)

$a = fun2(4,3)$
$3 = 3-4$
return -1

8. Consider the following method.

```
public void splat(String s)
{
  if (s.length() < 8)
    splat(s + s);
  System.out.println(s);
}
```

What is printed when splat("**") is called?

(A)   **

(B)   ****

(C)   ********

(D)   ********
      **

(E)   ********
      ****
      **

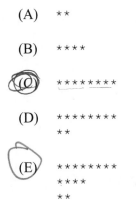

Questions 9 and 10 refer to the following method.

```java
public void printVals(String[] items, int k)
{
  if (k > 1)
  {
    printVals(items, k - 1);
    System.out.print(items[k] + " ");
    printVals(items, k - 2);
  }
}
```

Consider the following code segment.

```java
String[] names = {"Pat", "Joe", "Ann", "Cal", "Amy"};
printVals(names, names.length - 1);
```

9. What is printed when the code segment is executed?

    (A) Ann Cal Amy Ann
    (B) Ann Cal Amy Cal Ann
    (C) Ann Cal Joe Amy Joe Ann
    (D) Joe Ann Cal Joe Amy Joe Ann
    (E) Joe Ann Pat Cal Joe Amy Joe Ann Pat

10. How many calls to printVals are made, including the original call, when the code
    segment is executed?

    (A) 3
    (B) 5
    (C) 7
    (D) 8
    (E) 9

11. What is the result when the following code segment is compiled and executed?

```java
int m = 4, n = 5;
double d = Math.sqrt((m + n)/2);
System.out.println(d);
```

    (A) Syntax error "sqrt(double) in java.lang.Math cannot be applied to int"
    (B) 1.5 is printed
    (C) 2.0 is printed
    (D) 2.1213203435596424 is printed
    (E) ArithmeticException

12. Suppose a class `MyTest` has an instance variable score:

```
private int score = 0;
```

Which of the following could serve as a constructor in this class?

(A) `public MyTest() { }`
(B) `public int MyTest() { return score; }`
(C) `public MyTest(int s) { this = s; }`
(D) `public void MyTest(int s) { score = s; }`
(E) `public MyTest MyTest(int s) { score = s; return this; }`

13. Consider the following class `Athlete`.

```
public class Athlete
{
  private int numMedals;

  public int getRank() { return numMedals; }

  public int compareTo(Athlete other)
  {
    // return numMedals - other.numMedals;
    return getRank() - other.getRank();
  }

  < constructors and other methods not shown >
}
```

As you can see, the programmer has commented out direct references to `Athlete`'s instance variable `numMedals` in the `compareTo` method and replaced them with calls to the `getRank` method. What is the most compelling reason for doing this?

(A) To correct a syntax error: being private, neither `numMedals` nor `other.numMedals` is directly accessible in the method's code

(B) To correct a syntax error: being private, `other.numMedals` is not directly accessible in the method's code (`numMedals` is replaced with `getRank()` for consistency)

(C) To avoid possible problems later: if `other` happens to be an object of a subclass of `Athlete` in which `numMedals` is not used in calculating the rank, the original code would fail

(D) To improve run-time efficiency

(E) To achieve better encapsulation of the `Athlete` class

Questions 14 and 15 refer to the following classes.

```
public class Point
{
  private int x, y;

  public Point(int _x, int _y) { x = _x; y = _y; }

  public int getX() { return x; }
  public int getY() { return y; }

  public void move(int dx, int dy) { x += dx; y += dy; }
}

public class Polygon
{
  private ArrayList<Point> vertices;

  public Polygon()
  {
    vertices = new ArrayList<Point>();
  }

  public void add(Point p) { vertices.add(p); }

  /** Returns the x-coordinate of the k-th vertex
   *   (counting from 0)
   */
  public int getX(int k)
  { return < missing expression >; }

  /** Moves every vertex of the polygon horizontally by dx
   *   and vertically by dy
   */
  public void move(int dx, int dy)
  { < missing code > }
}
```

14. Which of the following could replace < *missing expression* > in the getX method of the
    Polygon class?

    (A) vertices[k].x
    (B) vertices.getX(k)
    (C) vertices.get(k).x
    (D) vertices.get(k).getX()
    (E) vertices.getX().get(k)

15. Which of the following could replace *< missing code >* in `Polygon`'s `move` method for it to work as described in the comment for this method?

I.
```
for (int k = 0; k < vertices.size(); k++)
{
    Point p = vertices.get(k);
    p.x += dx;
    p.y += dy;
}
```

II.
```
for (int k = 0; k < vertices.size(); k++)
    vertices.get(k).move(dx, dy);
```

III.
```
for (Point p : vertices)
    p.move(dx, dy);
```

(A) I only
(B) II only
(C) I and II only
(D) II and III only
(E) I, II, and III

16. Consider the following method from `ClassX`.

```
private int modXY(int x, int y)
{
    r = x / y;
    return x % y;
}
```

If `ClassX` compiles with no errors, which of the following must be true?

I.   r must have the type `double`.
II. r is not a local variable in the `modXY` method.
III. r must be a static variable in `ClassX`.

(A) I only
(B) II only
(C) I and II only
(D) II and III only
(E) I, II, and III

17. Consider the following code segment.

```
int[] factors = {2, 3, 4, 7, 2, 5};
int product = 1;

for (int i = 1; i < factors.length; i += 2)
{
    product *= (factors[i] % factors[i - 1]);
}
```

What is the value of product after the code segment is executed?

(A) 0
(B) 1
(C) 2
(D) 3
(E) 5

18. Consider the following class.

```
public class BuddyList
{
    /** Contains the names of buddies. */
    private ArrayList<String> buddies;

    public ArrayList<String> getBuddies()
    {
        return buddies;
    }

    < constructors, other fields and methods not shown >
}
```

If BuddyList myFriends is declared and initialized in some other class, a client of BuddyList, which of the following correctly assigns to name the name of the first buddy in the myFriends list?

```
I.   String name = myFriends.buddies[0];
II.  String name = myFriends.buddies.get(0);
III. String name = myFriends.getBuddies().get(0);
```

(A) I only
(B) II only
(C) III only
(D) I and II only
(E) II and III only

19. Consider the following method.

```
/** Returns the location of the target value
 *   in the array a, or -1 if not found.
 *   Precondition: a[0] ... a[a.length - 1] are
 *                 sorted in ascending order.
 */
public static int search(int[] a, int target)
{
  int first = 0;
  int last = a.length - 1;

  while (first <= last)
  {
    int middle = (first + last) / 2;
    if (target == a[middle])
      return middle;
    else if (target < a[middle])
      last = middle;
    else
      first = middle;
  }
  return -1;
}
```

This method fails to work as intended under certain conditions. If the array has five elements with the values 3, 4, 35, 42, 51, which of the following values of target would make this method fail?

(A) 3
(B) 4
(C) 35
(D) 42
(E) 51

2/21→7 6:15 - 6:45

20. The method

```
private void transpose(int[][] m)
{
  < implementation not shown >
}
```

flips the elements of m symmetrically over the diagonal. For example:

```
1 2 3            1 4 7
4 5 6   transpose  2 5 8
7 8 9    ——→      3 6 9
```

Which of the following implementations of transpose will work as intended?

I.
```
for (int r = 0; r < m.length; r++)
{
  for (int c = 0; c < m[0].length; c++)
  {
    int temp = m[r][c];
    m[r][c] = m[c][r];
    m[c][r] = temp;
  }
}
```

`[1][0] = [0][1]`
`[1][1]`

II.
```
for (int c = m[0].length - 1; c > 0; c--)
{
  for (int r = c-1; r >= 0; r--)
  {
    int temp = m[r][c];
    m[r][c] = m[c][r];
    m[c][r] = temp;
  }
}
```

`c = [2]`
`r = 1`
`temp = [1][2]`

III.
```
for (int c = 0; c < m[0].length - 1; c++)
{
  for (int r = c + 1; r < m.length; r++)
  {
    int temp = m[r][c];
    m[r][c] = m[c][r];
    m[c][r] = temp;
  }
}
```

(A) I only
(B) II only
(C) I and II only
(D) II and III only
(E) I, II, and III

21. Consider the following code segment.

```
String s = "ban";

ArrayList<String> words = new ArrayList<String>();
words.add(s);
words.add(s.substring(1));
words.add(s.substring(1, 2));

String total = "";

for (String w : words)
{
   total += w;
}
System.out.print(total.indexOf("an"));
```

What is printed when the code segment is executed?

(A) 1
(B) 2
(C) 3
(D) ana
(E) banana

22. Consider the following method.

```
public double goFigure(int n)
{
   n %= 7;
   return (double)(12 / n);
}
```

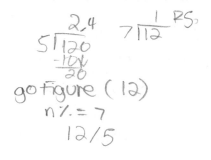

What is printed when the following code segment is executed?

```
int n = 12;
System.out.print(goFigure(n));
System.out.println(" " + n);
```

(A) 2.0 12
(B) 2.4 12
(C) 2.0 5
(D) 2.4 5
(E) 2.4 6

23. Consider the following code segment.

```
int n = 1, d = 1, s = 1;

while (n <= 5)
{
   System.out.print(s + " ");
   n++;
   d += 2;
   s += d;
}
System.out.println();
```

What is printed when the code segment is executed?

(A)   1 3 6 10 15
(B)   1 4 9 16 25
(C)   1 4 7 10 13
(D)   1 4 9 16
(E)   1 3 5 7

24. Consider the following classes.

```
public class A
{
   public A() { methodOne(); }

   public void methodOne() { System.out.print("A"); }
}
```

```
public class B extends A
{
   public B() { System.out.print("*"); }

   public void methodOne() { System.out.print("B"); }
}
```

What is printed when the following statement is executed?

```
A obj = new B();
```

(A)   *
(B)   *A
(C)   *B
(D)   A*
(E)   B*

25. Consider the following class.

```
public class Rectangle
{
  private int width, height;

  public Rectangle(int w, int h)
  {
    width = w;
    height = h;
  }

  public int getArea() { return width * height; }

  < other methods not shown >
}
```

Suppose this class also <u>overrides</u> `Object`<u>'s equals</u> method in such a way that the method returns `true` for `Rectangle` objects with the same area. Which of the following `equals` methods will accomplish this?

(A)
```
public int equals(int area)
{
  return getArea() - area;
}
```

(B)
```
public boolean equals(int area)
{
  return getArea() == area;
}
```

can't use Rectangle

(C)
```
public boolean equals(Rectangle other)
{
  return getArea() == other.getArea();
}
```

(D)
```
public boolean equals(Object other)
{
  return this.getArea() == other.getArea();
}
```

(E)
```
public boolean equals(Object other)
{
  return getArea() == ((Rectangle)other).getArea();
}
```

26. Consider the following incomplete method `cutToAverage`.

```
public double cutToAverage(double[] amps)
{
   double avg = 0.0;

   < missing code >

   return avg;
}
```

It first finds the average `avg` of the values in an array, then replaces every element that exceeds `avg` with `avg`. `cutToAverage` returns `avg`. Which of the following could replace < *missing code* > so that `cutToAverage` works as intended?

I.
```
for (double x : amps)
   avg += x;
avg /= amps.length;
for (double x : amps)
   if (x > avg)
      x = avg;
```

II.
```
for (int k = 0; k < amps.length; k++)
   avg += amps[k];
avg /= amps.length;
for (int k = 0; k < amps.length; k++)
   if (amps[k] > avg)
      amps[k] = avg;
```

III.
```
for (double x : amps)
   avg += x;
avg /= amps.length;
for (int k = amps.length - 1; k >= 0; k--)
   if (amps[k] > avg)
      amps[k] = avg;
```

(A) I only
(B) II only
(C) I and II only
(D) II and III only
(E) I, II, and III

27. Consider the following classes.

```
public class Lunch extends Meal
{
  public Lunch() { }

  <other constructors, methods, and instance variables not shown>
}

public class Pizza extends Lunch
{
  public Pizza() { }

  <other constructors, methods, and instance variables not shown>
}
```

Which of the following statements will cause a compile-time error?

(A) `Lunch pizza = new Lunch();`
(C) `Lunch pizza = new Pizza();`   *Pizza IS-A Lunch*
(B) `Meal pizza = new Lunch();`   *Lunch is-A meal*
(D) `Meal pizza = new Pizza();`
(E) None of the above

28. Consider the following method.

```
public int locate(String str, String oneLetter)
{
  int j = 0;
  while (j < str.length() &&
          str.substring(j, j+1).compareTo(oneLetter) < 0)
  {
    j++;
  }
  return j;
}
```

Which of the following must be true when the while loop terminates?

(A) `j == str.length()`
(B) `str.substring(j, j+1) >= 0`
(C) `j <= str.length() ||`
           `str.substring(j, j+1).compareTo(oneLetter) > 0`
(D) `j >= str.length() ||`
           `str.substring(j, j+1).compareTo(oneLetter) >= 0`
(E) `j >= str.length() &&`
           `str.substring(j, j+1).compareTo(oneLetter) >= 0`

Questions 29 and 30 refer to the following implementation of Mergesort.

```java
public class Mergesort
{
  /** Returns a new array that holds the values
   *   arr[m], arr[m+1], ... arr[n] arranged in ascending order
   *   Precondition: 0 <= m <= n < arr.length
   */
  public static int[] sort(int[] arr, int m, int n)
  {
    int[] result = new int[n - m + 1];

    if (m == n)
    {
      result[0] = arr[m];
    }
    else
    {
      int mid = (n + m) / 2;
      int[] result1 = sort(arr, m, mid);
      int[] result2 = sort(arr, mid + 1, n);
      result = merge(result1, result2);
    }

    return result;
  }

  /** Merges arr1 and arr2 in ascending order and returns the
   *   resulting array.
   *   Precondition: arr1 and arr2 are sorted in ascending order
   */
  private static int[] merge(int[] arr1, int[] arr2)
  { < implementation not shown > }
}
```

29. If int[] arr holds eight values and Mergesort(arr, 0, 7) is called, how many
    times in total will Mergesort's merge method be called?

    (A) 1
    (B) 3
    (C) 7
    (D) 8
    (E) 15

30. If `Mergesort.sort(arr, 0, 999)` takes on average 40 ms and
    `Mergesort.merge(arr1, arr2)` takes on average
    `0.01*(arr1.length + arr2.length)`, what is the average run time for
    `Mergesort.sort(arr, 0, 1999)`?

    (A) 50 ms
    (B) 100 ms
    (C) 160 ms
    (D) 170 ms
    (E) 180 ms

31. Consider the following code segment.

```
ArrayList<String> xyz = new ArrayList<String>();
xyz.add("X");
xyz.add("Y");
xyz.add("Z");

int count = 0;
for (String s1 : xyz)
{
   for (String s2 : xyz)
   {
     if (s1.equals(s2))
     {
       count++;
     }
   }
}

System.out.print(count);
```

X Y Z

What is the result when the code segment is compiled/executed?

    (A) 0 is printed
    (B) 1 is printed
    (C) 3 is printed
    (D) `NullPointerException`
    (E) Syntax error

32. A two-dimensional array `image` holds brightness values for pixels (picture elements) in an image. The brightness values range from 0 to 255. Consider the following method.

```
public int findMax(int[][] image)
{
  int[] count = new int[256];
  int i, iMax = 0;

  for (int r = 0; r < image.length; r++)
  {
    for (int c = 0; c < image[0].length; c++)
    {                    i ← value at [r][c]
      i = image[r][c];
      count[i]++;
    }                index of count @ i increased
  }

  for (i = 1; i < 256; i++)
  {
    if (count[i] > count[iMax])
      iMax = i;
  }

  return iMax;
}
```

What does this method compute?

(A) The column with the largest sum of brightness values in `image`
(B) The maximum brightness value for all pixels in `image`
(C) The most frequent brightness value in `image`
(D) The maximum sum of brightness values in any 256-by-256 square in `image`
(E) The maximum sum of brightness values in any 256 consecutive rows in `image`

33. What is the result when the following code segment is compiled/executed?

```
String a = "A";
String b = a;        // Line 1
String c = a + 1;    // Line 2
String d = b + "1";

System.out.println((c == d) + " " + c.equals(d));
```

(A) `false false` is printed
(B) `false true` is printed
(C) `true true` is printed
(D) Syntax error on Line 1
(E) Syntax error on Line 2

34. Consider the following class.

```
public class BankAccount
{
  private int balance;

  public BankAccount() { balance = 0; }
  public BankAccount(int amt) { balance = amt; }

  public int getBalance() { return balance; }
  public void makeDeposit(int amt) { balance += amt; }
}
```

What is printed when the following code segment in a client class is executed?

```
ArrayList<BankAccount> bank = new ArrayList<BankAccount>();
bank.add(new BankAccount());
bank.add(new BankAccount(5));
bank.add(new BankAccount(10));
bank.add(new BankAccount(15));

for (BankAccount customer : bank)
  customer.makeDeposit(10);
int total = 0;
for (BankAccount customer : bank)
  total += customer.getBalance();
System.out.println(total);
```

(A) 0
(B) 30
(C) 40
(D) 60
(E) 70

35. The statement

```
System.out.println(Integer.MAX_VALUE);
```

prints 2147483647, which is $2^{31}-1$. What is the result when

```
System.out.println(2*Integer.MAX_VALUE + 2);
```

is compiled/executed?

(A) 0 is printed
(B) 4294967296, which is 2^{32}, is printed
(C) ArithmeticException
(D) Syntax error: arithmetic overflow
(E) Syntax error: cannot apply the + operator to an Integer and an int

Questions 36-38 refer to the following classes.

```java
public class Party
{
  private ArrayList<String> theGuests;

  public Party() { theGuests = null; }

  public Party(ArrayList<String> guests) { theGuests = guests; }

  public void setGuests(ArrayList<String> guests)
  { theGuests = guests; }

  public String toString()
  { /* implementation not shown */ }
}

public class BDayParty extends Party
{
  private String theName;

  public BDayParty(String name, ArrayList<String> guests)
  { /* implementation not shown */ }

  public String getName() { return theName; }

  < other methods not shown >
}
```

36. Given

```java
ArrayList<String> guests = new ArrayList<String>();
guests.add("Amal");
guests.add("Ben");
guests.add("Candy");
```

which of the following declarations is NOT valid?

(A) `Party[] celebrations = new Party[2];`

(B) `Party[] celebrations =`
       `{new Party(guests), new Party()};`

(C) `BDayParty[] celebrations =`
       `{new BDayParty("Malika", guests), new Party(guests)};`

(D) `BDayParty[] celebrations =`
       `{new BDayParty("Ethan", guests),`
       ` new BDayParty("Henry", guests)};`

(E) All of the above are valid.

37. Consider the following constructor in the BDayParty class.

```
public BDayParty(String name, ArrayList guests)
{
   < missing statement >
   theName = name;
}
```

Which of the following statements can replace < *missing statement* > in this constructor?

  I.   theGuests = guests;

  II.   super(guests);

  III. setGuests(guests);

(A) I only
(B) II only
(C) I and II only
(D) II and III only
(E) I, II, and III

38. Suppose we have added the following methods to the Party class:

```
public String getOccasion() { return null; }
public String getMessage() { return "Happy"; }
public String greetings() { return getMessage() + " "
                                           + getOccasion(); }
```

and

```
BDayParty birthday = new BDayParty("Aaron", guests);
System.out.println(birthday.greetings());
```

prints

```
Happy Birthday Aaron
```

Which of the following is the smallest set of Party methods that would have to be overridden in the BDayParty class to make this happen?

(A) None
(B) getOccasion
(C) getMessage
(D) getOccasion and getMessage
(E) getOccasion, getMessage, and greetings

39. Consider the following code segment.

```
ArrayList<Integer> numbers = new ArrayList<Integer>();
numbers.add(0);
numbers.add(1);

for (int k = 1; k <= 3; k++)
{
  int n = numbers.size();
  for (int i = 0; i < n; i++)
    numbers.add(numbers.get(i) + 1);
}

int n = numbers.size();
System.out.println(n + " " + numbers.get(n - 1));
```

What is printed when the code segment is executed?

(A)   6 3
(B)   8 3
(C)   8 4
(D)   16 3
(E)   16 4

40. Consider the following method.

```
public int randomPoints(int n)
{
  return (int)(n * Math.random()) + 1;
}
```

Which of the following outputs is NOT possible when the statement

```
System.out.println(randomPoints(3) + randomPoints(3));
```

is executed?

(A)   2
(B)   3
(C)   4
(D)   6
(E)   All of the above are possible

Practice Exam #2

SECTION II

Time — 1 hour and 30 minutes
Number of questions — 4
Percent of total grade — 50

1. The class Bus is a simplified model of a bus schedule at a particular bus stop. You will write a constructor and a method of this class.

```
public class Bus
{
    /** Starting and ending times of the bus schedule
        (in minutes since midnight) at a particular bus stop */
    private int startTime, endTime;

    /** The interval between two consecutive buses (in minutes) */
    private int runInterval;

    /** Converts a string that represents time in the 24-hour
     *  format into minutes since midnight and returns the
     *  result.
     */
    private int toMinutes(String time)
    { /* implementation not shown */ }

    /** Constructs a Bus object with given starting and
     *  ending times and a given interval between two
     *  consecutive buses. The start and end strings represent
     *  time in the 24-hour format.
     */
    public Bus(String start, String end, int mins)
    { /* to be implemented in part (a) */ }

    /** Returns the wait time, in minutes, for the next bus
     *  from the given time, as described in part (b).
     */
    public int waitTime(String time)
    { /* to be implemented in part (b) */ }
}
```

(a) Write the constructor of the Bus class. Use the provided helper method toMinutes to convert the parameters String start and String end, which represent time in the 24-hour format, into minutes since midnight. For example, toMinutes("06:30") returns 390 (because $6 \cdot 60 + 30 = 390$) and toMinutes("18:30") returns 1110, so if a Bus object is constructed with parameters "06:30", "18:30", and 20, its instance variables startTime, endTime, and runInterval get the values 390, 1110, and 20, respectively.

Complete the constructor of the `Bus` class below.

```
/** Constructs a Bus object with given starting and
 *  ending times and a given interval between two
 *  consecutive buses. The start and end strings represent
 *  time in the 24-hour format.
 */
public Bus(String start, String end, int mins)
```

(b) The method `waitTime` of the `Bus` class takes one parameter, a string that represents the current time in the 24-hour format. The method returns the wait time, in minutes, for the next bus. If the current time exceeds the time of that day's final bus, the method returns –1. For example, if a `bus` object is constructed like this —

```
Bus bus = new Bus("6:00", "18:30", 20);
```

— then `bus.waitTime(time)` returns the following values:

time	Time in minutes since midnight	Next bus	bus.waitTime(time)
"5:20"	320	"6:00" => 360	40
"7:10"	430	"7:20" => 440	10
"7:20"	440	"7:20" => 440	0
"18:25"	1105	Last bus left at 18:20	-1
"18:40"	1120	No more buses	-1

Complete the `waitTime` method below. Call the `toMinutes` method to convert the `time` parameter into minutes since midnight.

```
/** Returns the wait time for the next bus from a given
 *  time. The parameter time is a string that represents
 *  time in the 24-hour format. If time exceeds the time
 *  of the final bus, the method returns -1.
 */
public int waitTime(String time)
```

For additional practice, implement the `toMinutes` method and provide a `main` method to test the code you wrote in Parts (a) and (b).

2. The class `EquationSolver` helps find an approximate solution for an equation $f(x) = 0$. (The function $f(x)$ is defined in a separate class `Fun`.) `EquationSolver`'s method `solve` looks for a solution on the specified interval $[a, b]$. It is known that the function f is continuous on $[a, b]$, $f(a) < 0$, and $f(b) \geq 0$. For example:

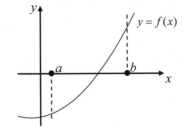

The `solve` method uses a "divide-and-conquer" algorithm to find the approximate solution. It takes the midpoint of the interval $[a, b]$, $m = \dfrac{a+b}{2}$, and examines $f(m)$. If $f(m) < 0$, a is set to m; otherwise b is set to m.

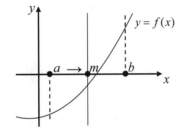

The process continues until the value of $b - a$ becomes smaller than the specified precision value. Then `solve` returns the midpoint of the last interval $[a, b]$.

`EquationSolver`'s constructor takes one `double` parameter, the desired precision of the solution. The `solve` method takes three parameters: an object of the type `Fun` (or of a subclass of `Fun`) that has a public method `double f(double x)`, and `double` values a and b. For example, if `EquationSolver` were constructed with the precision constant 0.000001 and $f(x)$ were defined as

```
public double f(double x)
{
   return Math.pow(x, 4) - 0.3;
}
```

(that is, $y = x^4 - 0.3$), then `solve` would return 0.7400828301906586, which is pretty close to the "exact" solution $0.3^{0.25} \approx 0.7400828044922853$.

Assume that the precondition $f(a) < 0$ and $f(b) \geq 0$ in the `solve` method is satisfied — no need to check for it.

Write the complete `EquationSolver` class, including a constructor that initializes the precision constant to a given value and the `solve` method described above. Your implementation must use the "divide-and-conquer" algorithm described above. **Do not use arrays, ArrayLists, or other data structures in your solution.**

For additional practice, supply a class `Fun` and define the `f(x)` method in it to return `Math.pow(x, 4) - r`, where `r` is a random number between 0 and 1. Also add a method that returns the "exact" solution, `Math.pow(r, 0.25)`. Test your `EquationSolver` class by calling the `solve` method several times and comparing the solutions produced by `solve` with the "exact" solutions. [*]

---

[*] Ordinarily, `Fun` would be an interface that specifies one method, `double f(double x)`, with different classes implementing that interface, but Java interfaces are not tested on AP CSA exams.

3. Apflix recommends movies to customers based on their previous selections. Clearly some movie matching mechanism is employed. A movie is described by a set of predefined features, such as genre, rating, director, lead actress, lead actor, and so on. A movie is represented by an object of the class `Movie`:

```
public class Movie
{
  /** Returns the list of features for this movie. */
  public ArrayList<String> getFeatures()
  {  /* implementation not shown */ }

  /** Returns the likeness score between this movie and other,
   *  as explained in part (a).
  public double likenessScore(Movie other)
  {  /* to be implemented in part(a) */  }

  /* fields, constructors, and other methods not shown */
}
```

The `getFeatures` method of the `Movie` class returns an `ArrayList<String>` whose elements represent the features of a movie. The sizes of the features lists are the same for all movies.

(a) The likeness score of two movies is defined as the number of matching features divided by the total number of features. For example:

movie1 features	["COM", "ROM", "PAL", "AFF", "PG"]
movie2 features	["DRA", "ROM", "PAL", "HOP", "PG"]
Total number of features	5
Number of matching features	3
movie1.likenessScore(movie2)	3/5 = 0.6

Complete the method `likenessScore` below.

```
/** Returns the likeness score between this movie and other.
 *  Precondition: The length of the features list is the
 *                same in this and other, and the features
 *                are listed in the same order in both
 *                movies.
 */
public double likenessScore(Movie other)
```

(b) An Apflix subscriber has a list of movies she has watched recently. Some of the movies on that list may not fit well with the rest (for example, a movie may have been ordered for a friend or a family member). Apflix's marketing department wishes to detect and remove such "outliers" from each subscriber's movie list.

An Apflix subscriber is represented by the class `ApflixSubscriber`:

```
public class ApflixSubscriber
{
    /** The list of movies watched recently by this subscriber */
    private ArrayList<Movie> movies;

    /** Returns an array of fit coefficients that correspond to
     *   movies in the subscriber's list; a coefficient for a
     *   movie indicates how well that movie fits with the rest
     *   of the movies in the list.
     */
    public double[] getFitCoefficients()
    {   /* implementation not shown */ }

    /** Removes outliers from the movies list, as explained
     *   below.
     */
    public void removeOutliers()
    {   /* to be implemented in part (b) */  }

    /* constructors and other fields and methods not shown */
}
```

The method `getFitCoefficients` returns an array of values that measure how well each movie in the list `movies` fits with the rest. The size of the array returned by `getFitCoefficients` is the same as the size of the `movies` list. The k-th element in the returned array is equal to the fit coefficient for the k-th movie.

Write the method `removeOutliers`. This method obtains an array of the fit coefficients for the `movies` list, calculates their average, and uses half of that value as a threshold. It then removes from the `movies` list all the elements whose fit coefficient is less than the threshold.

Complete the method `removeOutliers` below.

```
    /** Obtains the fit coefficients for the movies list,
     *   calculates their average, and removes from the
     *   movies list all the elements whose fit coefficient
     *   is less than half the average.
     *   Precondition: The size of the movies list is >= 2.
     */
    public void removeOutliers()
```

For additional practice, complete the `Movie` class, then implement the `getFitCoefficients` method of the `ApflixSubscriber` class. The fit coefficient for a movie M is defined as the average of the likeness scores between M and all the other movies in the list. Make sure that the likeness score for any pair of movies from the list is computed only once, but do not use any temporary arrays or other data structures.

4. A ski resort architect is using a program to help her lay out trails. The slope is represented as a two-dimensional array of integers, in which each element represents a location on the slope and holds the altitude at that location. The slope is modeled by the class SkiSlope.

```
public class SkiSlope
{
    /** The altitudes of locations on the slope */
    private int[][] alts;

    /** Returns the index of the element in the top row of alts
     *   that holds the greatest value of all the alts values in
     *   the top row.
     */
    public int summitLocation()
    { /* to be implemented in part (a) */ }

    /** Builds and returns the "steepest trail" on the slope,
     *   as explained in part (b).
     */
    public ArrayList<Integer> findSteepestTrail()
    { /* to be implemented in part (b) */}

    /* constructors and other fields and methods not shown */
}
```

(a)   The summit of the slope is the location in the top (index 0) row of the alts array that has the greatest value in that row. If several locations have the same greatest altitude, the summit is assumed to be the leftmost of them. Write the method summitLocation that finds the summit of the slope and returns the column index of the summit.

Complete the method summitLocation below.

```
/** Returns the index of the element in the top row of alts
 *   that holds the greatest value of all the alts values in
 *   the top row.
 */
public int summitLocation()
```

(b)   Write a method `findSteepestTrail` that builds and returns the "steepest trail" from the summit to the bottom. The "steepest trail" starts at the summit of the slope and proceeds down from one row to the next, ending at a location in the bottom row. On each step down, the trail proceeds to one of the two or three neighboring locations in the row below it: just below the current location or the one diagonally to the left or the one diagonally to the right, staying within the bounds of the `alts` array. Of the available two or three options, the method always chooses the location with the lowest altitude. If two or all three neighboring locations below the current one have the same smallest altitude, then any one of them may be chosen. The figure below shows an example of the altitude values on a slope and the locations that make up the "steepest trail."

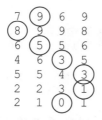

The method `findSteepestTrail()` for the slope returns an `ArrayList` of `Integer` objects whose values are the indices of the altitudes in the respective rows, starting with the location of the summit and ending with a location in the bottom row of the slope. In the above example, the indices of the circled locations are 1, 0, 1, 2, 3, 3, 2. Assume that the `findSummit` method from Part (a) works as specified, regardless of what you wrote there, and do not duplicate its code.

Complete the method `findSteepestTrail` below.

```
/** Builds and returns the "steepest trail" on the slope.
 *   The trail starts at the summit, in the top row. On each
 *   step, the trail proceeds to the neighboring location
 *   just below the current location or the one diagonally
 *   to the left or to the right (if available), always
 *   choosing the location with the lowest altitude. (If the
 *   altitude in two or three neighboring locations is the
 *   same, any one of them may be chosen.) Returns an
 *   ArrayList<Integer> that holds the indices of locations
 *   on the trail in consecutive rows, starting at the summit.
 */
public ArrayList<Integer> findSteepestTrail()
```

For additional practice, write a method `findZigzagTrail` that builds a trail that starts at the summit and proceeds down from one row to the next, always choosing the location with the greatest altitude in the row below it. Alternate between choosing the leftmost and the rightmost maximum location in consecutive rows: leftmost maximum in the top row, rightmost maximum in the next row, and so on. Write a helper method `leftAndRightMax` that returns a two-element array that holds the indices of the left maximum and the right maximum in a given array.

Practice Exam #3

SECTION I

Time — 1 hour and 30 minutes
Number of questions — 40
Percent of total grade — 50

1. Given the declarations

    ```
    int p = 5;
    int q = 3;
    ```

    which of the following expressions evaluate to 7.5?

    I.   `(double)p * (double)q / 2;`
    II. `(double)p * (double)(q / 2);`
    III. `(double)(p * q / 2);`

    (A) I only
    (B) II only
    (C) I and II only
    (D) I, II, and III
    (E) None of them

2. Consider the following code segment.

    ```
    String band = "anamanaguchi";

    System.out.println(band.substring(1, 4).
                        compareTo(band.substring(5, 8)));
    ```

    What is printed when the code segment is executed?

    (A) `true`
    (B) `false`
    (C) `0`
    (D) A negative integer
    (E) A positive integer

3. Consider the following class.

```
public class Sphere
{
  public static final double PI = 3.14159;

  public static double volume(int r)
  {
    return 4 / 3 * PI * Math.pow(r, 3);
  }
}
```

Which of the following statements about this code is true?

(A)   The class will not compile because no constructors are defined.
(B)   The class will not compile because PI cannot be declared public.
(C)   The class will not compile because the volume method is declared static.
(D)   Math.pow(r, 3) cannot be used because r is an int.
(E)   The class compiles with no errors but the volume method returns a smaller value than the expected $\frac{4}{3}\pi r^3$.

4. Consider the following code segment.

```
ArrayList<String> cities = new ArrayList<String>();
cities.add("Atlanta");
cities.add("Boston");
cities.add("Chicago");

for (String city : cities)
  city = city.substring(1);

System.out.println(cities);
```

What is printed when the code segment is executed?

(A)   [A, B, C]
(B)   [C, B, A]
(C)   [a, n, o]
(D)   [tlanta, oston, hicago]
(E)   [Atlanta, Boston, Chicago]

5. Consider the following method.

```
public String filter(String str, String pattern)
{
  int pos = str.indexOf(pattern);

  if (pos == -1)
    return str;
  else
    return filter(str.substring(0, pos) +
                  str.substring(pos + pattern.length()), pattern);
}
```

What is printed when the following statement is executed?

```
System.out.println(filter("papaya", "pa"));
```

(A) p
(B) pa
(C) ya
(D) aya
(E) paya

6. Consider the following statements.

```
String str = "\\*\n*\\";
System.out.println(str + " " + str.length());
```

What is printed when the statements are executed?

(A)
```
\*\n*\ 5
```
(B)
```
\**\*\" 6
```
(C)
```
\*\n*\ 8
```
(D)
```
\*
*\ 5
```
(E)
```
\\*
*\\ 7
```

7. Consider the following code segment.

```
int[] arr = {4, 3, 2, 1, 0};

for (int k = 1; k < arr.length; k++)
{
   arr[k-1] += arr[k];
}
```

Which of the following represents the contents of `arr` after the code segment has been executed?

(A)   4, 7, 5, 3, 1
(B)   4, 7, 9, 10, 10
(C)   7, 5, 3, 1, 0
(D)   7, 3, 2, 1, 0
(E)   10, 6, 3, 1, 0

8. Consider the following method.

```
public int countSomething(int[] arr)
{
   int m = arr[0];
   int count = 1;

   for (int k = 1; k < arr.length; k++)
   {
      int a = arr[k];
      if (a > m)
      {
        m = a;
        count = 1;
      }
      else if (m == a)
        count++;
   }

   return count;
}
```

For which of the following arrays will `countSomething` return 3?

(A)   `int[] arr = {0, 1, 1, 1, 1};`
(B)   `int[] arr = {1, 6, 5, 4, 0};`
(C)   `int[] arr = {1, 0, 5, 6, 1};`
(D)   `int[] arr = {3, 2, 1, 0, 5};`
(E)   None of the above

9. Consider the following code segment.

```
if (!somethingIsFalse())
    return false;
else
    return true;
```

Which of the following replacements for this code will produce the same result?

(A)   `return true;`
(B)   `return false;`
(C)   `return somethingIsFalse();`
(D)   `return !somethingIsFalse();`
(E)   None of the above

10. Assume that the `boolean` variables a, b, and c have been properly declared and initialized. Which of the following expressions is `true` if and only if NOT all three variables a, b, and c have the same value?

(A)   `a != b || b != c`
(B)   `a != b && b != c`
(C)   `a >= b && b >= c && c >= a`
(D)   `a > b || b > c || a > c`
(E)   `!(a == b || b == c || a == c)`

11. Consider the following method.

```
public void change(double[] nums, int n)
{
    for (int k = 0; k < n; k++)
    {
        nums[k] = 5.4;
    }
    n = 2;
}
```

What will be stored in `samples` and `len` after the following statements are executed?

```
double[] samples = {1.0, 2.1, 3.2, 4.3};
int len = samples.length;
change(samples, len);
```

(A)   samples contains `5.4, 5.4, 5.4, 5.4`; len is 2
(B)   samples contains `5.4, 5.4, 5.4, 5.4`; len is 4
(C)   samples contains `1.0, 2.1, 3.2, 4.3`; len is 4
(D)   samples contains `5.4, 5.4`; len is 2
(E)   samples contains `1.0, 2.1`; len is 2

12. Consider the following code segment.

```
for (int r = 1; r < mat.length; r++)
{
  for (int c = 1; c < mat[0].length; c++)
  {
    if ((r + c) % 2 == 0)
      mat[r][c] = 2 * mat[r - 1][c - 1] + c;
  }
}
System.out.println(mat[2][2]);
```

Suppose `mat` is declared as

```
int[][] mat = new int[3][4];
```

and holds the values

```
2 1 3 4
9 7 2 1
0 2 5 6
```

What is printed when the code segment is executed?

(A)   5
(B)   11
(C)   12
(D)   15
(E)   16

13. Consider the following code segment.

```
int num = 5;
while (num >= 0)
{
  num -= 2;
}
System.out.print(num);
```

What is printed when the code segment is executed?

(A)   -1
(B)   -2
(C)   0
(D)   2
(E)   21

14. What happens when the size of an `ArrayList<Integer>` numbers has reached its capacity and `numbers.add(0)` is called?

    (A) The program throws an `IndexOutOfBoundsException`.
    (B) `numbers` remains unchanged; `add` returns `false`.
    (C) The first element of `numbers` is set to hold an `Integer` object with the value 0. The size of `numbers` remains unchanged.
    (D) The values in `numbers` are shifted toward the beginning (with the first element overwritten), and an `Integer` object with the value 0 is appended at the end of `numbers`. The size of `numbers` remains unchanged.
    (E) A larger array is allocated to hold the elements of `numbers`; the values from the old `numbers` array are copied into the new array, and an `Integer` object with the value 0 is appended at the end of `numbers`. The size of `numbers` is incremented by 1.

15. Suppose an array `arr` contains 127 different random values arranged in ascending order, and the most efficient searching algorithm is used to find a target value. How many elements of the array will be examined when the target equals `arr[39]`?

    (A) 4
    (B) 5
    (C) 7
    (D) 63
    (E) 64

16. Consider the following statement.

    ```
    System.out.println(Math.pow(2, 3));
    ```

    What is the result when the statement is compiled/executed?

    (A) `8` is printed
    (B) `8.0` is printed
    (C) `9` is printed
    (D) Syntax error: "pow(double, double) in java.lang.Math cannot be applied to (int, int)"
    (E) `ArithmeticException` at run time

17. Consider the following code segment.

```
Integer n = 3;              // Line 1
Double x = 0.14;            // Line 2
System.out.println(n + x);  // Line 3
```

What is the result when the code segment is compiled/executed?

(A)   3 is printed
(B)   3.14 is printed
(C)   Syntax error on Line 1
(D)   Syntax error on Line 2
(E)   ArithmeticException on Line 3

18. Suppose ArrayList<Integer> numbers and ArrayList<String> names are created as follows:

```
ArrayList<Integer> numbers = new ArrayList<Integer>();
Integer x = 1;
numbers.add(x);
numbers.add(x);

ArrayList<String> names = new ArrayList<String>();
names.add(0, "Anya");
names.add(0, "Ben");
names.add(0, "Cathy");
```

Consider the following code segment.

```
for (Integer i : numbers)
{
  names.remove(i.intValue());
}
for (String name : names)
{
  System.out.print(name + " ");
}
```

What is the result when the code segment is executed?

(A)   Anya is printed
(B)   Cathy is printed
(C)   Cathy Anya is printed
(D)   Anya Cathy is printed
(E)   IndexOutOfBoundsException

19. Suppose we have two classes `Person` and `Student`, and the statements

```
double gpa = 3.8;
Person s = new Student("Isabella", gpa);
```

compile with no errors. Which of the following must be true?

I.   `Person` has a constructor that takes two parameters: a `String` and a `double`.
II. `Student` has a constructor that takes two parameters: a `String` and a `double`.
III. `Student` has private fields `String name` and `double gpa`.

(A) I only
(B) II only
(C) I and II only
(D) II and III only
(E) I, II, and III

20. The class `PlayList` provides methods that allow you to represent and manipulate a list of songs, but you are not concerned with how these operations work or how the list is stored in memory. You only know how to initialize and use `PlayList` objects and have no direct access to the implementation of the `PlayList` class or its private data fields. This is an example of:

(A) overriding
(B) inheritance
(C) encapsulation
(D) polymorphism
(E) method overloading

21. What is the result when the following code segment is executed?

```
Object[] nums = {null, null, null};
nums[0] = new Integer(2);
nums[1] = new Double(0.718);

System.out.println(nums[0].toString() +
        nums[1].toString() + nums[2].toString());
```

(A) `20.718` is printed
(B) `20.718null` is printed
(C) `NullPointerException`
(D) `StringIndexOutOfBoundsException`
(E) `ArrayIndexOutOfBoundsException`

Questions 22 and 23 refer to the following method.

```
private int product(int n)
{
  if (n <= 1)
    return 1;
  else
    return n * product(n-2);
}
```

22. What value does `product(6)` return?

    (A) 1
    (B) 8
    (C) 12
    (D) 48
    (E) 720

23. When you call `product(25)`, it returns –1181211311, a negative number. Which of the following best explains this result?

    (A) Integer arithmetic overflow
    (B) Logic error that shows up for odd values of `n`
    (C) Stack overflow error in recursive calls
    (D) Small range of integers in the Java Virtual Machine installed on your computer
    (E) A loss of precision in calculations

24. Consider the following code segment.

```
String abc = "ABCDEFGHIJKLMNOPQRSTUVWXYZ";
< missing statement >
System.out.println(abc.substring(k, k+1));
```

It is intended to print a randomly chosen letter of the alphabet. Any of the 26 letters can be chosen with equal probability. Which of the following can replace < *missing statement* > for the code to work that way?

    (A) int k = Math.random(25);
    (B) int k = Math.random(0, 25);
    (C) int k = Math.random(25) + 1;
    (D) int k = (int)(26*Math.random());
    (E) int k = (int)(25*Math.random()) + 1;

25. Consider the following method.

```
/** Rearranges the elements in words according to
 *  the values stored in an integer array indices,
 *  so that the element of words at index indices[k]
 *  is moved to the element at index k.
 *  Precondition: words.size() == indices.length
 */
public void permute(ArrayList<String> words, int[] indices)
{
  ArrayList<String> temp = new ArrayList<String>();
  < missing code >
}
```

For example, after executing the code segment

```
ArrayList<String> words = new ArrayList<String>();
words.add("I");
words.add("am");
words.add("Sam");

int[] indices = {2, 0, 1};
permute(words, indices);
```

words will become the list ["Sam", "I", "am"]. Which of the following code segments could replace < *missing code* > in the permute method?

I.
```
for (String word : words)
   temp.add(word);
for (int k = 0; k < indices.length; k++)
   words.set(k, temp.get(indices[k]));
```

II.
```
for (int j : indices)
   temp.add(words.get(j));
for (int k = 0; k < indices.length; k++)
   words.set(k, temp.get(k));
```

III.
```
while (words.size() > 0)
   temp.add(words.remove(0));
for (int j : indices)
   words.add(temp.get(j));
```

(A) I only
(B) II only
(C) I and II only
(D) II and III only
(E) I, II, and III

26. Consider the following class `Person` and its subclass `Friend`.

```
public class Person
{
  private String name;

  public Person(String nm) { name = nm; }

  public String getName() { return name; }
  public String toString { return getName(); }
}

public class Friend extends Person
{
  public Friend(String name) { super(name); }

  < methods not shown >
}
```

Which methods have to be defined in the `Friend` class for

```
System.out.println(new Friend("Li Min"));
```

to print `Li Min`?

(A)   No particular methods are needed
(B)   Only `getName()`
(C)   Only `toString()`
(D)   Both `getName()` and `toString()`
(E)   No combination of methods will work because `name` is undefined in `Friend`

27. Given two arrays of `double` values sorted in ascending order, one with 100 elements and the other with 10 elements, how many comparisons will it take in an optimal algorithm to merge these arrays into one sorted array, in the best case and in the worst case?

	Best case	Worst case
(A)	10	109
(B)	50	110
(C)	100	110
(D)	109	999
(E)	100	1000

28. Consider the following code segment, intended to find the position of an integer `targetValue` in `int[] a`.

```
int i = 0;
while (a[i] != targetValue)
{
   i++;
}
int position = i;
```

When will this code work as intended?

(A) Always
(B) Only when `targetValue == a[0]`
(C) Only when `0 <= targetValue < a.length`
(D) Only when `targetValue` equals `a[i]` for some `i` such that
     `0 <= i < a.length`
(E) Only when `targetValue` is not equal to `a[i]` for any `i` such that
     `0 <= i < a.length`

29. Consider the following method, intended to use Binary Search to find the location of `target` within `ArrayList<String> a`.

```
public int findLocation(ArrayList<String> a, String target)
{
   int first = 0, last = a.size() - 1;
   while (first <= last)
   {
      int middle = (first + last) / 2;
      int compResult = target.compareTo(a.get(middle));

      if (compResult == 0)
         return middle;
      if (compResult < 0)
         last = middle - 1;
      else
         first = middle + 1;
   }
   return -1;
}
```

This method may fail if it is applied to a list that is not sorted. For which of the following lists will `findLocation(a, "C")` return −1?

(A) `"A", "B", "C", "D", "E", "F", "G"`
(B) `"G", "F", "E", "D", "C", "B", "A"`
(C) `"A", "C", "D", "G", "E", "B", "F"`
(D) `"B", "A", "D", "C", "F", "E", "G"`
(E) `"D", "F", "B", "A", "G", "C", "E"`

30. Consider the following two implementations of the method
   getValue(double[] c, int n, double x) that computes and returns the value of
   $c_0 + c_1 x + c_2 x^2 + \ldots + c_n x^n$.

Implementation 1

```
double getValue(double[] c, int n, double x)
{
  double value = 0.0, powx = 1.0;

  for (int k = 0; k <= n; k++)
  {
    value += powx * c[k];
    powx *= x;
  }

  return value;
}
```

Implementation 2

```
public static double getValue(double[] c, int n, double x)
{
  double value = c[n];

  for (int k = n-1; k >= 0; k--)
  {
    value = value * x + c[k];
  }

  return value;
}
```

What is the total number of arithmetic operations on floating-point numbers (additions and multiplications combined) performed within the for loop in Implementation 1 and Implementation 2 when $n = 5$?

	Implementation 1	Implementation 2
(A)	10	5
(B)	12	6
(C)	15	10
(D)	18	10
(E)	18	12

31. Consider the following three code segments.

I.
```
int  i = 1;
while (i <= 10)
{
   System.out.print(i);
   i += 2;
}
```

II.
```
for (int i = 0; i < 5; i++)
{
   System.out.print(2*i + 1);
}
```

III.
```
for (int i = 0; i < 10; i++)
{
   i++;
   System.out.print(i);
}
```

Which of the three segments produce the same output?

(A) I and II only
(B) II and III only
(C) I and III only
(D) All three outputs are different.
(E) All three outputs are the same.

32. What is printed as a result of executing the following code segment?

```
ArrayList<String> digits = new ArrayList<String>();

for (int k = 0; k <= 9; k++)
   digits.add("" + k);

for (int k = 0; k <= 4; k++)
{
   String d1 = digits.remove(k);
   String d2 = digits.remove(k);
   digits.add(k, d1 + "+" + d2);
}

System.out.println(digits);
```

(A) [0+1, 1+2, 2+3, 3+4, 4+5]
(B) [0+1, 2+3, 4+5, 6+7, 8+9]
(C) [0+1, 1+2, 2+3, 3+4, 5, 6, 7, 8, 9]
(D) [0+1, 1+2, 2+3, 3+4, 4+5, 6, 7, 8, 9]
(E) [0+0, 1+1, 2+2, 3+3, 4+4, 5, 6, 7, 8, 9]

33. A class `Turtle` has a `void` method `forward(int d)` that moves the turtle forward by d units.

    A class `TurtleRace` has a list of `Turtle` objects:

    ```
    private ArrayList<Turtle> runners;
    ```

    `TurtleRace`'s method `move` is supposed to move all the turtles. Kim programmed it with a "for each" loop —

    ```
    public void move(int d)
    {
      for (Turtle t : runners)
        t.forward((int)(d*Math.random()));
    }
    ```

    — but Zane decided to replace that loop with a regular `for` loop:

    ```
    public void move(int d)
    {
      for (int i = 0; i < runners.size(); i++)
        runners.get(i).forward((int)(d*Math.random()));
    }
    ```

    What is a good reason for this change?

    (A) No good reason; Zane just wasn't sure how "for each" loops work.
    (B) The `for` loop with `get(i)` is more conventional programming style.
    (C) The "for each" loop didn't work because it cannot change objects in a list.
    (D) The `for` loop with `get(i)` is more efficient.
    (E) The "for each" loop won't work if the list `vertices` holds objects that belong to a subclass of `Point`.

34. Suppose class *D* extends class *B* and has one constructor. In which of the following situations must the first statement in *D*'s constructor be `super(...)`?

    (A) *B* has private fields
    (B) *B* has no constructors
    (C) *B* has only one constructor, which takes parameters
    (D) *B* has only one constructor, which takes no parameters
    (E) *D*'s constructor takes parameters

35. In a regular pentagon, the ratio of the length of a diagonal to the length of a side is equal to the Golden Ratio (defined as $\frac{1+\sqrt{5}}{2} \approx 1.618$). Consider the following class Pentagon, which represents a regular pentagon.

```
public class Pentagon
{
  public static final double GOLDEN_RATIO =
                            (1 + Math.sqrt(5.0)) / 2;
  private double side;

  public Pentagon (double x)
  {
    side = x;
  }

  public double getDiagonalLength()
  {
    return side * GOLDEN_RATIO;
  }
}
```

Which of the following code segments will compile with no errors and print the correct length of a diagonal in a regular pentagon with side 3.0?

```
I.        Pentagon p = new Pentagon(3);
          System.out.println(p.getDiagonalLength());

II.       System.out.println(3.0 * Pentagon.GOLDEN_RATIO);

III.      System.out.println(3/2 * (1 + Math.sqrt(5.0)));
```

(A) I only
(B) II only
(C) III only
(D) I and II only
(E) II and III only

Questions 36-39 refer to the following class `House` and its subclass `HouseForSale`.

```
public class House
{
  private int mySize;

  public House(int size) { mySize = size; }

  public int getSize() { return mySize; }

  public void setSize(int size) { mySize = size; }

  public int compareToOther(House other)
  {
    return getSize() - other.getSize();
  }
}

public class HouseForSale extends House
{
  private int myPrice;

  public HouseForSale(int size, int price)
  {
    < missing statement >
    myPrice = price;
  }

  public int getPrice() { return myPrice; }

  public int compareToOther(House other)
  {
    return getPrice() - ((HouseForSale)other).getPrice();
  }

  /* other constructors, methods, and fields not shown */
}
```

36. Which of the following is the most appropriate replacement for < *missing statement* > in `HouseForSale`'s constructor?

    (A) `mySize = size;`
    (B) `setSize(size);`
    (C) `super.setSize(size);`
    (D) `super(size);`
    (E) `super = new House(size);`

37. Suppose that while writing the `HouseForSale` class the programmer accidentally misspelled "compareToOther" in his code. What will happen when he tries to compile and run his class and the following statements in a client class?

```
HouseForSale house1 = new HouseForSale(2000, 129000);
HouseForSale house2 = new HouseForSale(1800, 149000);
System.out.println(house1.compareToOther(house2));
```

(A) The code compiles with no errors and prints `200`.
(B) The compiler fixes the spelling error based on the method name in the superclass; the code prints `-20000`.
(C) The compiler reports the syntax error "method compareToOther not found."
(D) The code compiles with no errors but throws a `NullPointerException`.
(E) The code compiles with no errors but throws a `ConcurrentModificationException`.

38. If the classes `House` and `HouseForSale` compile with no errors, which of the following declarations will result in a syntax error?

(A) `House[] houses = new House[2];`

(B) `HouseForSale[] houses = {new House(2000), new House(1800)};`

(C) `House[] houses = {new HouseForSale(2000, 129000),`
    `                   new HouseForSale(1800, 149000)};`

(D) `HouseForSale[] houses = {new HouseForSale(2000, 129000),`
    `                         new HouseForSale(1800, 149000)};`

(E) All of the above compile with no errors.

39. Which of the following is the most appropriate way to define the `getSize` method in `HouseForSale`?

(A) No definition is necessary, because the same code is already written in `House`.
(B) `public int getSize() { return mySize; }`
(C) `public int getSize() { return super.mySize; }`
(D) `public int getSize() { return super(mySize); }`
(E) `public int getSize() { return super.getSize(); }`

40. Which of the following code segments correctly traverses row-by-row a rectangular two-dimensional `int` array `m`?

(A)
```
for (int x : m)
{
   ...
}
```

(B)
```
for (int r : m)
{
  for (int c = 0; c < m.length; c++)
  {
    int x = m[r][c];
    ...
  }
}
```

(C)
```
for (int c = 0; c < m.length; c++)
{
  for (int r = 0; r < m[c].length; r++)
  {
    int x = m[r][c];
    ...
  }
}
```

(D)
```
for (int[] r : m)
{
  for (int c = 0; c < m[0].length; c++)
  {
    int x = r[c];
    ...
  }
}
```

(E)
```
for (int r = 0; r < m[0].length; r++)
{
  for (int c = 0; c < m.length; c++)
  {
    int x = m[r][c];
    ...
  }
}
```

Practice Exam #3

SECTION II

Time — 1 hour and 30 minutes
Number of questions — 4
Percent of total grade — 50

1. DNA sequencing and matching has become a standard technique in medical research, forensics, and recreational genealogy. A DNA molecule encodes genetic information as a sequence of nucleobases (or simply bases) of 4 kinds: adenine, cytosine, guanine, and thymine, denoted, respectively, by the letters A, C, G, and T. In this question you will work with strings that are sequences of these four letters.

    (a) Write a `boolean` method `isValidDNA` that checks whether a given string is a valid DNA string. A valid DNA string includes only the letters A, C, G, T. For example, `isValidDNA("GTACGTAATG")` should return `true`, while `isValidDNA("GXACGTAATG")` and `isValidDNA("GTAC_GTAATG")` should return `false`.

    Complete the `isValidDNA` method below.

    ```
    /** Checks whether str is a valid DNA string. Returns
     *   true if str contains only the letters A, C, G, or T;
     *   otherwise returns false.
     *   Precondition: str is not null and not empty.
     */
    public static boolean isValidDNA(String str)
    ```

    (b) A gene is a segment of DNA. A single gene can have hundreds, even thousands of bases; in our examples here we will use very short "genes." Write a method `matchTwoGenes` that takes two genes, gene1 and gene2, and attempts to find gene1 followed by gene2 in a given DNA string. If it finds gene1 followed by gene2, `matchTwoGenes` returns the gap (the number of letters) between gene1 and gene2 in the DNA string. The method always looks for the first occurrence of gene1 and the first occurrence of gene2, which must follow gene1. If one of the two genes is not found, or gene2 precedes gene1 or overlaps with gene1, then the method returns -1. The table below shows a few examples with the values returned by the calls to `matchTwoGenes(dna, "ACA", "ACG")`.

dna	Return	Reason
"GT**ACA**TAATG**ACG**GT" ⌞__⌟ 5 ⌞__⌟	5	
"GT**ACA**TAACAAG**ACG**GAC" ⌞__⌟ 7 ⌞__⌟	7	
"GT**ACAACG**GTAA" 0 1 2 3 4 5	0	
"AAT**ACG**TAATG**ACA**GT" ⌞__⌟ ⌞__⌟	–1	"ACG" found out of order
"GT**ACACG**AACAGT"	–1	"ACG" overlaps with "ACA"
"GT**ACA**TATTG**ACA**GT" ⌞__⌟	–1	"ACG" not found

Complete the method `matchTwoGenes` below.

```
/** Finds the first occurrence in a given DNA string of
 *  gene1 and gene2. Returns the gap between the matched
 *  genes if they are found in the correct order with no
 *  overlap; otherwise returns -1.
 *  Precondition: gene1 and gene2 are non-empty strings.
 */
public static int matchTwoGenes(String dna,
                        String gene1, String gene2)
```

⬇ For additional practice, write a method `matchGenes` that takes a DNA string and an `ArrayList` of genes (strings) and returns the sum of the gaps between the consecutive genes, if all of them are found in the DNA string in the correct order, with no overlaps. If one of the genes is not found or the order is wrong or two genes overlap, your method
⬆ should return -1.

2. This question involves an implementation of a system, represented by the class `Car`, that tracks a car's fuel usage and average gas mileage. The class `Car` defines a constant (a `final double` variable) that represents the size of the car's gas tank (in gallons). `Car`'s constructor initializes that constant to a given value of the type `double`. The constructor also sets the amount of fuel left in the tank to full tank.

The class `Car` provides the following methods:

- `getGasLeft` — returns the amount of gas left in the tank

- `fillUp` — resets the amount of fuel in the tank to full tank

- `logTrip` — takes two parameters: the number of miles driven on a trip and the amount of gas used, represented as a fraction of tank size, and updates the total number of miles driven and the total amount of gas used by the car (assume the car had enough gas for the trip)

- `mpg` — returns the average gas mileage in miles per gallon, rounded to the nearest integer

For example, the statements

```
Car car = new Car(12.0);
car.logTrip(65, 1.0/4);
car.logTrip(35, 1.0/8);
System.out.println("MPG: " + car.mpg() +
        "  Gas left: "  + car.getGasLeft() + " gallons");
```

print

```
MPG: 22  Gas left: 7.5 gallons
```

because the car has driven $65 + 35 = 100$ miles and used $12 \cdot \left(\frac{1}{4} + \frac{1}{8} \right) = 4.5$ gallons of gas (with 7.5 gallons remaining in the tank). The average gas mileage after the two trips is $\frac{100}{4.5} = 22.222 \approx 22$ miles per gallon.

Write the complete class `Car`, including the constructor and any required instance variables and methods. Your implementation must meet the specifications and conform to the above example.

For additional practice, write and test a `boolean` method `canMakeTrip(int miles)`, which returns `true` if the required amount of gas for the trip (based on the average mpg at the beginning of the trip) plus 10% does not exceed the amount of gas left in the tank.

3. All emails received by the Office of Complaints in Appaloosa County are assigned a priority rank from 0 to 9 and answered in order of priority; emails of higher priority are answered first; emails with the same priority are answered in the order in which they were received. In the Java application that handles email in Appaloosa, each message is represented by an object of the class `Message` whose `getPriority` method returns the priority of the message (an integer from 0 to 9, inclusive).

Messages of the same priority are held in a queue represented by an object of the class `Queue`. `Queue` has the following methods:

- `public void add(Message msg)` — adds `msg` at the end of the queue

- `public Message remove()` — removes and returns the first message from the queue

- `public boolean isEmpty()` — returns true if the queue is empty; false otherwise

An object of the `MessagePriorityQueue` class is used to store all incoming messages and retrieve them in order of priority, and in order of arrival from a queue of messages of the same priority. A `MessagePriorityQueue` object holds an array of ten queues, one for messages of each priority, from 0 to 9. The `MessagePriorityQueue` class also defines an instance variable that holds the total number of messages stored in all ten queues combined.

In this question you will write two methods of the `MessagePriorityQueue` class. An incomplete definition of this class is shown below.

```java
public class MessagePriorityQueue
{
  /** Array of queues; each queue holds messages of
   *  a particular priority. */
  private Queue[] queues;

  /** Total number of messages in all ten queues. */
  private int numMessages;

  /** Constructs a priority queue with ten empty queues,
   *  one for each priority.
   */
  public MessagePriorityQueue()
  { /* implementation not shown */ }

  /** Returns the total number of messages in all ten queues.
   */
  public int size()
  { /* implementation not shown */ }
```

```
/** Returns true if all ten queues are empty; otherwise returns
 *   false.
 */
public boolean isEmpty()
{ /* implementation not shown */ }

/** Adds a message to the priority queue, as described in
 *   part (a).
 */
public void add(Message msg)
{ /* to be implemented in part(a) */ }

/** Removes and returns the first message of the highest
 *   priority from this priority queue, as described in
 *   part (b).
 */
public Message remove()
{ /* to be implemented in part(b) */ }
}
```

(a) Write the method add(Message msg) of the MessagePriorityQueue class.
     This method retrieves the priority of msg and adds msg at the end of the queue that
     holds messages of that priority. add also increments numMessages.

     Complete the method add below.

```
/** Adds msg at the end of the queue that holds
 *   messages of the same priority as msg; increments the
 *   total number of messages stored in this priority queue.
 */
public void add(Message msg)
```

(b) Write the method remove of the MessagePriorityQueue class. If the priority
     queue is not empty, this method removes the first message of the highest priority
     and returns it; it also decrements numMessages. If the priority queue is empty,
     remove returns null.

     Complete the method remove below.

```
/** If this priority queue is not empty, removes and returns
 *   the first message of the highest priority from this
 *   priority queue and decrements the total number of
 *   messages in the priority queue; otherwise returns null.
 */
public Message remove()
```

For additional practice, write the class `Message`. Provide a constructor that accepts two parameters: the priority of the message and the text of the message. Include a suitable `toString` method.

Then write a class `Queue`. The easiest way to implement it is to simply derive `Queue` from `ArrayList<Message>`, adding one parameterless method `remove`, based on `ArrayList`'s `remove`.

Finally, implement the constructor and the `size` and `isEmpty` methods of the `MessagePriorityQueue` class, generate a few "complaint messages" of various priorities, and test your priority queue.

4. In a traffic modeling application, a segment of a highway is represented as a two-dimensional array of integers, in which each row represents one lane and each column represents a multilane cross-section at a given position. A value of 1 signifies a car is present, and a value of 0 signifies an empty slot. All cars move in the same direction. Cars can also make lateral moves ("switch lanes"). For example, the stretch of highway below has 4 lanes.

```
00000000
00010010
01001000
00100000
```

Direction of traffic

To simulate continuous traffic in a stretch of highway in the model, a car that goes out of bounds on the right reappears in the leftmost position of the same lane.

The model is implemented with the help of the class `Highway`. A partial definition of this class is shown below. You will write two methods of this class.

```java
public class Highway
{
  /** hwy[lane][x] = 1 if there is a car at position x
   *  in lane; hwy[lane][x] = 0 if there is no car. */
  private int[][] hwy;

  /** Constructs an empty Highway with a given number of
   *  lanes and a given length.
   */
  public Highway(int lanes, int length)
  { /* implementation not shown */ }

  /** Places a car in a given lane at a given position. */
  public void addCar(int lane, int x)
  { /* implementation not shown */ }

  /** Returns true if the car can switch to an adjacent lane
   *  -- see part (a).
   */
  public boolean canSwitchLane(int lane, int x, int dir)
  { /* to be implemented in part (a) */ }

  /** All cars in hwy attempt to switch lanes with
   *  the probability 0.1 up and the same probability
   *  down; all cars that can make such a lateral move
   *  do so.
   */
  public void moveAllSideways()
  { /* implementation not shown */ }
```

Continued ➥

```
/** Moves all cars in all lanes forward by one position;
 *   a car in the last (rightmost) position moves into the
 *   first position (position 0) in the same lane.
 */
public void moveAllForward()
{ /* to be implemented in part (b) */ }
}
```

(a) Write the `boolean` method `canSwitchLane` of the `Highway` class. A car at
     `hwy[lane][x]` can move in direction -1 (up) if `lane-1` exists and there are no
     cars at position x in any lanes above the current lane (lanes `lane-1`, `lane-2`, and
     so on).   A car can move in direction +1 (down) if `lane+1` exists and there are no
     cars at position x in any lane below (lanes `lane+1`, `lane+2`, and so on). In the
     example below, the cars that can change lanes are shown in bold.

Can move up ↑	Can move down ↓
dir = -1	dir = 1
01000010	01000010
00**0**10010	00010**0**10
01001**00**1	01**0**01001
001**0**1000	00111000

     Complete the method `canSwitchLane` below.

```
/** A car can switch to an adjacent lane if that lane is
 *   within hwy bounds and there are no cars at the same
 *   position in other lanes in the direction of the lateral
 *   move.
 */
public boolean canSwitchLane(int lane, int x, int dir)
```

(b) Write the method `moveAllForward` of the `Highway` class. In this simplified
     version of the model, each car moves forward by one position. A car in the last
     position (rightmost column) is placed into the same lane in the leftmost position
     (column 0). <u>You may not use any temporary arrays or lists.</u> If a temporary array or
     list is used, your solution may not receive full credit.

     Complete the method `moveAllForward` below.

```
/** Moves all cars in all lanes forward by one position;
 *   a car in the last (rightmost) position moves into the
 *   first position (position 0) in the same lane.
 */
public void moveAllForward()
```

For additional practice, write the constructor and the methods of the `Highway` class
whose code is not shown. Then implement a more sophisticated version of
`moveAllForward` in which each car moves halfway toward the current position of the
next car in the same lane. (If a car has no other cars in front of it, use the first car in its
lane as the "next" car.) Do not use any temporary arrays or lists.

Practice Exam #4

SECTION I

Time — 1 hour and 30 minutes
Number of questions — 40
Percent of total grade — 50

1. Consider the following statements.

```
double x = 2.5, y = 1.99;
System.out.println((int)(x/y) + (int)(x*y));
```

   What is printed when the statements are executed?

   (A) 0
   (B) 3
   (C) 4
   (D) 4.0
   (E) 5

2. Which of the following expressions will evaluate to `true` when x and y are `boolean` variables with different values?

   I.   `(x || y) && (!x || !y)`
   II. `(x || y) && !(x && y)`
   III. `(x && !y) || (!x && y)`

   (A) I only
   (B) II only
   (C) I and II only
   (D) II and III only
   (E) I, II, and III

3. Which of the following statements will result in a syntax error?

   (A) `String x = "123";`
   (B) `Integer x = "123";`
   (C) `Object x = "123";`
   (D) `String[] x = {"123"};`
   (E) None of the above

4. Consider the following code segment.

```
String abc = "AAABBBCCC";
String abc1 = abc.substring(0, abc.length() - 1);

abc1 = abc1.substring(1, abc1.length());
System.out.println(abc.indexOf(abc1));
```

What is printed when the code segment is executed?

(A)   -1
(B)   0
(C)   1
(D)   7
(E)   StringIndexOutOfBoundsException

5. Consider the following code segment.

```
int x = < integer value >, y = < another integer value >;

while (x > y && x % y != 0)
{
   x -= y;
}
```

Which of the following conditions will always be true after the while loop, regardless of the initial values of x and y?

(A)   x < y
(B)   x < y || x % y != 0
(C)   x <= y && x % y != 0
(D)   x <= y || x % y == 0
(E)   x >= y && x % y == 0

6. In OOP, programmers often arrange classes into inheritance hierarchies instead of implementing isolated classes. Which of the following is NOT a valid reason for doing so?

(A)   More general classes at the top of the hierarchy can be extended in the project or reused in other projects.
(B)   Methods of a superclass can often be reused in its subclasses without duplication of code.
(C)   Objects of different subclasses can be passed as parameters to a method designed to accept objects of the superclass.
(D)   Objects of different subclasses can be stored in the same array.
(E)   All of the above are valid reasons for using inheritance hierarchies.

7. The following method is intended to remove from `ArrayList<Integer> list` all elements whose value is less than zero.

```
public void removeNegatives(ArrayList<Integer> list)
{
  int i = 0, n = list.size();

  while (i < n)
  {
    if (list.get(i) < 0)
    {
      list.remove(i);
      n--;
    }
    i++;
  }
}
```

For which lists of `Integer` values does this method work as intended?

(A) Only an empty list
(B) Only lists that do not contain negative values in consecutive positions
(C) Only lists in which all the negative values occur before all the positive values
(D) Only lists in which all the positive values occur before all the negative values
(E) All lists

8. Consider the following code segment.

```
int[] arr = {1, 2, 3, 4, 5, 6, 7, 8};

for (int k = 1; k <= 6; k += 2)
{
  arr[7] = arr[k];
  arr[k] = arr[k+1];
  arr[k+1] = arr[7];
}
```

Which of the following represents the contents of `arr` after the code segment has been executed?

(A) 1 3 2 5 4 7 6 6
(B) 1 3 2 5 4 7 6 8
(C) 2 1 4 3 6 5 8 7
(D) 2 1 4 3 6 5 7 8
(E) 2 1 4 3 6 5 7 5

Questions 9 and 10 refer to the method `smile` below.

```
public static void smile(int n)
{
  if (n == 0)
    return;

  for (int k = 1; k <= n; k++)
  {
    System.out.print("smile!");
  }

  smile(n-1);
}
```

9. What is printed when `smile(4)` is called?

(A) `smile!`
(B) `smile!smile!`
(C) `smile!smile!smile!`
(D) `smile!smile!smile!smile!`
(E) `smile!smile!smile!smile!smile!smile!smile!smile!smile!smile!`

10. When `smile(4)` is called, how many times will `smile` actually be called, including the initial call?

(A) 2
(B) 3
(C) 4
(D) 5
(E) 10

11. Consider the following code segment.

```
Integer year = 2020;
System.out.println(year.compareTo(2021));
```

What is the result when the code segment is compiled/executed?

(A) Syntax error
(B) A positive integer is printed
(C) A negative integer is printed
(D) `true` is printed
(E) `false` is printed

12. Consider the following method.

```
private int swap(int a, int b)
{
  if (a < b)
  {
    b = a;
    a = b;
  }
  return b - a;
}
```

What are the values of the variables a, b, and c after the following statements are executed?

```
int a = 2, b = 5;
int c = swap(a, b);
```

(A) 2, 5, 0
(B) 2, 5, 3
(C) 2, 5, –3
(D) 2, 2, 0
(E) 5, 2, 3

13. What is printed when the following code segment is executed?

```
int sum = 0, d = -1;

for (int count = 10; count > 0; count--)
{
  sum += d;

  if (d > 0)
  {
    d++;
  }
  else
  {
    d--;
  }
  d = -d;
}

System.out.println(sum);
```

(A) 0
(B) 5
(C) -5
(D) 10
(E) -10

14. Consider the following incomplete method, which shuffles a list of `Card` objects so that any card can end up at any index in the list `deck` with equal probability.

```
public void shuffle(ArrayList<Card> deck)
{
  int n = deck.size();
  while (n > 1)
  {
    < missing statement >

    Card temp = deck.set(k, deck.get(n-1));
    deck.set(n-1, temp);
    n--;
  }
}
```

Which of the following can replace < *missing statement* > so that the method works as intended?

(A)   `int k = Math.random(n);`
(B)   `int k = Math.random(deck.size());`
(C)   `int k = Math.random(deck.size() - 1);`
(D)   `int k = (int)(n * Math.random());`
(E)   `int k = (int)((n-1) * Math.random());`

15. The method

```
public void addStars(ArrayList<String> words)
```

is intended to append `"*"` at the end of each string in `words`. Which of the following implementations of `addStars` will work?

```
I.    for (String word : words)
         word += "*";

II.   for (int k = 0; k < words.size(); k++)
         words.set(k, words.get(k) + "*");

III.  for (int k = 0; k < words.size(); k++)
         words.add(words.remove(k) + "*");
```

(A)   I only
(B)   II only
(C)   I and II only
(D)   II and III only
(E)   I, II, and III

16. Suppose a class `Solid` has a method `getVolume()` that returns 0. Two classes, `Cube` and `Pyramid`, extend `Solid`. Which Java feature makes it possible for the following code segment to print the correct values for the volume of a pyramid and a cube?

```
Solid[] solids = new Solid[2];
Solids[0] = new Cube(100);
Solids[1] = new Pyramid(150, 100);

System.out.println("Cube: " + solids[0].getVolume());
System.out.println("Pyramid: " + solids[1].getVolume());
```

(A) abstraction
(B) encapsulation
(C) polymorphism
(D) modularity
(E) method overloading

17. Consider the following method.

```
public boolean examine(String[] letters)
{
  int count = 0;

  for (String letter1 : letters)
  {
    for (String letter2 : letters)
    {
      if (letter1.equals(letter2))
        count++;
    }
  }

  return count > 0;
}
```

What will `examine` return for the following arrays?

```
String[] letters1 = {"A", "B", "C"};
String[] letters2 = {"A", "B", "B"};
String[] letters3 = {"A", "A", "B"};
```

	letters1	letters2	letters3
(A)	true	true	true
(B)	true	true	false
(C)	false	true	true
(D)	false	false	true
(E)	false	false	false

18. Consider the following classes.

```
public class APTestResult
{
  private String subject;
  private int score;

  public int getScore()
  {
    return score;
  }

  /* constructors and other methods not shown */
}

public class APScholar
{
  private String name;
  private int id;
  private ArrayList<APTestResult> exams;

  public int getExamResult(k)
  {
    return exams.get(k);
  }

  /* constructors and other methods not shown */
}
```

Given

```
APScholar[] list = new APScholar[100];
```

which of the following expressions correctly represents the third AP score of the first APScholar in list?

(A)   list[0].exams[2].getScore()
(B)   list[2].exams.getScore()
(C)   list[2].getExamResult().getScore()
(D)   list[0].getExamResult().getScore(2)
(E)   None of the above

19. What is printed when the following code segment is executed?

```
String[] xy = {"X", "Y"};
String[] yx = xy;
yx[0] = xy[1];
yx[1] = xy[0];

System.out.println(xy[0] + xy[1] + yx[0] + yx[1]);
```

(A) XXXX
(B) YYYY
(C) XYYX
(D) XYXY
(E) XYYY

20. Consider the following class Toy.

```
public class Toy
{
  private String name;

  public Toy (String nm) { name = nm; }
  public String toString() { return name; }

  public void meet(Toy other)
  {
    System.out.println("Hello " + other);
  }
}
```

Suppose the class Barbie has a no-arguments constructor. Which of the following code segments compile without syntax errors if Barbie extends Toy, but cause a syntax error if Barbie does not extend Toy?

    I.   Toy kenny = new Toy("Ken");
              Barbie barb = new Barbie();
              kenny.meet(barb);

    II.   Toy barb = new Barbie();
              Toy kenny = new Toy("Ken");
              barb.meet(kenny);

    III.   Barbie barb = new Barbie();
              Barbie barb2 = new Barbie();
              barb.meet(barb2);

(A) I only
(B) II only
(C) I and II only
(D) II and III only
(E) I, II, and III

21. Suppose `m` is a two-dimensional array of size 4 by 4, with all its elements initialized to zeros. The method `fill` is defined as follows:

```
public void fill(int[][] m)
{
  int n = m.length;

  for (int i = 1; i < n - 1; i++)
  {
    for (int j = 1; j < n - 1; j++)
      m[i][j] = 1;
  }
}
```

What values will be stored in `m` after `fill(m)` is called?

(A)   0000
      0000
      0000
      0000

(B)   1100
      1100
      0000
      0000

(C)   0000
      0110
      0110
      0000

(D)   1110
      1110
      1110
      0000

(E)   1111
      1111
      1111
      1111

22. Classes `Salsa` and `Swing` are subclasses of `Dance`. If the calls

```
perform(new Salsa());
perform(new Swing());
```

are both valid, which of the following headers of the `perform` method(s) in the `DanceSchool` class will compile successfully?

  I.   Two methods:

```
public void perform(Salsa dance)
public void perform(Swing dance)
```

  II.   `public void perform(Dance dance)`

  III.   `public void perform(Object dance)`

(A)   I only
(B)   II only
(C)   I and II only
(D)   II and III only
(E)   I, II, and III

23. Suppose *a*, *b*, and *c* are positive integers under 1000, and *x* satisfies the formula

$$\frac{a}{b} = \frac{c}{x}$$

The integer value *d* is obtained by truncating *x* to an integer. Which of the following code segments correctly calculate *d*?

  I.   `d = c * b / a;`

  II.   ```
int temp = c * b;
d = temp / a;
```

  III.       ```
int temp = b / a;
d = c * temp;
```

(A)   I only
(B)   II only
(C)   I and II only
(D)   II and III only
(E)   I, II, and III

24. Suppose a class `Particle` has the following fields defined.

```
public class Particle
{
  public static final int START_POS = 100;
  private double velocity;

  private boolean canMove()
  { /* implementation not shown */ }

  /* constructors, other fields and methods not shown */
}
```

Which of the following is true?

(A)   Java syntax rules wouldn't allow us to use the name `startPos` instead of `START_POS`.

(B)   Java syntax rules wouldn't allow us to make `velocity` public.

(C)   Both `velocity` and `START_POS` can be changed by one of `Particle`'s methods.

(D)   A statement

```
double pos = START_POS + velocity;
```

in `Particle`'s `canMove` method would result in a syntax error.

(E)   None of the above

25. Consider the following method.

```
private double compute(int x, int y)
{
  double r = 0;

  if (!(y == 0 || x/y <= 2))
    r = 1 / ((x - 2*y) * (2*x - y));

  return r;
}
```

For which of the following values of x and y will `compute(x, y)` throw an exception?

(A)   x = 0,   y = 0
(B)   x = 1,   y = 2
(C)   x = 2,   y = 1
(D)   x = 3,   y = 5
(E)   None of the above

26. Consider the following method.

```
/** Returns the number of zeros in s.
 *  Precondition: s.length() = 31; s consists of several
 *                0's followed by several 1's
 *                (s can also be all 0's or all 1's).
 */
public int countZeros(String s)
{
  int i = 0, j = 30;
  while (i <= j)
  {
    int k = (i + j) / 2;
    if (s.substring(k, k+1).equals("0"))
      i = k + 1;
    else
      j = k - 1;
  }
  return i;
}
```

How many iterations through the `while` loop will be made in the best and the worst case?

	Best case	Worst case
(A)	1	5
(B)	4	5
(C)	5	5
(D)	1	15
(E)	4	15

27. Consider the following code segment.

```
int x = (int)Math.pow(2, 5);

for (int k = 1; k <= 3; k++)
  x *= (2*x);

System.out.println(x);
```

What is the result when the code segment is compiled/executed?

(A) Syntax error: "method pow in class Math cannot be applied to given types"
(B) 3125000 is printed $(= 5^8 \cdot 2^3)$
(C) 8388608 is printed $(= 2^{23})$
(D) 140737488355328 is printed $(= 2^{47})$
(E) None of the above

28. Consider the following method.

```
public String encrypt(String word)
{
  int pos = word.length() / 2;

  if (pos >= 1)
  {
    word = encrypt(word.substring(pos)) +
            encrypt(word.substring(0, pos));
  }

  return word;
}
```

Which of the following strings is returned by encrypt("SECRET")?

(A)   TERCES
(B)   TSECRE
(C)   RETSEC
(D)   CESTER
(E)   ETRECS

29. Consider the following code segment.

```
int[] nums = new int[8];
nums[0] = 0;
int n = 1;

while (n < nums.length)
{
  int k;

  for (k = n; k < 2*n; k++)
    nums[k] = nums[k-n] + 1;

  n = k;
}
```

Which of the following represents the contents of nums after the code segment has been executed?

(A)   0 1 1 1 1 1 1 1
(B)   0 1 0 1 0 1 0 1
(C)   0 1 1 2 1 2 2 3
(D)   0 1 2 3 1 2 3 4
(E)   0 1 2 3 4 5 6 7

30. Consider the following class.

```
public class Game
{
  private static int bestScore;
  private int score;
  private String player;

  < constructors and methods not shown >
}
```

Which of the following constructors or methods in Game will cause a syntax error?

I.   `public static void resetScore()`
      `{ score = 0; bestScore = 0; }`

II.   `public Game()`
      `{ score = 0; bestScore = 0; }`

III. `public void setPlayer(String name)`
      `{ player = name; }`

(A) I only
(B) II only
(C) I and II only
(D) II and III only
(E) I, II, and III

31. What is printed when the following code segment is executed?

```
int[] factors = {2, 3, 5};
ArrayList<Integer> products = new ArrayList<Integer>();
products.add(1);

for (int f : factors)
{
  int n = products.size();
  for (int k = 0; k < n; k++)
    products.add(f * products.get(k));
}

int n = products.size();
System.out.print(n + " " + products.get(n-2) +
                      " " + products.get(n-1));
```

(A) 4 3 5
(B) 4 6 15
(C) 8 10 15
(D) 8 10 30
(E) 8 15 30

Questions 32 and 33 refer to the following class `SortX`.

```java
public class SortX
{
  public static void sort(String[] items)
  {
    int n = items.length;

    while (n > 1)
    {
      sortHelper(items, n - 1);
      n--;
    }
  }

  private static void sortHelper(String[] items, int last)
  {
    int m = last;

    for (int k = 0; k < last; k++)
    {
      if (items[k].compareTo(items[m]) > 0)
        m = k;
    }

    String temp = items[m];
    items[m] = items[last];
    items[last] = temp;
  }
}
```

32. Suppose `names` is an array of `String` objects:

```java
String[] names =
          {"Dan", "Ada", "Claire", "Evan", "Boris"};
```

If `SortX.sort(names)` is running, what is the order of the values in `names` after two complete iterations through the `while` loop in the `sort` method?

(A)   `"Boris"`, `"Ada"`, `"Claire"`, `"Dan"`, `"Evan"`
(B)   `"Ada"`, `"Claire"`, `"Boris"`, `"Dan"`, `"Evan"`
(C)   `"Ada"`, `"Boris"`, `"Claire"`, `"Evan"`, `"Dan"`
(D)   `"Ada"`, `"Claire"`, `"Dan"`, `"Evan"`, `"Boris"`
(E)   None of the above

33. If `items` contains five values and `SortX.sort(items)` is called, how many times, total, will `items[k].compareTo(items[m])` be called in the `sortHelper` method?

(A)   5
(B)   10
(C)   15
(D)   25
(E)   Depends on the values in `items`

34. Consider the following method.

```
/** Returns the number of times the digit d occurs in the
 *  decimal representation of n.
 *  Precondition: n and d are non-negative integers.
 */
private int findDigit(int n, int d)
{
  int count = 0;

  < statement 1 >

  while (n > 0)
  {
    if (n % 10 == d)
    {
      count++;
    }
    < statement 2 >
  }

  return count;
}
```

Which of the following could replace < *statement 1* > and < *statement 2* > to make `findDigit` work as described in the comment for this method?

	< *statement 1* >	< *statement 2* >
(A)	`if (n == 0) return 1;`	`n /= 10;`
(B)	`if (n == 0) return 1;`	`d *= 10;`
(C)	`if (d == 0) count++;`	`n -= n % 10;`
(D)	`if (n == 0 && d == 0) count++;`	`n /= 10;`
(E)	`if (n == 0 && d != 0) return 0;`	`n *= 10;`

Questions 35-37 **involve reasoning about classes and objects used in an implementation of a library catalog system.**

An object of the class `BookInfo` represents information about a particular book, and an object of the class `LibraryBook` represents copies of a book on the library's shelves.

```
public class BookInfo
{
  private String title;
  private String author;
  private int numPages;

  < constructors not shown >

  public String toString()
  {
    return title + " by " + author;
  }

  public String getTitle() { return title; }

  public int getNumPages() { return numPages; }
}

public class LibraryBook
{
  private BookInfo info;
  private int numCopies;    // Number of copies on shelf

  < constructors not shown >

  public int getNumCopies() { return numCopies; }

  public void setNumCopies(int num) { numCopies = num; }

  public BookInfo getInfo() { return info; }

  /** If there are copies on shelf, decrements
   *  the number of copies left and returns true;
   *  otherwise returns false.
   */
  public boolean checkOut() { /* implementation not shown */ }
}
```

35. If `catalog` is declared in a client class as

    ```
    LibraryBook[] catalog;
    ```

    then which of the following statements will correctly print

    title by *author*

    for the third book in `catalog`?

    I.   `System.out.println(catalog[2]);`

    II. `System.out.println(catalog[2].getInfo());`

    III. `System.out.println(catalog[2].getInfo().toString());`

    (A) I only
    (B) II only
    (C) I and II only
    (D) II and III only
    (E) I, II, and III

36. Consider the following method from another class, a client of `LibraryBook`.

    ```
    /** Returns the total number of pages in all
     *  books in catalog that are on the shelves.
     */
    public int totalPages(LibraryBook[] catalog)
    {
      int count = 0;

      for (LibraryBook bk : catalog)
      {
        < statement >
      }
      return count;
    }
    ```

    Which of the following replacements for *< statement >* completes the method as intended?

    (A) `count += bk.numCopies * bk.info.numPages;`
    (B) `count += bk.getNumCopies() * bk.getNumPages();`
    (C) `count += bk.(numCopies * info.getNumPages());`
    (D) `count += bk.getNumCopies() * bk.getInfo().getNumPages();`
    (E) None of the above

37. Which of the following code segments will correctly complete the `checkOut()` method of the `LibraryBook` class?

I.
```
if (getNumCopies() == 0)
{
  return false;
}
else
{
  setNumCopies(getNumCopies() - 1);
  return true;
}
```

II.
```
int n = getNumCopies();
if (n == 0)
{
  return false;
}
else
{
  setNumCopies(n - 1);
  return true;
}
```

III.
```
if (numCopies == 0)
{
  return false;
}
else
{
  numCopies--;
  return true;
}
```

(A) I only
(B) II only
(C) I and II only
(D) I and III only
(E) I, II, and III

38. Consider the following method.

```java
public int[][] makeCounts(int n)
{
  int[][] counts = new int[3][n];
  counts[0][0] = 0;
  counts[1][0] = 0;
  counts[2][0] = 1;

  for (int k = 1; k < n; k++)
  {
    counts[0][k] = counts[0][k-1] + counts[1][k-1];
    counts[1][k] = counts[1][k-1] + counts[0][k-1] +
                                    counts[2][k-1];
    counts[2][k] = counts[2][k-1] + counts[1][k-1];
  }
  return counts;
}
```

What values are in the array returned by `makeCounts(5)`?

(A)
```
0   0   1   1   1
0   1   1   1   1
1   1   1   1   1
```

(B)
```
0   0   1   2   3
0   1   2   3   4
1   2   3   4   5
```

(C)
```
0   0   1   3   6
0   1   2   5   8
1   1   4   7   9
```

(D)
```
0   0   1   3   8
0   1   2   5   12
1   1   2   4   9
```

(E)
```
0   1   3   9   27
0   1   3   9   27
1   1   3   9   27
```

39. What is printed when the following code segment is executed?

```
ArrayList<Integer> lst = new ArrayList<Integer>();

for (int k = 1; k <= 6; k++)
  lst.add(k);

for (int k = 0; k < 3; k++)
{
    Integer i = lst.remove(k);
    lst.add(i);
}
for (Integer i : lst)
  System.out.print(i);
```

(A)   123456
(B)   246135
(C)   456123
(D)   456321
(E)   IndexOutOfBoundsException

40. Consider the following method.

```
public int mysteryCount(int[] p)
{
  int count = 0;
  for (int i = 0; i < p.length; i++)
  {
    count++;
    int j = p[i];
    while (j != i)
    {
      j = p[j];
      count++;
    }
  }
  return count;
}
```

Given

```
int[] arr = {0, 2, 3, 1};
```

what will mysteryCount(arr) return?

(A)   2
(B)   3
(C)   5
(D)   10
(E)   13

Practice Exam #4

Time — 1 hour and 30 minutes
Number of questions — 4
Percent of total grade — 50

1. The class `Cipher` provides methods to encrypt and decrypt a message using a simple substitution cipher.

```java
public class Cipher
{
    private static final String abc = "ABCDEFGHIJKLMNOPQRSTUVWXYZ";

    /** Returns a new string as described in part (a).
     *  Precondition: All letters in text are uppercase;
     *                0 < key > 26.
     */
    public static String encrypt(String text, int key)
    { /* to be implemented in part (a) */ }

    /** Returns a new string as described in part (b) */
    public static String decrypt(String code, int key)
    { /* to be implemented in part (b) */ }
}
```

(a) Write a method `encrypt` that takes a string `text` and a positive integer `key` as parameters and replaces each letter in `text` with the letter in the `abc` string shifted by `key` positions. If the index of the substitution letter exceeds 25, then wrap-around occurs back through the beginning of the `abc` string. For example, if `key` is 3, then 'A' becomes 'D', 'B' becomes 'E', ..., 'W' becomes 'Z', 'X' becomes 'A', 'Y' becomes 'B', and 'Z' becomes 'C'. Assume that all letters in `text` are uppercase. All the characters that are not letters remain unchanged.

Complete the method `encrypt` below.

```java
/** Returns a new string in which each letter in text is
 *  replaced with the letter whose index in abc is equal
 *  to the index of the original letter plus key, with
 *  wraparound, if needed, back to the beginning of abc.
 *  All the characters in text that are not letters remain
 *  unchanged.
 *  Precondition: all letters in text are uppercase;
 *                0 < key < 26.
 */
public static String encrypt(String text, int key)
```

(b)   Write a method `decrypt` that restores the original message from the encrypted message generated by the `encrypt` method above. For example, if `key` is 3, then 'B' in the encrypted message corresponds to 'Y' in the original message. Notice that the decryption algorithm is exactly the same as the encryption algorithm if you use a modified key, so there is no need to replicate the code from the `encrypt` method from Part (a). Assume that the `encrypt` method in Part (a) works as specified, regardless of what you wrote there.

Complete the method `decrypt` below.

```
/** Returns a new string in which each letter in code is
 *   replaced with the letter whose index in abc is equal
 *   to the index of the letter minus key, with
 *   wrap-around at index 0.
 *   Precondition: All letters in code are uppercase;
 *                 0 < key < 26
 */
public static String decrypt(String code, int key)
```

For additional practice, modify the `Cipher` class to accommodate both uppercase and lowercase letters in `text` and `code`, preserving the case of each letter. For even more practice, find on the Internet the description of the Vigenère cipher and implement the `encrypt` and `decrypt` methods for it.

2.   The College Board gives awards to students who are successful on AP exams:

   - **AP Scholar**: Received grades of 3 or higher on three or more AP Exams

   - **AP Scholar with Honor**: Received an average grade of at least 3.25 on all AP Exams taken, and grades of 3 or higher on four or more of these exams

   - **AP Scholar with Distinction**: Received an average grade of at least 3.5 on all AP Exams taken, and grades of 3 or higher on five or more of these exams

These awards are summarized in the following table:

	AP Scholar	AP Scholar with Honor	AP Scholar with Distinction
Average grade on <u>all</u> AP exams taken, at least	No effect	3.25	3.5
Minimum grade that counts toward an award	3	3	3
Minimum number of exams not below the minimum grade	3	4	5

Notice that a student may receive low grades on some AP exams and still qualify for any one of the above awards.

The class `APStudent` provides methods that help to determine the award level for a student:

   - `addExam` — takes a given grade (an `int`) as a parameter and updates this `APStudent`'s instance variables

   - `awardLevel` — returns the award level of this `APStudent` based on all the added exams

The award level returned by `awardLevel` is represented by an integer: 0 for no award, 1 for AP Scholar, 2 for AP Scholar with Honor, and 3 for AP Scholar with Distinction.

The `APStudent` class does not define a constructor — it relies on the default no-arguments constructor.

For example, the statements

```
APStudent s = new APStudent();
s.addExam(2);
System.out.print(s.awardLevel() + " ");
s.addExam(4);
s.addExam(5);
System.out.print(s.awardLevel() + " ");
s.addExam(3);
System.out.print(s.awardLevel() + " ");
s.addExam(4);
System.out.print(s.awardLevel() + " ");
s.addExam(3);
System.out.print(s.awardLevel() + " ");
s.addExam(1);
System.out.print(s.awardLevel() + " ");
System.out.println();
```

print

```
0  0  1  2  3  1
```

Write the complete APStudent class, including the required instance variables and the two methods described above. Your implementation must meet the specifications and conform to the above example. **Do not use arrays, ArrayLists, or other data structures in your solution.**

For additional practice, write a class APStudentWithName as a subclass of APStudent. Supply a constructor that takes the student's name as a parameter and a toString method that returns that name. Write and test a method of a client class of APStudentWithName that takes an ArrayList of APStudentWithName objects and returns an ArrayList of names of the students from the list who qualify for the AP Scholar with Distinction award.

3. In computerized monitoring of an electrocardiogram (also called ECG or EKG) one of the tasks is detecting the most prominent spikes, called R-peaks, in the signal.

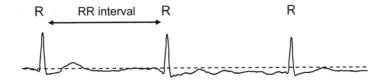

Measuring the time intervals between consecutive R-peaks allows the ECG device to compute the patient's heart rate.

In this question you will write two methods of the class ECG that help make a list of all R-peaks and calculate the patient's heart rate.

In a computer system, the ECG voltage signal is digitized at a certain sampling rate and the resulting values are stored in a "voltage" array. For example, a sampling rate of 300 means that 300 samples are obtained and stored every second. An integer constant SAMPLING_RATE in the ECG class indicates how many consecutive elements in the voltage array represent one second of an ECG recording.

We are not concerned with the magnitudes of R-peaks here, only with the times when they occur. Knowing the sampling rate, we can compute the time interval between two R-peaks from their indices in the voltage array.

A partial definition of the ECG class is shown below.

```
public class ECG
{
    /** ECG sampling rate in samples taken per second. */
    private static final int SAMPLING_RATE = 300;

    /** Minimum possible distance between R-peaks. */
    private static final int DELTA = SAMPLING_RATE / 10;

    /** Returns true if an R-peak is detected at index k;
     *  otherwise returns false.
     */
    private static boolean isRpeak(double[] v, int k)
    { /* implementation not shown */ }

    /** Returns an ArrayList of indices of all consecutive
     *  R-peaks in v, as described in part (a).
     */
    public static ArrayList<Integer> findRpeaks(double[] v)
    { /* to be implemented in part (a) */ }
```

Continued ☞

```
/** Returns the heart rate in beats per minute obtained from
 *   a list of indices of R-peaks.
 *   Precondition: rPeakPositions.size() >= 2
 */
public static int heartRate(ArrayList<Integer> rPeakPositions)
{ /* to be implemented in part (b) */ }

/* other methods not shown */
}
```

(a)   Write the method `findRpeaks(double[] v)`. This method returns an
      ArrayList of the indices of all R-peaks found in a given voltage array `v`,
      preserving their order in time. Call `isRpeak(v, k)` to decide whether there is an
      R-peak in `v` at index `k`. The implementation of the algorithm used by `isRpeak` is
      not shown. This algorithm examines the values in `v` in a certain interval around `k`.
      Start looking for R-peaks at `k = DELTA` and finish at `k = v.length-1-DELTA` to
      leave room for `isRpeak` to do its job. Also, when an R-peak is detected at index `k`,
      look for the next R-peak starting from `k+DELTA` (to avoid detecting the same R-
      peak multiple times).

      Complete the method `findRpeaks` below.

```
/** Returns an ArrayList of indices of all consecutive
 *   R-peaks in v between v[DELTA] and v[v.length-1-DELTA].
 *   An R-peak is determined by a call to the method isRpeak.
 *   R-peaks must be at least DELTA apart.
 */
public static ArrayList<Integer> findRpeaks(double[] v)
```

(b)   Write the method `heartRate` that takes a list of indices of R-peaks in the voltage
      array and returns the patient's heart rate in beats per <u>minute</u>, rounded to the nearest
      integer. The heart rate is derived from the average length of RR-intervals (distances
      between consecutive R-peaks) in the list. To obtain the average distance, take the
      distance between the first and the last R-peak (the difference between the last and
      the first elements of the list) and divide it by the number of RR-intervals represented
      by the list.

      Use `SAMPLING_RATE` to convert the indices into real time. For example, if the
      average length of RR-intervals is 250 (indices) and `SAMPLING_RATE` is
      300 (indices/second), then the average length of the RR-interval is
      $250/300 = 5/6$ seconds, which corresponds to $60 \cdot 6 / 5 = 72$ beats per minute.

      Complete the method `heartRate` below.

```
/** Returns the heart rate in beats per minute obtained from
 *   rPeakPositions, the list of the indices of R-peaks.
 *   Precondition: rPeakPositions.size() >= 2
 */
public static int heartRate(ArrayList <Integer> rPeakPositions)
```

For additional practice, implement the `isRpeak(int k)` method. This method returns `true` if there is an R-peak at index `k` in the voltage array `v`; otherwise it returns `false`. Use the following simplified algorithm for detecting R-peaks: there is an R-peak at `k` in `v` if the following three conditions are satisfied:

1. `v[k] > 1.0`

2. `v[k]` is equal to the maximum value among `v[j]` for all `j` in the interval `k - DELTA ≤ j ≤ k + DELTA`, where `DELTA` is a constant defined in `ECG`.

3. `v[j]` is negative somewhere on the interval `k - DELTA ≤ j ≤ k` and also somewhere on the interval `k ≤ j ≤ k + DELTA`.

Implement two private methods `max` and `min` in `ECG` to facilitate detection of R-peaks.

Write a test program that reads the first 2000 values from the file `"ecg.dat"`, downloadable from this book's companion website. Your program should be able to detect R-peaks at 40, 290, 541, 791, 1029, 1266, 1502, 1734, and 1969 and yield a heart rate of 75.

4. Seats in a movie theater are modeled by a two-dimensional array of `boolean` values: `true` represents an occupied seat and `false` represents a vacant seat. Row number 0 represents the row of seats closest to the screen.

In Part (a) we assume that the most desirable seats are in the rectangular area of width `w` and "height" `h`, centered in front of the screen (middle of the row), in the rows numbered 2 to `h+1`. Both `w` and the number of seats in each row are even numbers. For example:

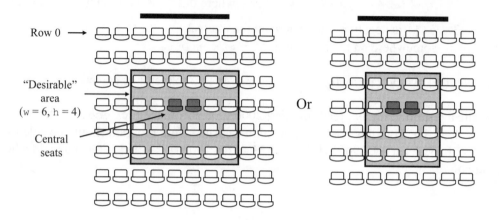

You will write a method that returns the number of vacant seats in the "desirable" area.

In Part (b), we introduce a different idea: the "best two seats" are in the center of the central row of the seats array. If the number of rows in the theater is even, and there are two "central" rows, then the best seats are in the one that is closer to the screen. (In the above examples, the two central seats happen to be within the "desirable" area, but this is not required.) You will write a method that finds a pair of adjacent vacant seats that are closest to the "best two seats."

(a) Write a static method `vacantGoodSeats` that takes a two-dimensional array representing the seats in a movie theater and `w` and `h`, the width and "height" of the "desirable" seating area, and returns the number of vacant seats in that area.

Complete the method `vacantGoodSeats` below.

```
/** Returns the number of vacant seats in the "desirable"
 *   area of the seats array: the h rows starting from row 2
 *   and the w contiguous seats in the center of each row.
 *   Precondition: The entire "desirable" area fits within
 *                 the seats array; w and the number of seats
 *                 in each row are even numbers.
 */
public static int vacantGoodSeats(boolean[][] seats,
                                  int w, int h)
```

(b)   The class `Location` has a constructor that takes two parameters, `row` and `col`, and a method

```
public double distanceFrom(Location other)
```

that returns the distance from this location to `other`. Write a method `bestTwoSeats` that takes a two-dimensional array of seats, as described above, and finds the location of a pair of adjacent <u>vacant</u> seats closest to the center of the theater. The distance is measured from the left seat in the found pair of seats to the left seat in the central pair of seats. `bestTwoSeats` returns the location of the left seat in the found pair. If a pair of adjacent vacant seats is not found, `bestTwoSeats` returns `null`.

Complete the method `bestTwoSeats` below.

```
/** Returns the location of a pair of vacant seats closest
 *  to the central pair of seats. The central pair is
 *  in the middle of the center row; if the number of rows
 *  is even, the "center" row is the one closer to the
 *  screen. The location of a pair of seats is defined
 *  as the row and column of the left seat in the pair
 *  (the seat with the smaller column index). Returns
 *  null if a pair of adjacent vacant seats is not found.
 */
public static Location bestTwoSeats(boolean[][] seats)
```

For additional practice, implement the `Location` class. Make the distance between seats equal to the absolute value of the difference in rows plus the absolute value of the difference in columns.

Practice Exam #5

SECTION I

Time — 1 hour and 30 minutes
Number of questions — 40
Percent of total grade — 50

1. Consider the following code segment.

```
double x = 5*4/2 - 5/2*4;
System.out.println(x);
```

What is printed when the code segment is executed?

(A) 0
(B) 1
(C) 0.0
(D) 1.0
(E) 2.0

2. Consider the following method and code segment in the same class.

```
public void process(String s)
{
  s = s.substring(2, 3) + s.substring(1, 2) +
                              s.substring(0, 1);
}

String s = "ABCD";
process(s);
System.out.println(s);
```

What is printed when the code segment is executed?

(A) ABCD
(B) CBA
(C) CDBCA
(D) CDBCAB
(E) StringIndexOutOfBoundsException

3. Assume that `int` variables x and y have been properly declared and initialized. The
    expression

    ```
    !(x > y && y <= 0)
    ```

    is equivalent to which of the following?

    (A) `x <= y || y > 0`
    (B) `x > y && y <= 0`
    (C) `x > y || y < 0`
    (D) `x <= y && y <= 0`
    (B) `!(x <= y) || (y > 0)`

4. Consider the following method.

    ```
    public int guess(int num1, int num2)
    {
      if (num1 % num2 == 0)
        return num2;
      else
        return guess(num2, num1 % num2);
    }
    ```

    What is the value of `num` after the following statement is executed?

    ```
    int num = (6 * 14) / guess(6, 14);
    ```

    (A) 6
    (B) 12
    (C) 28
    (D) 42
    (E) 84

5. Consider the following code segment.

    ```
    ArrayList<String> words = new ArrayList<String>();
    words.set(0, "ANT");
    ```

    What is the result when the code segment is executed?

    (A) `NullPointerException`
    (B) `IndexOutOfBoundsException`
    (C) The size of `words` remains 0 and nothing is added to `words`
    (D) The size of `words` becomes 1 and the element at index 0 becomes `"ANT"`
    (E) The size of `words` becomes 10 and the element at index 0 becomes `"ANT"`

6. Assume that `String` variables `str1` and `str2` have been properly declared and initialized. Which of the following `boolean` expressions evaluate to `true` if and only if `str1` and `str2` hold the same values?

> I. `str1 == str2`
>
> II. `str1.equals(str2)`
>
> III. `str1.compareTo(str2) == 0`

(A) I only
(B) II only
(C) I and II only
(D) II and III only
(E) I, II, and III

7. Consider the following code segment.

```
int[] nums = new int[51];

for (int k = 0; k < nums.length; k++)
  nums[k] = 1;

for (int k = 3; k <= 50; k += 3)
  nums[k] = 0;

for (int k = 5; k <= 50; k += 5)
  nums[k] = 0;
```

How many elements in the array `nums` have the value 0 after this code has been executed?

(A) 23
(B) 25
(C) 26
(D) 27
(E) 28

8. Which of the following methods are equivalent (always return the same value for the same values of input parameters)?

I.
```
public boolean fun(int a, int b, int c)
{
   if (a >= b)
     if (b >= c)
        return true;
     else
        return false;
   else
     return false;
}
```

II.
```
public boolean fun(int a, int b, int c)
{
   if (a >= b && b >= c)
     return true;
   else
     return false;
}
```

III.
```
public boolean fun(int a, int b, int c)
{
   return a >= b || b >= c;
}
```

(A) I and II only
(B) I and III only
(C) II and III only
(D) All three are equivalent
(E) All three are different

9. Consider the following method.

```
/** Precondition: amt represents a positive value in dollars
 *                and cents (for example, 1.15 represents
 *                one dollar and fifteen cents).
 */
private int process(double amt)
{
   return (int)(amt * 100 + 0.5) % 100;
}
```

Which of the following best describes its return value?

(A) The cent portion in amt
(B) The number of whole dollars in amt
(C) amt converted into cents
(D) amt rounded to the nearest dollar
(E) The smallest number of whole dollars that is greater than or equal to amt

10. Consider the following method with two missing statements.

```
/** Returns the sum of all positive odd values
 *   among the first n elements of arr.
 *   Precondition: 1 <= n <= arr.length.
 */
public static int addPositiveOddValues(int[] arr, int n)
{
   int sum = 0;

   < statement 1 >
   {
     < statement 2 >
       sum += arr[i];
   }
   return sum;
}
```

Which of the following are appropriate replacements for < *statement 1* > and < *statement 2* > so that the method works as specified?

	< *statement 1* >	< *statement 2* >
(A)	`for (int i = 1; i < n; i += 2)`	`if (arr[i] > 0)`
(B)	`for (int i = 0; i < n; i++)`	`if (arr[i] > 0 &&` `          arr[i] % 2 != 0)`
(C)	`for (int i = 1; i <= n; i += 2)`	`if (arr[i] > 0)`
(D)	`for (int i = 0; i <= n; i++)`	`if (arr[i] % 2 != 0)`
(E)	None of the above	

11. Consider the following code segment.

```
int n = IO.readInt();    // read an int value
n = Math.abs(n);

while (n >= 2)
{
   n = n/2 - 1;
}
System.out.println(n);
```

Which of the following represents the list of all possible outputs?

(A) 0
(B) -1, 0
(C) 0, 1
(D) -1, 1
(E) -1, 0, 1

12. Consider the following code segment.

```
int x = (int)(2*Math.random()) + (int)(2*Math.random());
System.out.println(x);
```

Which of the following could be printed by the code segment?

(A) 0 only
(B) 2 only
(C) 0 and 2 only
(D) 1 and 2 only
(E) 0, 1, and 2

13. Esther wants to write a method swap that swaps two integer values. Which of the following three ways of representing the values and corresponding methods successfully swap the values?

I.
```
/** a and b are Integer objects that represent
 *   the values to be swapped
 */
public static void swap(Integer a, Integer b)
{
    Integer temp = a; a = b; b = temp;
}
```

II.
```
/** a[0] and a[1] contain the values to be swapped */
public static void swap(int[] a)
{
    int temp = a[0]; a[0] = a[1]; a[1] = temp;
}
```

III.
```
/** a[0] and b[0] contain the values to be swapped */
public static void swap(int[] a, int[] b)
{
    int temp = a[0]; a[0] = b[0]; b[0] = temp;
}
```

(A) I only
(B) II only
(C) I and II only
(D) II and III only
(E) I, II, and III

14. Consider the following method with missing code.

```
public void zeroSomething(int[][] m)
{
   int numRows = m.length;
   int numCols = m[0].length;

   < missing code >
}
```

Which of the following three versions of < *missing code* > are equivalent, that is, result in the same values for a given two-dimensional array m?

I.
```
for (int k = 0; k < numRows; k++)
{
   m[k][0] = 0;
   m[k][numCols - 1] = 0;
}
for (int k = 0; k < numCols; k++)
{
   m[0][k] = 0;
   m[numRows - 1][k] = 0;
}
```

II.
```
for (int k = 0; k < numRows - 1; k++)
{
   m[k][0] = 0;
   m[numRows - k - 1][numCols - 1] = 0;
}
for (int k = 0; k < numCols - 1; k++)
{
   m[0][numCols - k - 1] = 0;
   m[numRows - 1][k] = 0;
}
```

III.
```
for (int k = 0; k < numCols; k++)
{
   m[0][k] = 0;
   m[numRows - 1][k] = 0;
}
for (int[] r : m)
{
   r[0] = 0;
   r[numCols - 1] = 0;
}
```

(A)   All three are equivalent
(B)   I and II only
(C)   II and III only
(D)   I and III only
(E)   All three are different

15. Consider the following method, which prints a message depending on whether the equation $x^2 + bx + c = 0$ has a positive solution.

```
public static void positiveSolution(double b, double c)
{
  double d2 = b*b - 4*c;

  < missing code >
}
```

Which of the following replacements for < *missing code* > are equivalent to each other, that is, produce the same outcome given any values of parameters b and c?

I.
```
double x = (-b + Math.sqrt(d2)) / 2;
if (d2 >= 0 && x > 0)
  System.out.println("Has a positive solution");
else
  System.out.println("No positive solutions");
```

II.
```
if (d2 >= 0)
{
  double x = (-b + Math.sqrt(d2)) / 2;
  if (x > 0)
    System.out.println("Has a positive solution");
}
else
  System.out.println("No positive solutions");
```

III.
```
double x = -1.0;
if (d2 >= 0)
  x = (-b + Math.sqrt(d2)) / 2;
if (x > 0)
  System.out.println("Has a positive solution");
else
  System.out.println("No positive solutions");
```

(A) I and II only
(B) I and III only
(C) II and III only
(D) All three are equivalent
(E) All three are different

16. Consider the following class definitions.

```
public class Airplane
{
  private int fuel;

  public Airplane() { fuel = 0; }
  public Airplane(int g) { fuel = g; }

  public void addFuel() { fuel++; }
  public String toString() { return fuel + " "; }
}

public class Jet extends Airplane
{
  public Jet(int g) { super(2*g); }
}
```

What is the result when the following code is compiled/executed?

```
Airplane plane = new Airplane(4);
Airplane jet = new Jet(4);

System.out.print(plane);
plane.addFuel();
System.out.print(plane);

System.out.print(jet);
jet.addFuel();
System.out.print(jet);
```

(A)   A syntax error, "undefined addFuel," is reported for the `jet.addFuel();`
      statement.
(B)   The code compiles and runs with no errors; the output is 4 5 4 5
(C)   The code compiles and runs with no errors; the output is 4 5 5 6
(D)   The code compiles and runs with no errors; the output is 4 5 8 9
(E)   The code compiles and runs with no errors; the output is 8 9 9 10

17. What is printed when the following statement is executed?

```
int x = 1024;
System.out.println((1 - 2*x) / x);
```

(A)   -2
(B)   -1
(C)   0
(D)   1
(E)   2

Questions 18 and 19 refer to the following method `process`.

```
public void process(int[] a)
{
  for (int i = 1; i < a.length; i++)   // Line 1
  {
    int current = a[i];                // Line 2
    int j = 0;                         // Line 3

    while (a[j] < current)             // Line 4
    {
      j++;                             // Line 5
    }

    for (int k = i; k > j; k--)        // Line 6
    {
      a[k] = a[k-1];                   // Line 7
    }

    a[j] = current;                    // Line 8
  }
}
```

18. The algorithm implemented in the method `process` is best described as:

   (A)   Mergesort
   (B)   Insertion Sort
   (C)   Selection Sort
   (D)   A faulty implementation of Binary Search
   (E)   A faulty implementation of a sorting algorithm

19. Given

```
int[] a = {24, 16, 68, 56, 32};
```

   what will be the result after the statement on Line 8 in `process` completes for the second time?

   (A)   The values in `a` are 16, 24, 68, 56, 32
   (B)   The values in `a` are 16, 24, 32, 56, 68
   (C)   The values in `a` are 24, 16, 32, 56, 68
   (D)   The code has failed with an `ArrayIndexOutOfBoundsException` on Line 4
   (E)   The code has failed with an `ArrayIndexOutOfBoundsException` on Line 8

20. The two versions of the `search` method shown below are both intended to return `true` if `ArrayList<Object> list` contains the target value; otherwise they are supposed to return `false`.

Version 1

```
public boolean search(ArrayList<Object> list, Object target)
{
  for (Object x : list)
  {
    if (target.equals(x))
      return true;
  }
  return false;
}
```

Version 2

```
public boolean search(ArrayList<Object> list, Object target)
{
  boolean found = false;

  for (Object x : list)
  {
    if (target.equals(x))
      found = true;
  }
  return found;
}
```

Which of the following statements about the two versions of `search` is true?

(A) Only Version 1 works as intended.
(B) Only Version 2 works as intended.
(C) Both versions work as intended; Version 1 is often more efficient than Version 2.
(D) Both versions work as intended; Version 2 is often more efficient than Version 1.
(E) Both versions work as intended; the two versions are always equally efficient.

21. What is the best description of the return value of the method `propertyX` below?

```
/** Precondition: v.length >= 2
 */
public boolean propertyX(int[] v)
{
  boolean flag = false;

  for (int i = 0; i < v.length - 1; i++)
  {
    flag = flag || (v[i] == v[i+1]);
  }

  return flag;
}
```

(A) Returns `true` if the elements of `v` are sorted in ascending order, `false` otherwise
(B) Returns `true` if the elements of `v` are sorted in descending order, `false` otherwise
(C) Returns `true` if `v` has two adjacent elements with the same value, `false` otherwise
(D) Returns `true` if `v` has two elements with the same value, `false` otherwise
(E) Returns `true` if all elements in `v` have different values, `false` otherwise

22. Consider the following method.

```
/** Returns the greatest common divisor of a and b.
 * Precondition: a > 0 and b > 0
 */
public static int gcd(int a, int b)
{
  int d = a;
  if (b < d)
    d = b;

  while (a % d != 0 || b % d != 0)
    d--;

  return d;
}
```

How many times will modulo division be performed when `gcd(12, 15)` is called?

(A) 14
(B) 20
(C) 24
(D) 27
(E) 30

23. Consider the following recursive method.

```
public static void printSomething(int n)
{
  if (n > 0)
    printSomething(n-1);

  for (int k=1; k <= n; k++)
    System.out.print(k);
}
```

What is printed when `printSomething(4)` is called?

(A) 1234
(B) 1231234
(C) 1121231234
(D) 1234123121
(E) 4444333221

24. Suppose the class `Text` has a constructor that takes one parameter of `String` type. `Text` also has a static method `translate`:

```
public static Text translate(Text t) { /* code not shown */ }
```

The class `Greeting` extends `Text` and has a constructor that takes one parameter of `String` type. Which of the following code segments in a client class of `Text` and `Greeting` will compile with no errors?

I.   ```
        Text greeting = new Text("Hello");
        Text translation = Text.translate(greeting);
        ```

II.     ```
        Text greeting = new Greeting("Hello");
        Text translation = Text.translate(greeting);
        ```

III.   ```
        Greeting greeting = new Greeting("Hello");
        Text translation = Text.translate(greeting);
        ```

(A)  I only
(B)  I and II only
(C)  I and III only
(D)  II and III only
(E)  I, II, and III
        ```

25. Consider the following method.

```
/** Returns the index of searchVal, if found in list;
 *  otherwise returns -1
 */
public int binarySearch(ArrayList<String> list,
                                      String searchVal)
{
  int first = 0, last = list.size() - 1;

  while (first <= last)
  {
    int mid = (first + last) / 2;

    if (searchVal.compareTo(list.get(mid)) < 0)
      last = mid - 1;
    else if (searchVal.compareTo(list.get(mid)) > 0)
      first = mid + 1;
    else
      return mid;      // Statement 1
  }
  return -1;           // Statement 2
}
```

We want to modify this method: if `searchVal` is not already in the list, we want `binarySearch` to return the position where it can be inserted to keep the list sorted. Which of the following could be used for *Statement 1* and *Statement 2*?

	Statement 1	*Statement 2*
(A)	return mid;	return mid;
(B)	return mid;	return first;
(C)	return mid;	return last;
(D)	return mid - 1;	return first;
(E)	return mid - 1;	return last;

26. The statement

```
System.out.println(Integer.MAX_VALUE);
```

prints `2147483647`. What does the following statement print?

```
System.out.println(Integer.MAX_VALUE / 10 + 1);
```

(A) Nothing: it causes a syntax error
(B) 214748365.7
(C) 214748365.0
(D) 214748365
(E) Nothing: it causes an `ArithmeticException`

27. Consider the following code segment.

```
int[][] t = new int[2][3];

for (int i = 0; i < t.length; i++)
{
  for (int j = 0; j < t[0].length; j++)
  {
    t[i][j] = i + j + 1;
  }
}
```

What is the result when the code segment is executed?

(A)   t holds the values

```
1 2 3
4 5 6
```

(B)   t holds the values

```
1 2 0
2 3 0
```

(C)   t holds the values

```
1 2 3
2 3 4
```

(D)   t holds the values

```
3 4 5
4 5 6
```

(E)   ArrayIndexOutOfBoundsException

28. Consider the following two recursive versions of the method `choose(n, k)`.

Version 1

```
public static int choose(int n, int k)
{
  if (k == 0)
    return 1;
  else
    return choose(n, k-1) * (n-k+1)/k;
}
```

Version 2

```
public static int choose(int n, int k)
{
  if (k < 0 || k > n)
    return 0;
  else if (n == 0)
    return 1;
  else
    return choose(n-1, k-1) + choose(n-1, k);
}
```

When `choose(4, 2)` is called, how many times total, including the original call, will `choose` be called in each version?

	Version 1	Version 2
(A)	2	7
(B)	2	19
(C)	3	7
(D)	3	19
(E)	3	27

29. What is the outcome when the following code is compiled/executed?

```
ArrayList<Integer> numbers = new ArrayList<Integer>();
numbers.add(1);
numbers.add(2);
numbers.add(3);
numbers.add(4);

for (int x : numbers)
{
  if (x % 2 == 0)
    numbers.add(5);
}
System.out.println(numbers);
```

(A) Syntax error
(B) `IndexOutOfBoundsException`
(C) `ConcurrentModificationException`
(D) `[1, 2, 3, 4, 5, 5]` is printed
(E) `[5, 5, 1, 2, 3, 4]` is printed

30. Consider the following class.

```
public class Question
{
  private boolean answer;

  public void flip(Question q)
  {
    < missing statement >
  }

  /* constructors and other methods not shown */

}
```

Which of the following could replace < *missing statement* > in the `flip` method so that it compiles with no errors?

   I.   `answer = !answer;`
   II.   `answer = !q.answer;`
   III. `q.answer = !q.answer;`

(A) None
(B) I only
(C) II only
(D) I and II only
(E) All three

Questions 31-34 use the classes `Track` and `CD`:

```java
public class Track
{
  private String name;
  private int duration;

  public Track(String nm, int dur)
  {
    name = nm;
    duration = dur;
  }

  public String getName() { return name; }
  public int getDuration() { return duration; }
}

public class CD
{
  private String title;
  private String band;
  private int numTracks;
  private ArrayList<Track> tracks;

  public CD(String t, int n)
  {
    title = t;
    numTracks = n;
  }

  /** Initializes all the instance variables and copies
   *  all the data from songs into tracks.
   */
  public CD(String t, String b, int n, ArrayList<Track> songs)
  {
    title = t;
    band = b;
    numTracks = n;

    < missing code >
  }

  public int totalPlayTime()
  { /* implementation not shown */ }

  /** Returns duration of the k-th track.
   *  Precondition: 1 <= k <= numTracks.
   */
  public int getDuration(int k)
  { /* implementation not shown */ }

  /* other methods not shown */
}
```

31. Which of the following declarations is INVALID?

    (A)   `Track tune = new Track();`
    (B)   `Track tune = new Track("Help", 305);`
    (C)   `Track[] playList = new Track[20];`
    (D)   `CD top = new CD("throwing copper", 13);`
    (E)   `CD[][] rack = new CD[3][40];`

32. Which of the following expressions correctly refers to the duration of the *k*-th track inside CD's method `totalPlayTime`?

    (A)   `getDuration(k);`
    (B)   `tracks[k-1].duration;`
    (C)   `tracks.getDuration(k);`
    (D)   `tracks.get(k-1).duration;`
    (E)   `getDuration(tracks[k-1]);`

33. Consider the following code segment.

```
Track t = new Track("lightning crashes", 200);
ArrayList<Track> tracks = new ArrayList<Track>();  // Line **

for (int count = 1; count <= 13; count++)
{
   tracks.add(t);
}

CD live = new CD("throwing copper", "live", 13, tracks);
System.out.println(live.totalPlayTime());
```

What is the result when the code segment is compiled/executed?

    (A)   Syntax error on Line **
    (B)   Run-time `IndexOutOfBoundsException`
    (C)   0 is printed
    (D)   200 is printed
    (E)   2600 is printed

34. Which of the following can replace < *missing code* > in the CD class's constructor so that it works as specified?

I.
```
for (Track t : songs)
    tracks.add(t);
```

II.
```
tracks = new ArrayList<Track>();
for (Track t : songs)
    tracks.add(t);
```

III.
```
tracks = new ArrayList<Track>();
for (int i = 0; i < songs.size(); i++)
    tracks.set(i, songs.get(i));
```

(A)   I only
(B)   II only
(C)   I and II only
(D)   II and III only
(E)   I, II, and III

35. Consider the following class.

```
public class Counter
{
  private int count = 0;

  public Counter() { count = 0; }
  public Counter(int x) { count = x; }             // Line 1
  public int getCount() { return count; }          // Line 2
  public void setCount(int c) { int count = c; }   // Line 3
  public void increment() { count++; }             // Line 4
  public String toString() { return "" + count; }  // Line 5
}
```

The test code

```
Counter c = new Counter();
c.setCount(3);
c.increment();
System.out.println(c.getCount());
```

is supposed to print 4, but the class has an error. What is actually printed, and which line in the class definition should be changed to get the correct output, 4?

(A)   0, Line 1
(B)   1, Line 3
(C)   0, Line 4
(D)   3, Line 4
(E)   36, Line 5

36. Consider the following class.

```
public class Matrix
{
  private int[][] m;

  /** Initializes m to a square n-by-n array with all
   *   the elements on the diagonal m[k][k] equal to 0 and
   *   all other elements equal to 1
   */
  public Matrix(int n)
  {
    m = new int[n][n];

    < missing code >
  }

  < other constructors and methods not shown >
}
```

Which of the following could replace < *missing code* > in `Matrix`'s constructor so that it compiles with no errors and works as specified?

I.
```
for (int r = 0; r < n; r++)
   for (int c = 0; c < n; c++)
      m[r][c] = 1;
for (int k = 0; k < n; k++)
   m[k][k] = 0;
```

II.
```
for (int r = 0; r < n; r++)
   for (int c = 0; c < n; c++)
      if (r != c)
         m[r][c] = 1;
```

III.
```
for (int c = 0; c < n; c++)
   for (int r = 0; r < n; r++)
      if (r == c)
         m[r][c] = 0;
      else
         m[r][c] = 1;
```

(A) I only
(B) II only
(C) I and II only
(D) II and III only
(E) I, II, and III

Questions 37 and 38 are based on the following information.

Ashanti has decided to write and test her own version of the `indexOf` method, which takes two strings as parameters:

```
/** Returns the first index k such that word.substring(k)
 *  starts with str; if no such k found, returns -1.
 *  Precondition: word != null, str != null.
 */
public int indexOf(String word, String str)
{
  int n = str.length();
  for (int k = 0; k <= word.length() - n; k++)
    if (word.substring(k, k + n).equals(str))
      return k;
  return -1;
}
```

37. What will happen if Morgan calls Ashanti's `indexOf` method as follows?

```
    int i = indexOf("Hello", null);
```

(A) `i` will be set to 0
(B) `i` will be set to –1
(C) `NullPointerException`
(D) `StringIndexOutOfBoundsException`
(E) `ConcurrentModificationException`

38. Ashanti also wrote the test method `findWord` —

```
public String findWord(ArrayList<String> words, String str)
{
  for (String word : words)
    if (indexOf(word, str) >= 0)
      return word;
  return null;
}
```

— and created a list of strings `continents` with the values

```
["Africa", "America", "Antarctica", "Asia", "Australia",
"Europe"]
```

How many times will the method `equals` be called in Ashanti's `indexOf` code when `findWord(continents, "tar")` is called?

(A) 1
(B) 3
(C) 12
(D) 15
(E) 36

39. Consider the following code segment.

```
ArrayList<Integer> list = new ArrayList<Integer>();
list.add(1);
list.add(2);

for (int i = 1; i <= 3; i++)
{
  list.add(i, i);
}

System.out.println(list);
```

What is the result when the code segment is executed?

(A) `[1, 1, 2, 2, 3]` is printed
(B) `[1, 1, 2, 3, 2]` is printed
(C) `[1, 2, 1, 2, 3]` is printed
(D) `[1, 2, 3, 1, 2]` is printed
(E) `IndexOutOfBoundsException`

40. Consider the following method.

```
public void reduce(int[] arr, int len)
{
  for (int k = 0; k < len; k++)
  {
    arr[k]--;
  }

  len--;
}
```

What is printed when the following code segment is executed?

```
int[] counts = {3, 2, 1, 0};
int len = 3;
reduce(counts, len);

for (int c : counts)
{
  System.out.print(c + " ");
}

System.out.println(len);
```

(A) 2 1 0 -1 2
(B) 2 1 0 -1 3
(C) 2 1 0 0 2
(D) 2 1 0 0 3
(E) 2 1 1 0 3

Practice Exam #5

Time — 1 hour and 30 minutes
Number of questions — 4
Percent of total grade — 50

1. A high school Casino Night event offers a game of chance in which a player can buy a ticket to have a low-probability chance at winning a fixed prize. (All tickets and prizes are in the fictional *Darsek* currency). The class GameOfChance models this game. You will write two methods of this class.

```
public class GameOfChance
{
  /** Returns true if a game is won; otherwise returns false.
   */
  private static boolean win()
  { /* implementation not shown */ }

  /** Returns the average amount won or lost
   *   after playing n games, given the price of one ticket
   *   and the size of the prize.
   */
  public static double averageAmt(int prize,
                                 double ticketPrice, int n)
  { /* to be implemented in part (a) */ }

  /** Returns the prize size (a multiple of 5) that makes
   *   the game worth playing, based on the average return
   *   after 100 games, as modeled by the averageAmt method.
   */
  public static int prizeWorthPlaying(double ticketPrice)
  { /* to be implemented in part (b) */ }
}
```

(a) Write the `averageAmt` method. The method takes three parameters: the size of the prize, the ticket price, and the number of games played. `averageAmt` calls the `win` method for each game played to determine whether a game was won or lost: `win` returns `true` to indicate that a game was won and `false` if a game was lost. The price of one ticket is subtracted from the total for each game played, regardless of whether the game was won or lost. For example, `averageAmt(15, 1.0, 10)` will call `win()` ten times. If none of these calls return `true`, then `averageAmt` will return $(0 - 10 \cdot 1.0)/10 = -1.0$; if, however, exactly one of the ten calls to `win` returns `true`, then `averageAmt` will return $(15 - 10 \cdot 1.0)/10 = 0.5$.

Complete the `averageAmt` method below.

```
/** Returns the prize size (a multiple of 5) that makes
 *  the game worth playing, based on the average return
 *  after 100 games, as modeled by the averageAmt method.
 */
public static double averageAmt(int prize,
                               double ticketPrice, int n)
```

(b) Write the `prizeWorthPlaying` method of the `GameOfChance` class. This method tries different values of `prize`, in increments of 5 — 5, 10, 15, and so on — until the size of the prize makes it worth playing the game, given the price of one ticket. `prizeWorthPlaying` relies on the result of `averageAmt` for 100 games: it needs to be positive to make the game worth playing. For example, if `averageAmt(15, 1.7, 100)` returns -0.2 and `averageAmt(20, 1.7, 100)` returns 1.1, then `prizeWorthPlaying(1.7)` will return 20.

Complete the `prizeWorthPlaying` method below.

```
/** Returns the prize size (a multiple of 5) that makes
 *  it worth playing, based on the average return after
 *  100 games, as modeled by the averageAmt method.
 */
public static int prizeWorthPlaying(double ticketPrice)
```

For additional practice, implement the `win` method. Make it return `true` randomly with the probability 0.05. See if the value returned by `prizeWorthPlaying` makes sense with your `win` method and a ticket price of $1.00 — it should usually be between 15 and 25.

2. You can purchase any number of apples at Papas Orchards, but every six purchased are priced as five. For example, if the price of each apple is 69 cents and you purchase 34 apples, your total cost will be 29 * $0.69 = $20.01, because 30 apples are priced as 25. The class `ApplesPurchase` helps calculate the cost of your purchase at Papas.

The constructor of the `ApplesPurchase` class takes two `int` parameters: the price of one apple in cents and the number of apples purchased. `ApplesPurchase` has three methods:

- `totalCost` — takes no parameters; returns the total cost of the purchase in cents.

- `toDollarsAndCents` — returns a `String` that represents a given `int` parameter `cents` as dollars and cents, with a dollar sign, at least one digit for dollars, a decimal point, and two digits after the decimal point.

- `toString` — returns a string with the summary of the purchase (in the same format as the one shown in the example below).

For example,

```
ApplesPurchase purchase1 = new ApplesPurchase(79, 1);
System.out.println(purchase1);
ApplesPurchase purchase2 = new ApplesPurchase(50, 12);
System.out.println(purchase2);
ApplesPurchase purchase3 = new ApplesPurchase(69, 34);
System.out.println(purchase3);
```

in a client class of `ApplesPurchase` should print

```
1 apples at $0.79 each: $0.79
12 apples at $0.50 each: $5.00
34 apples at $0.69 each: $20.01
```

Do not duplicate code from `totalCost` and `toDollarsAndCents` in your `toString` method; call these methods instead.

Write a complete `ApplesPurchase` class, including the required instance variables and the constructor and three methods described above. Your implementation must meet the specifications, and the format of the output must conform to the above example.

For additional practice, derive a class `ApplesPurchaseWithPie` from `ApplesPurchase` to provide a way to add an apple pie to the purchase. Apple pies should be available in two sizes, small (`"S"`) and large (`"L"`). Pass the price of the large pie as a parameter to `ApplesPurchaseWithPie`'s constructor. Compute the price of the small pie as 75% of the large pie price, rounded to the nearest cent. Override `ApplesPurchase`'s `totalCost` and `toString` methods.

3. In an international ballroom dancing competition, competitors are scored by a panel of judges on a scale from 0 to 100. The final score for each couple is computed as the average of the scores from all the judges (possibly excluding the highest score and/or the lowest score in some cases, as explained in Part (b)).

(a) Write a method `findMaxAndMin` of the `BallroomScoring` class. This method takes an `ArrayList<Integer>` scores as a parameter and returns an array of length two, where the first element is the maximum value in `scores` and the second element is the minimum value in `scores`.

Complete the method `findMaxAndMin` below.

```
/** Returns an array of two elements in which
 *   the first element is the maximum value in scores and
 *   the second element is the minimum value in scores.
 *   Precondition: scores.size() > 0; 0 <= all scores <= 100
 */
public static int[] findMaxAndMin(ArrayList<Integer> scores)
```

(b) Write a method `averageScore` of the `BallroomScoring` class that takes an `ArrayList<Integer>` scores as a parameter and computes and returns the average score. However, if the size of the list `scores` is 6 or greater and the maximum value occurs only once in the array, that value is excluded from computing the average. The same is done for the minimum value.

The `BallroomScoring` class has a private method

```
private static int countOccurrences(ArrayList<Integer> scores,
                                                    int target)
```

that returns the number of occurrences of `target` in `scores`. In writing `averageScore`, call the `countOccurrences` method. Also assume that the method `findMaxAndMin` from Part (a) works as specified, regardless of what you wrote there. You may not receive full credit if instead of calling these two methods you re-implement their functionality here.

Complete the method `averageScore` below.

```
/** Returns the average of the values in scores. However,
 *   if the size of the scores list is not less than 6 and
 *   the largest value occurs only once in scores, that value
 *   is excluded from computing the average; the same for
 *   the smallest value.
 *   Precondition: scores.size() >= 3
 */
public static double averageScore(ArrayList<Integer> scores)
```

For additional practice, implement the `countOccurrences` method.

Then implement a computer model for a ballroom dancing competition. The competition includes several dance events, and several couples participate in all the events. Each event is scored by a panel of eight judges. Generate the judges' scores as random integers from 90 to 99. Calculate the average score for each couple in each event by calling the `averageScore` method from Part (b). Then add up the couple's average scores in all events and round the sum to the nearest integer to get the couple's final score.

Determine the maximum total score among all the couples, and find the number of couples that share first place.

Whenever possible, use the appropriate methods of the `BallroomScoring` class — do not duplicate their code.

4.   In chess, a queen can move vertically, horizontally, and diagonally on an 8-by-8 chessboard. The picture below shows all the positions on the board that a queen can reach from its current position.

Squares on the chessboard are often labeled with a letter and a digit, but we will just treat a chessboard as a two-dimensional array and use indices, as in Java, counting from zero. So the upper-left corner of the board is in row 0, column 0, and the position of the queen in the above picture is row 5, column 3.

(a)   Write a method oneQueen that takes two integer parameters, the row and column of a queen on a chessboard, and generates and returns an 8-by-8 two-dimensional array of boolean values in which the queen's position and all the positions that the queen can reach from it are set to true, and all the other positions are set to false.

Complete the method oneQueen below.

```
/** Returns an 8-by-8 boolean two-dimensional array in which
 *   the element at row, col and all the elements that
 *   represent positions reachable by a queen placed at row,
 *   col are set to true, and all the other elements are set
 *   to false.
 *   Precondition: 0 <= row < 8; 0 <= col < 8
 */
public static boolean[][] oneQueen(int row, int col)
```

(b)   Write a method twoQueens that takes four integer parameters — the row and column of the first queen on a chessboard, followed by the row and column of the second queen — and generates and returns an 8-by-8 two-dimensional array of boolean values in which the elements that correspond to both queens' positions and all the positions reachable by one or both queens are set to true, and all the other elements are set to false. In writing this method, do not duplicate your code from oneQueen; instead, call that method twice, once for each queen, and combine the two boards returned by these calls. Assume that the method oneQueen from Part (a) works as specified, regardless of what you wrote there.

Complete the method twoQueens below.

```
/** Returns an 8-by-8 boolean two-dimensional array in which
 *   the element at row1, col1, the element at row2, col2,
 *   and all the elements that represent positions reachable
 *   by a queen placed at row1, col1 as well as positions
 *   reachable by a queen placed at row2, col2 are set to
 *   true, and all the other elements are set to false.
 *   Precondition: 0 <= row1 < 8; 0 <= col1 < 8;
 *                 0 <= row2 < 8; 0 <= col2 < 8
 */
public static boolean[][] twoQueens(int row1, int col1,
                                    int row2, int col2)
```

For additional practice, write a boolean method that takes an ArrayList of positions of several queens and returns true if there is a position on the board that none of the queens can reach; otherwise your method should return false. Use only two variables of the boolean[][] type.

Answers and Solutions

Exam #1 ~ Multiple Choice

1. A	11. E	21. C	31. D
2. A	12. B	22. A	32. B
3. D	13. B	23. E	33. A
4. C	14. D	24. D	34. A
5. B	15. C	25. E	35. A
6. A	16. D	26. D	36. C
7. B	17. D	27. C	37. B
8. B	18. C	28. C	38. B
9. D	19. B	29. C	39. B
10. A	20. E	30. E	40. E

Notes:

1. `17/5` gives 3; `3 % 3 = 0`; `85 % 3 = 1`.

2. This is equivalent to `(a && !b) || (!a && b)`.

3. `\\` in `"yes\\no"` represents one backslash character, and `\n` in `"\no"` represents the newline character. `"yes\\no"` does not include a newline character.

4. `s1 = "BCD"`, so `printSomething(s1)` cannot print any A's. The only "A" is printed in the `println` statement for the original string. `printSomething(s)` prints 1 letter if n is 1, 1 + 2 + 1 = 4 letters if n is 2, 4 + 3 + 4 = 11 letters if n is 3, and 11 + 4 + 11 = 26 letters if n is 4.

5. The smallest possible value of x is 0, when `Math.random()` returns a number close to 0 (any number < 1/16). The largest possible value of x is 2, when `Math.random()` returns a number close enough to 1 (any number > 9/16).

6. Strings are usually compared using the `equals` method, not `==`, unless you want to establish that two strings are exactly the same object, or when you are comparing a `String` reference to `null`. (The `String` class has a constructor that creates a copy of a string, but constructing a copy using the `new` operator, as in `str2 = new String(str1)`, is rarely, if ever, useful. Strings are immutable, and there are no problems when more than one reference points to the same string, so you can just copy a reference to the string, as in `str2 = str1`.)

7. A cast to `int` truncates the `double` value 31415.9 toward zero.

8. To compare two strings you must use `compareTo`, which returns an `int`.

9. The base cases, n <= 2, are implicit in this method: the for loop will never be entered. So fun(2) returns 2. fun(3) returns $2 \cdot 2 = 4$. fun(4) returns $2 \cdot 2 \cdot 4 = 16$. fun(5) returns $2 \cdot 2 \cdot 4 \cdot 16 = 256$.

10. The code in Choices B, C, and E creates a new object of the type Test and works with it. All three will compile fine and display 2020. (In Choice C first the empty string is concatenated with 20, then the result is again concatenated with 20.) The code in Choice D works, because year is declared static and it is accessible in all instance and static methods of the class, including main. Choice A won't compile, because this, the reference to an object whose constructor or method is running, is undefined in a static method, such as main.

11. When one of the operands in the + operator is a string, the other is converted into a string, and the two strings are concatenated. The + operators are applied from left to right.

12. At the end of an iteration, i is 3, then 4, then 5; k changes from 0 to 3 to 7 to 12.

13. A Monster object keeps track of the biggest (lexicographically) string passed to its feed method. In this case it happens to be "Two". x is initialized to null by default, then updated as necessary to bigger values. NullPointerException does not occur, due to short-circuit evaluation.

14. a and b refer to the same array. After the assignments, its values are
    a[0] = b[0] = 2; a[1] = b[1] = 1.

15. Let's trace the values of the variables a and b:

	a	b
Before the for loop	1	2
After the first iteration	2	3
After the second iteration	3	2

    (Interestingly, this sequence of *a*, *b* pairs is periodic, with the period 5.)

16. mystery(0, 16) prints 0, then calls mystery(5, 15); that call prints 5, then calls mystery(10, 14); that call prints 10, then calls mystery(15, 13); that call prints 15 and quits.

17. This is a pretty standard way to reverse an array.

18. Either way, a > 10. Try a = 15 with b = 10 and b = 20.

19. In Choice B, the compiler would report an error.

20. count is not incremented.

21. list.remove(i) shifts the subsequent elements to the left by one, so only every other element is removed.

22. The code segments in Options II and III essentially fail the same way: in both of them "*" is appended to a local variable, not an element of letters.

23. Replacing `Cake` with `PricedItem` is neither encapsulation nor modularity.

24. Option I was already guaranteed — no change is necessary for that.

25. The statement `s = t;` has no effect in this code. The last element of `list` is set in turn to the first element, then the second element, and then to its own value, so it remains equal to the second element.

26. The three friends are created with the sum of their miles equal to 30000. The "for each" loop gives 1000 additional miles to each friend. It is often said that you cannot modify the elements of a list (an array or an `ArrayList`) in a "for each" loop. It is true that you cannot replace an element in the list, but if the list holds mutable objects, you can change the state of an element by calling one of its mutator methods.

27. `url.indexOf(...)` sets `pos` to 0; `url.substring(0,0)` returns an empty string.

28. Choice A: `Animal` is not necessarily a `Mammal`; Choice B: `Mammal` must have a constructor that takes a `String` parameter; Choice D: No relation to the situation; Choice C works.

29. `msg[0]` has not been initialized (`null`), so you cannot call its methods.

30. Selection Sort finds the largest element among 2000, then among the remaining 1999, and so on.

31. By default, an array is initialized with 0.0 values, so Option I doesn't work. Option III works with a "for each" outer loop, which produces each row, and a regular inner loop to set the values in that row. We cannot use an inner "for each" loop in Option III because we need to set the values of the elements.

32. Choices D and E do not work, because `amps` is private in `Sample`.

33. The concept of "privacy" applies to the whole class, not a particular object, so Choice A works.

34. After the first pass through the outer loop: `counts` holds 0, 2, 3, 4, 5, 1; 1 swap.
    After the second pass through the outer loop: `counts` holds 0, 1, 3, 4, 5, 2; 1 swap.
    After the third pass through the outer loop: `counts` holds 0, 1, 2, 4, 5, 3; 1 swap.
    And so on.

35. With 160,000 numbers, it will take 18 ms to sort each half. Then merging together the two sorted halves with 80,000 numbers in each of them takes $40 - 2 \cdot 18 = 4$ ms. For 320,000 elements, it will take $2 \cdot 40$ ms to sort each half and $2 \cdot 4$ (twice as long) to merge the sorted halves with 160,000 numbers in each, for a total of $2 \cdot 40 + 8 = 88$ ms.

36. Option II does not necessarily work: consider {2, 3, 4, 0, 1, 5, 6, 7, 8} and `target = 3`.

37. In this code segment, we add to `lst` the next number that is not evenly divisible by any of the numbers already in the list. This results in the list of the first five primes.

38. Notice that `Game`'s `getPlayer(k)` returns `players.get(k-1)`. Choices C and D don't work because `players` is private in `Game`; Choice E doesn't work because `Game` has no method `getPlayers`.

39. Option I doesn't work because `Game` has no constructor that takes three parameters. Option II is fine. Option III doesn't work because `super(...)`, a call to a superclass's constructor, must be the first statement in the subclass's constructor.

40. There are no tricks in this question: Options I, II, and III are all fine.

Answers and Solutions

Exam #1 ~ Free Response

1. (a)

```
public static boolean isValid(String  password)
{
  return password.length() >= 8 && password.length() <= 16 &&
      hasUpper(password) && hasLower(password) &&
      hasDigit(password);
}
```

(b)

```
public static String makePassword(String phrase, int n)
{
  String password = makePasswordLetters(phrase);

  if (n == 0)
  {
    password += 0;
  }
  else
  {
    while (n != 0)
    {
      password += n % 10;
      n /= 10;
    }
  }

  if (isValid(password))
    return password;
  else
    return null;
}
```

2.

```java
public class Shopping
{
  private final int maxDistance;

  private int totalStores;
  private double sumOfPrices;

  private String bestStoreName;
  private double bestPrice;
  private int bestDistance;

  public Shopping(int distance)
  {
    maxDistance = distance;
    totalStores = 0;            ¹
    sumOfPrices = 0.0;
    bestStoreName = null;
  }

  public void addShoppingOption(String name, double price,
                                          int distance)
  {
    totalStores++;
    sumOfPrices += price;
    if (distance <= maxDistance &&
            (bestStoreName == null || price < bestPrice))
    {
      bestStoreName = name;
      bestPrice = price;
      bestDistance = distance;
    }
  }

  public double streetPrice()
  {
    return 0.01 * (int)(100*sumOfPrices / totalStores + 0.5);  ²
  }

  public String toString()
  {
    return bestStoreName + " " + bestPrice + " " +
                                        bestDistance;
  }
}
```

Notes:

1. This and the two subsequent statements are optional, because instance variables get default values: 0 for `int`s, 0.0 for `double`s, `null` for objects.

2. Convert to cents, round, then convert back to dollars.

3. (a)

```
public boolean isValidArrangement()
{
  for (int i = 0;  i < numCards;  i++)
  {
    int count = 0;

    for (int j = 0;  j < numCards;  j++)
      if (cards[i].equals(cards[j]))
        count++;

    if (count != 2)
      return false;
  }
  return true;  ¹
}
```

(b)

```
public void removeCard(int k)
{
  for (int j = k+1;  j < numCards;  j++)
    cards[j-1] = cards[j];

  numCards--;
}
```

(c)

```
public boolean openTwoCards(int k1, int k2)
{
  if (cards[k1].equals(cards[k2]))
  {
    removeCard(k2);  ²
    removeCard(k1);
    return true;
  }
  else
    return false;
}
```

Notes:

1. `return true` only outside of the outer `for` loop.

2. It is important to remove the cards in the correct order, because when a card is removed, the subsequent cards shift to the left.

4. (a)

```
public static boolean isComplete(int[][] m)
{
  int n = m.length;

  for (int i = 0; i < n; i++)
  {
    if (m[i][i] != 0)
      return false;
  }

  for (int i = 0; i < n; i++)
  {
    for (int j = 0; j < i; j++)  1
    {
      if (m[i][j] != 1 || m[j][i] != 1)
        return false;
    }
  }
  return true;
}
```

(b)

```
public static int[][] makeAdjacencyMatrix(
        ArrayList<String> vertices, String edges)
{
  int n = vertices.size();
  int[][] m = new int[n][n];  2

  for (int i = 0; i < n; i++)
  {
    for (int j = 0; j < n; j++)
    {
      String letter1 = vertices.get(i);
      String letter2 = vertices.get(j);
      if (edges.indexOf(letter1 + letter2) >= 0)
      {
        m[i][j] = 1;
        m[j][i] = 1;
      }
    }
  }
  return m;
}
```

Notes:

1. From the beginning of the row up to but not including the diagonal.

2. The elements of m get 0 values by default.

Answers and Solutions

Exam #2 ~ Multiple Choice

1. B	11. C	21. A	31. C
2. C	12. A	22. A	32. C
3. D	13. C	23. B	33. B
4. C	14. D	24. E	34. E
5. B	15. D	25. E	35. A
6. C	16. B	26. D	36. C
7. A	17. D	27. E	37. D
8. E	18. C	28. D	38. B
9. A	19. E	29. C	39. E
10. E	20. D	30. B	40. E

Notes:

1. "`&& z`" in Choice B gives it away.

2. Take, for instance, a = 2 and b = 1. The given expression evaluates to 4 because 3/2 is truncated to 1. The expression in Choice A gives 5. The expression in Choice B gives 2, because 1/2 is truncated to 0. The expression in Choice C gives `2 + 2*(1) = 4`, and, in general, is equivalent to the given expression.

3. `\\` represents one backslash; `\"` represents a quotation mark; `substring(1)` gets rid of the leading backslash.

4. a and b are references to the same array; c is a reference to a different array with the same values as the initial values in a. When a changes, c remains unchanged.

5. `s.substring(1, 4)` is `"LAS"`; index of `"A"` in it is 1.

6. The code adds 2, 4, 8, 16, and 32 to the elements of v, respectively. `v[4]`, the last element, becomes 33.

7. `b = fun2(a, b)` sets b to 4, a remains 3 (because a and b are passed to `fun2` by value); then `a = fun2(b, a)` sets a to −1, b remains 4.

8. The last thing `splat("**")` does is display `"**"`, which eliminates Choices B and C.
   `splat("**")` calls `splat("****")`, then prints `**`.
   `splat("****")` calls `splat("********")`, then prints `****`.
   `splat("********")` prints `********`.

9. `printVals(names, 0)` and `printVals(names, 1)` do nothing.
   `printVals(names, 2)` prints `"Ann"`.
   `printVals(names, 3)` prints `"Ann"`, then `"Cal"`.
   `printVals(names, 4)` prints `"Ann"`, then `"Cal"`, then `"Amy"`, then `"Ann"`.

10. `printVals(names, 2)` results in $1 + 1 + 1 = 3$ calls.
    `printVals(names, 3)` results in $1 + 3 + 1 = 5$ calls.
    `printVals(names, 4)` results in $1 + 5 + 3 = 9$ calls.

11. `(m + n)/2` evaluates to 4.

12. A constructor does not return a value and has no return type. This eliminates Choices B, D, and E. In Choice C, `this` refers to an object of the type `MyTest`; you cannot assign an integer to it. The answer is A. (This no-argument constructor does nothing, which is OK.)

13. It might seem fanciful to think of a subclass not using the instance variables of its superclass. However, the "Decorator" design pattern suggests just that. (This pattern would use a "wrapper" class, say `DecoratedAthlete`, that <u>both</u> extends `Athlete` and has an `Athlete` object as an instance variable, and a method of `DecoratedAthlete` calls the corresponding method of the embedded `Athlete` object, while the instance variables of `DecoratedAthlete` itself — other than the embedded `Athlete` — are unused.)

14. Choices A and C don't work, because `x` is private in `Point`.

15. The code in Options II and III does the same thing. Option III works, because `Point` objects are mutable, and we can change the state of a mutable object in a "for each" loop by calling one of its mutator methods. Option I doesn't work because `x` is private in `Point`.

16. `r` does not have to be a `double` (`x/y` results in an `int` anyway); `r` can be either a static variable or an instance variable in `ClassX`.

17. `product = (3%2) * (7%4) * (5%2) = 1 * 3 * 1`.

18. Options I and II do not work, because `buddies` is private in `BuddyList`.

19. The code goes into an infinite loop when `first` is 3 and `last` is 4.

20. In Option I, the loops go "too far," swapping `m[r][c]` and `m[c][r]` twice.

21. Before the loop, `words` contains `["ban", "an", "a"]`; the `for` loop concatenates all the elements together to make `"banana"`. The first occurrence of `"an"` in `"banana"` is at index 1.

22. `12%7` gives 5; `(double)(12/5)` results in 2.0; `n` remains unchanged, because it is passed to `goFigure` by value.

23. Trace the values of the variables:

```
    n     d     s
 ===========
    1     1     1
    2     3     4
    3     5     9
    4     7    16
    5     9    25
```

The loop runs five times, for n = 1, 2, 3, 4, 5.

24. The sequence of calls: B's constructor ==> A's constructor ==> B's methodOne (not A's methodOne, due to polymorphism) ==> print "B" in B's methodOne ==> print "*", finishing B's constructor.

25. The correct signature for equals is in Choices D and E, but in D a cast of other into a Rectangle is missing.

26. Option I does not work, because in the second "for each" loop, x acts like a local variable; you cannot replace the value of an array element using a "for each" loop.

27. Lunch IS-A Meal, and Pizza IS-A Lunch and IS-A Meal. All of the choices from A to D are valid declarations.

28. Using De Morgan's Laws, negate the condition in the while loop.

29. 4 times for each pair plus 2 times for each quadruplet plus 1 time at the top level.

30. 40 ms + 40 ms to sort both halves + 0.01 * 2000 = 20 ms to merge them.

31. Each of the 3 elements equals only itself.

32. findMax first counts the number of times each brightness value occurs in image, then finds the largest count.

33. There is no problem with Line 1. When the + operator is applied to a string and an integer, the integer is converted into a string, so there is no syntax error on Line 2. The == operator, when applied to two objects, compares the addresses of the objects, which in this case are different. c.equals(d) compares the values of c and d, which are the same.

34. It is often said that a "for each" loop cannot change the values in a list. This is true only when the list holds values of a primitive data type or immutable objects. A mutable object in the list can be changed by calling one of its mutator methods. Here the list first holds four bank accounts with balances 0, 5, 10, and 15. Then 10 is added to each balance.

35. The statement compiles with no problems, so Choices D and E do not apply. `Integer.MAX_VALUE` is the largest possible value of the `int` type. The value of `2*Integer.MAX_VALUE + 2`, which equals 2^{32}, exceeds the `int` range, so the number in Choice B cannot be printed. Java does not catch the arithmetic overflow error and just prints an incorrect result, `0`. (In Java, an `int` value is always held in four bytes, which is 32 bits. The result here is 0 because the high-order bit in the binary representation of 2^{32}, which is 1 followed by 32 zeros, is lost — only the 32 zeros remain.)

36. We can't make a `Party` object an element of the `BDayParty[]` array: not every party is a birthday party.

37. `theGuests` is private in `Party`.

38. The method `getOccasion` must be defined, and it should return
    `"Birthday " + getName();`

39. Starting with `[0, 1]`, we double the size of the `numbers` list in each iteration through the outer loop, and the value of the last element of `numbers` is incremented by 1. So, after three iterations, the size of `numbers` becomes 16 and the last element becomes 4.

40. The two consecutive calls to `randomPoints(3)` may return different numbers in the range from 1 to 3, inclusive.

Answers and Solutions

Exam #2 ~ Free Response

1. (a)

```
public Bus(String start, String end, int mins)
{
  startTime = toMinutes(start);  ¹
  endTime = toMinutes(end);
  runInterval = mins;
}
```

(b)

```
public int waitTime(String time)
{
  int now = toMinutes(time);
  int nextBus = startTime;

  while (nextBus < now)  ²
    nextBus += runInterval;

  if (nextBus > endTime)
    return -1;

  return nextBus - now;
}
```

Notes:

1. It is OK to call public or private instance methods of the class from its constructors.

2. Of course it is possible to calculate the expected next bus arrival time using arithmetic, but it is much easier to use a loop.

2.

```
public class EquationSolver
{
  private final double precision;

  public EquationSolver(double e)
  {
    precision = e;
  }

  public double solve(Fun fun, double a, double b)
  {
    while (b - a > precision)
    {
      double m = (a + b) / 2;
      double y = fun.f(m);  [1]

      if (y > 0)
        b = m;
      else
        a = m;
    }
    return (a + b) / 2;
  }
}
```

Notes:

1. `fun` is not a function but an object that has a method `f`.

3. (a)

```
public double likenessScore(Movie other)
{
  ArrayList<String> features1 = this.getFeatures();
  ArrayList<String> features2 = other.getFeatures();
  int n = features1.size();
  int count = 0;

  for (int i = 0; i < n; i++)
    if (features1.get(i).equals(features2.get(i)))  ¹
      count++;

  return (double)count / n;  ²
}
```

(b)

```
public void removeOutliers()
{
  double[] coefficients = getFitCoefficients();

  double sum = 0.0;
  for (double c : coefficients)
    sum += c;

  double threshold = (sum / coefficients.length) / 2;

  for (int k = coefficients.length - 1; k >= 0; k--)  ³
    if (coefficients[k] < threshold)
      movies.remove(k);
}
```

Notes:

1. Not

    ```
    if (features1.get(i) == features2.get(i)))
    ```

2. Don't forget to cast count or n to double first.

3. Remove the elements starting from the end.

4.   (a)

```
public int summitLocation()
{
  int iMax = 0;

  for (int i = 1; i < alts[0].length; i++)
  {
    if (alts[0][i] > alts[0][iMax])
      iMax = i;
  }
  return iMax;
}
```

(b)

```
public ArrayList<Integer> findSteepestTrail()
{
  ArrayList<Integer> trail = new ArrayList<Integer>();

  int col = summitLocation();
  trail.add(col);

  for (int row = 1; row < alts.length; row++)
  {
    int nextCol = col;
    if (col > 0 && alts[row][col-1] < alts[row][nextCol])
      nextCol = col - 1;

    if (col < alts[0].length - 1 &&
                  alts[row][col+1] < alts[row][nextCol])
      nextCol = col + 1;

    col = nextCol;
    trail.add(col);
  }
  return trail;
}
```

Answers and Solutions

Exam #3 ~ Multiple Choice

1. A	11. B	21. C	31. E
2. E	12. C	22. D	32. B
3. E	13. A	23. A	33. A
4. E	14. E	24. D	34. C
5. C	15. A	25. E	35. D
6. D	16. B	26. A	36. D
7. C	17. B	27. A	37. A
8. E	18. B	28. D	38. B
9. C	19. B	29. B	39. A
10. A	20. C	30. D	40. D

Notes:

1. In Option II, `(double)(q / 2)` evaluates to 1.0; in Option III, `(double)(p * q / 2)` evaluates to 7.0.

2: `band.substring(1, 4)` is `"nam"`; `band.substring(5, 8)` is `"nag"`.

3. `4/3` yields 1.

4. A "for each" loop cannot change the values in an `ArrayList` of strings because `String` objects are immutable.

5. `filter` makes a new string from `str` with all the occurrences of `pattern` in `str` removed one by one.

6. `\\` represents one backslash, and `\n` represents the newline character. So `str` actually consists of 5 characters: `\`, `*`, *<newline character>*, `*`, `\`.

7. The last element remains unchanged, which eliminates Choices A and B.

8. `countSomething` returns the number of times the maximum value occurs in the array. If a new maximum is found, the count is reset to 1.

9. Suppose `somethingIsFalse` returns `true`. Then the `else` clause is executed in the code segment and it returns `true`, and so does the statement in Choice C.

10. It is easier to negate each of the expressions (using De Morgan's Laws when necessary) and check whether the result is equivalent to "all three values are the same." In Choice A, `!(a != b || b != c)` is the same as `(a == b && b == c)`, which is `true` if and only if `a == b` and `b == c` and `a == c`.

11. n remains unchanged, because it is passed to `change` by value. The `change` method does change the values in `samples`, because the method gets a copy of the reference to `samples`.

12. `mat[0][0]` remains equal to 2, `mat[1][1]` becomes `2*2 + 1 = 5`; `mat[2][2]` becomes `2*5 + 2 = 12`.

13. The last iteration starts with `num` = 1.

14. `ArrayList` implements extendable arrays. Once the capacity of an `ArrayList` is reached, a bigger underlying array is created, the values from the old array are copied into the new one, and the old array is discarded.

15. Binary Search will look at `arr[63]`, `arr[31]`, `arr[47]`, and `arr[39]`.

16. In `Math.pow(2, 3)`, 2 and 3 are promoted into `doubles`; the result is a `double` equal to $2^3 = 8$.

17. All the lines are OK due to autoboxing and unboxing. `n + x` is converted to a `double`, and `println` displays the `double` value with a decimal point.

18. `numbers` holds two elements: two copies of an `Integer` with value 1. `names` holds `["Cathy", "Ben", "Anya"]`. Then the element at index 1 is deleted twice from `names`.

19. Option I is false because a `Student` object is constructed here, not a `Person` object. This leaves Choices B and D. Option III is false because this code does not tell us anything about private fields.

20. Encapsulation, which is also called information hiding.

21. `nums[2]` is not assigned a value, so it remains `null`. A call to `null.toString()` raises a `NullPointerException`.

22. `product` returns $6 \cdot 4 \cdot 2$.

23. When an `int` value gets out of range, it might be interpreted as negative because the sign bit gets set to 1. In Java the range of integers is the same on all platforms, four bytes, so Choice E is wrong.

24. `Math.random` takes no parameters and returns a random `double` in the range $0 \le x < 1$. In Choice E, 'A' will never be chosen.

25. In Options I and III, we copy `words` into `temp`, then reconstitute `words` according to the values in `indices`. In Option II, we build `temp` according to the values in `indices`, then copy it back into `words`. All three options work.

26. The class `Friend` inherits the instance variable `name` and the `toString` method from `Person`.

27. In the best case, all the values in the shorter array are smaller than the first value in the longer array. We need 10 comparisons to establish that. In the worst case, neither array "runs out of values," so we need one comparison for each element of the resulting array, except the last one.

28. If `targetValue` is not in `a`, the `while` loop eventually causes an `ArrayIndexOutOfBoundsException`.

29. In Choice B, after the first comparison with `"D"` in the middle, `findLocation` will continue searching in the left half of the array.

30. Implementation 1 has two multiplications and one addition in each of the 6 iterations, 18 operations total. Implementation 2 has one addition and one multiplication in each of the 5 iterations, 10 operations total.

31. All three print 13579. In Option III, the loop is entered with $i = 0, 2, 4, 6$, and 8.

32. The code first adds `"0"`, `"1"`, `"2"`, ..., `"9"` to `digits`, then replaces each of the 5 pairs of elements `"a"`, `"b"` with `"a+b"`.

33. Choice C refers to a situation in which an array holds values of a primitive data type, or an array or list holds immutable objects. In these situations you cannot change the array or list values in a "for each" loop. If objects are mutable, as the `Turtle` objects are here, you can change an object by calling its mutator method. The proposition in Choice D is simply not true for an `ArrayList` (and the opposite is true for a `LinkedList`).

34. If a subclass's constructor does not begin with a call `super(...)`, the superclass's no-args constructor is called by default, and it must exist.

35. Option III doesn't work, because `3/2` evaluates to 1.

36. Since `House` doesn't have a no-args constructor, `super(someInt)` must be the first statement in its subclass's constructor.

37. Superclass's `compareToOther` method will be called, which returns the difference in sizes, `2000 - 1800 = 200`.

38. We cannot assign a `House` to a `HouseForSale` (because not every house is for sale).

39. `getSize` is inherited from `House`.

40. The "for each" loops in Choices A and B are wrong because `m` is not a one-dimensional array. Choice C is wrong because the outer loop has to iterate over the first index (the Java convention is that the first index is row, the second is column). Choice E is wrong because the number of rows is `m.length` and the number of columns is `m[0].length`.

Answers and Solutions

Exam #3 ~ Free Response

1. (a)

```java
public static boolean isValidDNA(String dna)
{
  String DNAletters = "ACGT";

  for (int  i = 0; i < dna.length(); i++)
    if (DNAletters.indexOf(dna.substring(i, i+1)) < 0) ¹
      return false;

  return true;
}
```

    (b)

```java
public static int matchTwoGenes(String dna,
                              String gene1, String gene2)
{
  int i1 = dna.indexOf(gene1);
  if (i1 < 0)
    return -1;

  int i2 = dna.indexOf(gene2);
  if (i2 < i1 + gene1.length())
    return -1;

  return i2 - i1 - gene1.length();
}
```

Notes:

1. `if (DNAletters.indexOf(DNAstring.charAt(i)) < 0)`
    is not in the Java AP subset but is also acceptable.

2.

```
public class Car
{
  private final double TANK_SIZE;
  private int totalMilesDriven;
  private double totalGasUsed;
  private double gasLeft;

  public Car(double tankSize)
  {
    TANK_SIZE = tankSize;
    totalMilesDriven = 0;  ¹
    totalGasUsed = 0;
    gasLeft = TANK_SIZE;
  }

  public double getGasLeft()
  {
    return gasLeft;
  }

  public void fillUp()
  {
    gasLeft = TANK_SIZE;
  }

  public void logTrip(int miles, double tankFraction)
  {
    totalMilesDriven += miles;
    double gas = tankFraction * TANK_SIZE;
    totalGasUsed += gas;
    gasLeft -= gas;

  }

  public int mpg()
  {
    return (int)(totalMilesDriven / totalGasUsed + 0.5);  ²
  }
}
```

Notes:

1. This and the next statement are optional because instance variables get default values: 0 for `int`s, 0.0 for `double`s.

2. This strategy of rounding a `double` to the nearest integer is expected in solutions to AP questions.

3.   (a)

```
public void add(Message msg)
{
  queues[msg.getPriority()].add(msg);
  numMessages++;
}
```

   (b)

```
public Message remove()
{
  for (int prio = queues.length - 1; prio >= 0; prio--)  ¹
  {
    Queue q = queues[prio];

    if (!q.isEmpty())
    {
      numMessages--;
      return q.remove();  ²
    }
  }
  return null;
}
```

Notes:

1. Look for the first non-empty queue starting at the highest priority.

2. This parameterless `remove` is a method of `Queue`. The class `Queue` may simply extend `ArrayList<Message>`:

```
public class Queue extends ArrayList<Message>
{
  public Message remove() { return remove(0); }
}
```

4. (a)

```
public boolean canSwitchLane(int lane, int x, int dir)
{
  int lanes = hwy.length;
  int newLane = lane + dir;

  if (newLane < 0 || newLane >= lanes)
    return false;

  while (newLane >= 0 && newLane < lanes)
  {
    if (hwy[newLane][x] != 0)
      return false;
    newLane += dir;
  }
  return true;
}
```

(b)

```
public void moveAllForward()
{
  int xMax = hwy[0].length - 1;

  for (int lane = 0; lane < hwy.length; lane++)
  {
    int saved = hwy[lane][xMax];

    for (int x = xMax; x > 0; x--) [1]
      hwy[lane][x] = hwy[lane][x-1];

    hwy[lane][0] = saved;
  }
}
```

Notes:

1. Going backward from the end of the lane, shifting the elements of hwy forward.

Answers and Solutions

Exam #4 ~ Multiple Choice

1. E	11. C	21. C	31. E
2. E	12. A	22. E	32. A
3. B	13. B	23. C	33. B
4. C	14. D	24. E	34. D
5. D	15. B	25. E	35. D
6. E	16. C	26. C	36. D
7. B	17. A	27. E	37. E
8. A	18. E	28. A	38. D
9. E	19. B	29. C	39. B
10. D	20. C	30. A	40. D

Notes:

1. `1 < x/y < 2` and `4 < x*y < 5`; truncated to integers gives $1 + 4 = 5$.

2. Applying one of De Morgan's Laws, we can see that the expressions in Options I and II are equivalent. The expression in Option III is `true` when x ≠ y, the same as I and II.

3. Can't convert a `String` into an `Integer` this way — not allowed in Java.

4. `abc1` is first set to `"AAABBBCC"`, then to `"AABBBCC"`; it is a substring of `abc`, starting at index 1.

5. Use De Morgan's Laws: `!(x > y && x % y != 0)` is the same as `(x <= y || x % y == 0)`.

6. Inheritance hierarchies are at the heart of OOP for the reasons listed in the question.

7. `list.remove(i)` shifts to the left all the subsequent elements. Therefore, it is a mistake to increment `i` when an element is removed: the subsequent element won't be examined.

8. `arr[0]` is never changed, which leaves us with Choices A and B. On the last iteration, `arr[7]` is assigned the value of `arr[5]`, which is 6.

9. `smile(4)` prints `"smile!"` 4 times, then calls `smile(3)`, and so on. The total number of times `"smile!"` will be printed is $4 + 3 + 2 + 1 = 10$.

10. `smile` is called in succession with parameters 4, 3, 2, 1, and 0.

11. The statements compile fine due to autoboxing: 2021 is converted into an `Integer` object. `compareTo` returns an `int`, not a `boolean`; in this case it returns a negative integer (actually –1), because 2020 is less than 2021.

12. First of all, `a` and `b` are passed to `swap` by value, so `swap` cannot change their values. This rules out Choices D and E. Inside `swap`, `a` and `b` act as local variables. The assignment `b = a` makes them equal, so `swap` returns 0.

13. $0 - 1 + 2 - 3 + 4 - \ldots + 10 = 0 + (-1 + 2) + (-3 + 4) + \ldots (-9 + 10) = 5$

14. The shuffling algorithm is similar to Selection Sort. In each iteration through the `while` loop, a random card among the first n is selected and swapped with the n-th card.

15. The "for each" loop in Option I does not work, because `word` is a copy of the string in `words`. The copy is modified but the value in the list remains unchanged. Option II with indices and `get` and `set` is the correct way of doing this. Option III is trickier: at first it seems it might work, but actually it does not. Suppose `words` has just two elements: `["A", "B"]`. After the first iteration, `words` becomes `["B", "A*"]`. `k` becomes 1, so after the second iteration, `words` becomes `["B", "A**"]`. To make it work, replace `words.remove(k)` with `words.remove(0)`.

16. This is a typical example of polymorphism.

17. `examine` returns `true` even when all the letters in the array are different, because in the inner `for` loop each letter is also compared to itself.

18. `list[0]`, not `list[2]`, holds a reference to the first `APScholar`, so Choices B and C are off base. Choice D cannot be right, because the `getExamResult` method, not the `getScore` method, takes an integer parameter. Choice A is more plausible, but it doesn't work, because `exams` is private in `APScholar`.

19. `yx` and `xy` refer to <u>the same array</u>, so `yx[0]` and `xy[0]` are both set to `"Y"` after the assignment `yx[0] = xy[1]`.

20. `kenny.meet(barb)` in Option I (third line) and `Toy barb = new Barbie()` in Option II (first line) work if and only if `Barbie` extends `Toy`. The code in Option III works fine even when `Barbie` is not a subclass of `Toy`, as long as `Barbie` has its own method `meet(Barbie other)`.

21. The elements in the 2-by-2 square in the middle are set to 1.

22. Option I works: we simply have two overloaded versions of the `perform` method. Options II and III are valid because `Salsa` IS-A `Dance` IS-A(n) `Object`, and `Swing` IS-A `Dance` IS-A(n) `Object`.

23. Take, for instance, $a = 2, b = 1, c = 2$. The code in Option III gives 0 instead of 1.

24. In Choice C, a method cannot change `START_POS`, because it is declared `final`.

25. Simplify using De Morgan's Laws and notice short-circuit evaluation.

26. This is basically a Binary Search algorithm. We need 1 iteration for one element, 2 iterations for three elements, 3 iterations for seven elements, 4 iterations for 15 elements, and 5 iterations for 31 elements. There is no "best" or "worst" case.

27. x is first set to 2^5. After the first iteration, x becomes 2^{11}; after the second iteration, x becomes 2^{23}; after the third iteration, x would become 2^{47}, as in Choice D, but this overflows the integer range in Java.

28. `encrypt("SEC")` returns `"CES"`; `encrypt("RET")` returns `"TER"`.

29. On each iteration through the `while` loop, the code takes the elements from 0 to `n-1` and repeats that segment of the array, adding 1 to each element. Thus `{0, ...}` becomes `{0, 1, ...}`, then `{0, 1, ...}` becomes `{0, 1, 1, 2, ...}`, then `{0, 1, 1, 2, ...}` becomes `{0, 1, 1, 2, 1, 2, 2, 3}`. Note that `nums[k]` is the number of binary digits equal to 1 in the binary representation of `k`. The sequence can grow in the same manner up to any power of 2. (The infinite sequence formed like this is a "fractal" sequence: if you take every second element, starting from 0, you will get the same sequence!)

30. In Option I, you cannot access an instance variable `score` from a static method. You can, of course, access static variables in constructors and instance methods.

31. After the first iteration through the outer "for each" loop, with `f = 2`, the `products` list will hold `[1, 2]`. After the second iteration, with `f = 3`, the `products` list will hold `[1, 2, 3, 6]`. After the third iteration, with `f = 5`, the `products` list will hold `[1, 2, 3, 6, 5, 10, 15, 30]`.

32. `SortX` implements Selection Sort. First `"Boris"` is swapped with `"Evan"`, then `"Boris"` is swapped with `"Dan"`.

33. $4 + 3 + 2 + 1 = 10$

34. `n /= 10` is the correct choice for < *statement 2* > (to eliminate the rightmost digit). This leaves only Choices A and D. If $n = 0$, the return should be 1 only when $d = 0$, so Choice A is wrong.

35. `LibraryBook` does not override `Object`'s `toString` method, so Option I is out. Options II and III are equivalent and both work.

36. Choice A doesn't work, because `numCopies` and `info` are private in `LibraryBook`.

37. It is your choice to use the `getNumCopies` and `setNumCopies` methods or to manipulate the `numCopies` variable directly within the `LibraryBook` class.

38. The value of an element in a given column is set to the sum of the values of its two or three neighbors in the previous column.

39. When the *k*-th element is removed from the list in the second `for` loop, the subsequent elements are shifted to the left, and their indices are decremented by one. As a result, this loop removes every other element — values 1, 3, and 5, at the original indices 0, 2, and 4. These values are added at the end of the list.

40. For each element `p[i]`, `mysteryCount` adds to `count` the length of the cycle `p[p[p...[i]...]] = i`. This is 1 for the first element and 3 for each of the other three elements.

Answers and Solutions

Exam #4 ~ Free Response

1. (a)

```
public static String encrypt(String text, int key)
{
  String code = "";
  for (int i = 0; i < text.length(); i++)
  {
    String letter = text.substring(i, i+1);  ¹
    int j = abc.indexOf(letter);
    if (j >= 0)  ²
    {
      j = (j + key) % 26;   // The index of the substitute
                            //    letter
      code += abc.substring(j, j+1);
    }
    else
    {
      code += letter;
    }
  }
  return code;
}
```

(b)

```
public static String decrypt(String code, int key)
{
  return encrypt(code, 26 - key);  ³
}
```

Notes:

1. `String letter = text.charAt(i);`
    is not in the Java AP subset but is also acceptable.

2. Encrypt only uppercase letters.

3. Because `key` must be > 0, we cannot write `encrypt(code, -key)`.

2.

```
public class APStudent
{
  private static final int MIN_GRADE = 3;  ¹

  private int totalExams;
  private int goodExams;   // grade of 3 or higher
  private int sumOfGrades;

  public void addExam(int grade)
  {
    totalExams++;
    sumOfGrades += grade;
    if (grade >= MIN_GRADE)
      goodExams++;
  }

  public int awardLevel()
  {
    if (totalExams == 0)  ²
      return 0;

    double averageGrade = (double)sumOfGrades / totalExams;

    if (goodExams >= 5 && averageGrade >= 3.5)  ³
      return 3;
    else if (goodExams >= 4 && averageGrade >= 3.25)
      return 2;
    else if (goodExams >= 3)
      return 1;
    else
      return 0;
  }
}
```

Notes:

1. Using a symbolic constant rather than 3 makes your code self-documenting.

2. This special case must be handled separately.

3. The if-else sequence should go from the highest to the lowest award.

3.   (a)

```
public static ArrayList<Integer> findRpeaks(double[] v)
{
  ArrayList<Integer> rPeakPositions =
                              new ArrayList<Integer>();

  int k = DELTA;
  while (k < v.length - DELTA)
  {
    if (isRpeak(v, k))
    {
      rPeakPositions.add(k);
      k += DELTA;
    }
    else
      k++;
  }
  return rPeakPositions;
}
```

(b)

```
public static int heartRate(ArrayList<Integer> rPeakPositions)
{
  int first = rPeakPositions.get(0);
  int last = rPeakPositions.get(rPeakPositions.size() - 1);
  double avgDistance = (double)(last - first) /
                          (rPeakPositions.size() - 1); [1]
  return (int)(60 * SAMPLING_RATE / avgDistance + 0.5);
}
```

Notes:

1. If rPeakPositions has *n* elements, then there are *n* - 1 RR-intervals between the first and the last R-peaks.

4.   (a)

```
public static int vacantGoodSeats(boolean[][] seats,
                                              int w, int h)
{
  int count = 0;

  for (int r = 2; r <= 1 + h; r++)
    for (int c = (seats[0].length - w)/2;
              c < (seats[0].length + w)/2; c++)
      if (seats[r][c] == false)
        count++;

  return count;
}
```

(b)

```
public static Location bestTwoSeats(boolean[][] seats)
{
  Location center = new Location((seats.length - 1)/2,
                              seats[0].length/2 - 1);
  Location bestLocation = null;

  for (int r = 0; r < seats.length; r++)
  {
    for (int c = 0; c < seats[0].length - 1; c++)
    {
      if (!(seats[r][c] || seats[r][c+1]))  [1]
      {
        Location loc = new Location(r, c);
        if (bestLocation == null || loc.distanceFrom(center) <
                        bestLocation.distanceFrom(center))  [2]
          bestLocation = loc;
      }
    }
  }
  return bestLocation;
}
```

Notes:

1. Or:
```
          if (seats[r][c] == false && seats[r][c+1] == false)
```

2. A NullPointerException does not happen here due to short-circuit evaluation.

Answers and Solutions

Exam #5 ~ Multiple Choice

1. E	11. C	21. C	31. A
2. A	12. E	22. A	32. A
3. A	13. D	23. C	33. E
4. D	14. A	24. E	34. B
5. B	15. E	25. B	35. B
6. D	16. D	26. D	36. E
7. A	17. B	27. C	37. C
8. A	18. B	28. E	38. C
9. A	19. A	29. C	39. B
10. B	20. C	30. E	40. D

Notes:

1. `5*4/2 = (5*4)/2` evaluates to 10. `5/2*4 = (5/2)*4` evaluates to 8. The result is converted into a `double` at the end.

2. Strings are immutable; a method cannot change a `String` object.

3. Use a De Morgan's Law.

4. You might notice that `guess` implements Euclid's Algorithm for finding the greatest common divisor.

5. When `words` is created, its size is 0. Trying to access the first element in `words` raises an `IndexOutOfBoundsException`.

6. `d` is set to the smallest of `a` and `b`, here 12. Then, due to short-circuit evaluation, `%` is applied twice for `d = 12, 6, 4, 3` and once for `d = 11, 10, 9, 8, 7, 5`.

7. Every third element from 3 to 48 is set to 0 — 16 elements. Every fifth element from 5 to 50 is set to 0 — 10 elements. The total is $10 + 16 = 26$. But we counted the 15th, the 30th, and the 45th elements twice. $26 - 3 = 23$.

8. The `fun` implementations in Options I and II are equivalent: both return `true` when `a >= b >= c`. This leaves us with Choices A and D. Options II and III are different, because II has `&&` and III has `||`.

9. `% 100` leaves the last 2 digits.

10. Array indices start from 0; need for `arr[i]` to be both positive and odd.

11. `n` remains greater than or equal to 2, until it is eventually reduced to either 0 or 1.

12. Each of the two addends can have the value 0 or 1, independently. Their sum can have the values 0, 1, or 2 (actually, 1 will be twice as likely as 0 or 2).

13. Option I won't work: in it `swap` receives and swaps <u>copies</u> of references to the objects. An array is passed to a method as a copy of a reference to the original array, so both Option II and Option III will work.

14. All three code segments set the values on the border of the array `m` to 0.

15. The code in Option I will crash right away in `Math.sqrt` if `d2` is negative. The code in Option II prints nothing if `d2` is positive but `x` is not positive. The code in Option III always prints the correct message.

16. `Jet` inherits `addFuel` from `Airplane`. `plane` is created with fuel 4 and `jet` is created with fuel 8.

17. The ratio is a negative number between –2 and –1; it is truncated toward 0.

18. The `while` loop finds the correct spot to insert `current`; the inner `for` loop shifts the elements in `a` to the right to make room.

19. `a[1]` and `a[2]` have been inserted into the correct places, so the first three elements in `a` must now be in ascending order.

20. The first version quits as soon as the target value is found; the second version always scans the whole array.

21. The `boolean` variable `flag` "accumulates" the values of the Boolean expressions `v[i] == v[i+1]`, that is, it remains `true` once one of these expressions is `true`.

22. In Option 1, the expression compares the references to (the addresses of) `str1` and `str2`.

23. The last thing `printSomething(4)` does is print `1234`, so we can eliminate Choices D and E. Prior to that, it calls `printSomething(3)`. `printSomething(3)` calls `printSomething(2)`, which prints something that ends with `12`. `printSomething(3)` then prints `123`, so the output of `printSomething(3)` ends with `12123`. The output of `printSomething(4)` ends with `121231234`.

24. The only statements that can potentially cause an incompatible types problem are

    ```
    Text greeting = new Greeting("Hello");
    ```

    in Option II and

    ```
    Text translation = Text.translate(greeting);
    ```

    in Option III. Both work, because `Greeting` extends `Text`.

25. "`return mid;`" must remain unchanged for the method to work when `searchVal` is in `list`. Try a list of size 1 to see where to insert `searchVal`: at the beginning, both `first` and `last` are 0; after the loop, `mid` is undefined and `last` becomes –1 when `searchVal < list.get(0)`, so `last` cannot be used as the insert position.

26. The data type of `Integer.MAX_VALUE` is int, so `Integer.MAX_VALUE / 10` is truncated to an integer and gives `214748364`. `Integer.MAX_VALUE / 10 + 1` gives `214748365`.

27. The nested `for` loops correctly traverse the entire array and fill all its elements in a diagonal pattern, starting with 1 in the upper-left corner.

28. In Version 1, `choose(4, 2)` calls `choose(4, 1)`, which in turn calls `choose(4, 0)` — three calls total. In Version 2, there is a branching progression of calls —

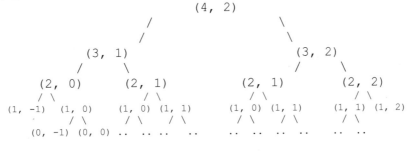

     — 27 calls total.

29. If you add or remove elements while traversing an `ArrayList` with a "for each" loop, the code will throw a `ConcurrentModificationException`.

30. The concept of privacy applies to the class as a whole. Any method of a class has access to private fields of all objects of that class.

31. `Track` does not have a no-args constructor.

32. `duration` is private in `Track`, so Choices B and D are wrong.

33. `tracks` holds 13 copies of the same track of duration 200.

34. Option I fails to create `ArrayList tracks`. Option III attempts to set a non-existing element, which would cause an `IndexOutOfBoundsException`.

35. A call to `Counter`'s `setCount` method has no effect, because `setCount` introduces and sets a local variable `count`, as opposed to modifying the field `count`. The code prints 1. The correct method would be

```
public void setCount(int c) { count = c; }  // Line 3
```

36. The code in Option I first sets all the elements to 1, then sets the elements on the diagonal to 0. The code in Option II works, because when an array is created with the `new` operator, its elements are set to default values, zeros for an `int` array. The code in Option III checks whether the element is on the diagonal or not and sets it accordingly. All three work.

37. The statement `int n = str.length()` will raise a `NullPointerException`.

38. 4 times for `"Africa"`, 5 times for `"America"`, and 3 times for `"Antarctica"`.

39. `[] => [1] => [1, 2] => [1, 1, 2] => [1, 1, 2, 2] => [1, 1, 2, 3, 2]`.

40. `arr` is passed as a reference to the original array; `len` is passed by value.

Answers and Solutions

Exam #5 ~ Free Response

1. (a)

```
public static double averageAmt(int prize,
                        double ticketPrice, int n)
{
  double total = 0;

  for (int k = 1; k <= n; k++)
  {
    total -= ticketPrice;
    if (win())
      total += prize;
  }
  return total/n;
}  1
```

(b)

```
public static int prizeWorthPlaying(double ticketPrice)
{
  int prize = 5;

  while (averageAmt(prize, ticketPrice, 100) < 0)
    prize += 5;

  return prize;
}  2
```

Notes:

1. Or:

```
public static double averageAmt(int prize,
                        double ticketPrice, int n)
{
  double total = -n*ticketPrice;

  for (int k = 1; k <= n; k++)
    if (win())
      total += prize;
  return total/n;
}
```

2. Because averageAmt depends on random returns from win, this method can return different values in different runs.

2.

```
public class ApplesPurchase
{
  private int applePrice;
  private int apples;

  public ApplesPurchase(int cents, int howMany)
  {
    applePrice = cents;
    apples = howMany;
  }

  public int totalCost()
  {
    int sixes = apples / 6;
    return applePrice * (apples - sixes);
  }

  private String toDollarsAndCents(int cents)
  {
    int dollars = cents/100;
    cents -= 100*dollars;

    if (cents >= 10)
      return "$" + dollars + "." + cents;
    else
      return "$" + dollars + ".0" + cents;
  } 1

  public String toString()
  {
    String applePriceStr = toDollarsAndCents(applePrice);
    String totalCostStr = toDollarsAndCents(totalCost());
    return apples + " apples at " + applePriceStr +
            " each: " + totalCostStr + " total";
  }
}
```

Notes:

1. This is a simple way to format cents into dollars and cents, which might be expected on an AP exam. There are several other ways, of course — outside of the AP Java subset. For example:

```
import java.text.DecimalFormat;
...
  private String toDollarsAndCents(int cents)
  {
    DecimalFormat money = new DecimalFormat("$0.00");
    return money.format((double)cents/100);
  }
```

3.   (a)

```
public static int[] findMaxAndMin(ArrayList<Integer> scores)
{
  int[] maxmin = {0, 100};

  for (Integer s : scores)
  {
    if (s > maxmin[0])
      maxmin[0] = s;
    if  (s < maxmin[1])  1
      maxmin[1] = s;
  }
  return maxmin;
}
```

(b)

```
public static double averageScore(ArrayList<Integer> scores)
{
  int sum = 0, count = 0;

  for (Integer s : scores)
  {
    sum += s;
    count++;
  }

  if (count >= 6)
  {
    int[] maxmin = findMaxAndMin(scores);
    for (int m : maxmin)  2
    {
      if (countOccurrences(scores, m) == 1)
      {
        sum -= m;
        count -= 1;
      }
    }
  }
  return (double)sum / count;
}
```

Notes:

1.   Not `else if` here, because `maxmin[1]` needs to be updated the first time.

2.   It is easier to handle both maximum and minimum scores in one loop.

4. (a)

```
public static boolean[][] oneQueen(int row, int col)
{
  boolean[][] board = new boolean[8][8];  ¹

  for (int k = 0; k < 8; k++)
  {
    board[row][k] = true;
    board[k][col] = true;
  }

  for (int k = -7; k < 8; k++)  ²
  {
    int r, c;

    r = row + k;
    c = col + k;
    if (0 <= r && r < 8 && 0 <= c && c < 8)
      board[r][c] = true;

    r = row + k;
    c = col - k;
    if (0 <= r && r < 8 && 0 <= c && c < 8)
      board[r][c] = true;
  }
  return board;
}
```

(b)

```
public static boolean[][] twoQueens(int row, int col,
                                    int row2, int col2)
{
  boolean[][] board = oneQueen(row, col);
  boolean[][] board2 = oneQueen(row2, col2);

  for (int r = 0; r < 8; r++)
  {
    for (int c = 0; c < 8; c++)
      board[r][c] = board[r][c] || board2[r][c];  ³
  }

  return board;
}
```

Notes:

1. The elements of `board` are initialized to `false` by default.

2. It is easier to scan the longest possible diagonal and check whether the square falls within the board than to figure out the exact limit in each direction.

3. For some reason, Java does not support the compound assignment ||=.

Index

Index to Free-Response Questions
in Practice Exams

	Exam	Question	Page	Solution
AP Scholar awards	4	2	*219*	*288*
Apflix movie matching	2	3	*163*	*273*
Apples purchase	5	2	*253*	*296*
Ballroom competition scoring	5	3	*254*	*297*
Bus schedule	2	1	*159*	*271*
Car gas mileage	3	2	*189*	*280*
DNA strings	3	1	*187*	*279*
Equation solver	2	2	*161*	*272*
ECG	4	3	*221*	*289*
Game of chance	5	1	*251*	*295*
Graphs	1	4	*134*	*266*
Highway	3	4	*193*	*282*
Memory Lane game	1	3	*131*	*265*
Passwords	1	1	*127*	*263*
Priority queue	3	3	*190*	*281*
Queens on chessboard	5	4	*256*	*298*
Shopping options	1	2	*130*	*264*
Ski slope design	2	4	*165*	*274*
Substitution cipher	4	1	*217*	*287*
Theater seats	4	4	*224*	*290*

Java Methods

and other
math and computer science books and
e-books from Skylight Publishing

www.skylit.com/orderform.pdf

www.skylit.com
sales@skylit.com
Toll free: 888-476-1940
Fax: 978-475-1431

Skylight Publishing, 9 Bartlet Street, Suite 70, Andover, MA 01810